LOTS OF PARKING

LAND USE IN
A CAR CULTURE

JOHN A. JAKLE AND KEITH A. SCULLE

UNIVERSITY OF VIRGINIA PRESS
Charlottesville and London

Publication of this volume was assisted by a grant from
the Graham Foundation for Advanced Studies in the Fine Arts.

UNIVERSITY OF VIRGINIA PRESS
Printed in the United States of America on acid-free paper

First published 2004

1 3 5 7 9 8 6 4 2

LIBRARY OF CONGRESS CATALOGING-IN-PUBLICATION DATA
Jakle, John A.
    Lots of parking : land use in a car culture / John A. Jakle
and Keith A. Sculle.
        p.   cm.
    Includes bibliographical references and index.
    ISBN 0-8139-2266-6 (Cloth : alk. paper)
    1. Parking lots — Landscape architecture.   2. Parking
lots — Design and construction.   3. Parking lots — United
States — History.   I. Sculle, Keith A.   II. Title.
    TL175.J34 2004
    711'.73 — dc22

                                                2003021181

This book is published in association with the
CENTER FOR AMERICAN PLACES
Santa Fe, New Mexico, and Staunton, Virginia
(www.americanplaces.org).

FOR
THE FRUSTRATED MOTORIST,
THE HARRIED METER MAID,
THE DUTIFUL PARKING LOT ATTENDANT

CONTENTS

PREFACE

This is a book about parking and its impact on America, especially its impact on the American built environment. Does it stretch the imagination to think that something so commonplace should deserve the emphasis of a book? Is life's never-ending search for a place to park not time consuming enough without having to spend more time reading about it? Parking, we would have our readers fully appreciate, has become an essential fact in American life. Just look around. Where don't you see automobiles? And, accordingly, where isn't parking necessarily close at hand? America's geography has been fully impacted by the logistics of car storage. It is not just the motor vehicle in motion that underpins life in America today. It is, as well, the motor vehicle at rest. Parking fully impacts how we create and use places in our modern world. For Americans, parking lots and parking garages have become absolutely essential. The country would not function without them.

Our title, *Lots of Parking*, is, of course, a play on words. By its adoption we imply that parking lots (and parking garages also) are everywhere in America, given the nation's substantial embrace of the automobile and automobility. And yet most Americans, we suspect, sense that there still is not enough parking. Where is that empty parking space when you need it?!

Automobile use impacts the structuring of built environment and people's thinking about that structuring. To be set and sustained in motion, cars necessitate rights-of-way conducive to speed and ease of fast maneuverability. But so also do parked cars make demands. Indeed, the space needed for vehicle storage in America equals, if not exceeds, that for vehicular movement, although we tend not to think of it quite that way. The urban freeway, for example, serves readily to symbolize modern America's reliance on automobiles. That such motorways are often congested, with cars moving slowly (if at all) much of time, does not diminish the power of the freeway's liberating idealization. The "open road" is how most Americans like to conceptualize the motorcar's potential. "Life in the fast lane" is what many if not most American's like to claim. On the other hand, parking lots and garages have come to symbolize relatively little good or bad. Parking hardly captures the imagination, except, perhaps, when an immediate lack of parking space frustrates.

Solid assessment of the automobile's impact on American landscapes requires a parking, as well as a motoring, orientation. It is not a matter of just "getting there." It is, as well, a matter of "parking there." Parking dominates both at one's point of departure and at one's destination. To park (or not to park) is the question that anchors every trip by car. Without places to park, motoring, even fast motoring, matters little.

In the chapters that follow, we outline the history of parking in America. Our work is structured topically but is written in such a way as to bring the reader along chronologically from early- to late-twentieth-century considerations. Our focus is decidedly urban, with big cities being favored over small. We ask the following kinds of questions: How has parking impacted urban land use, especially commercial and institutional land use? What have been parking's prevailing landscape or architectural expressions over time? To what extent has parking influenced urban development and redevelopment, especially in business districts?

Unfortunately, space does not allow our full consideration of residential parking, especially concerned with the domestic garage. Our focus is very much commercial and institutional parking beyond the nation's residential neighborhoods.

In the introduction, parking's landscape implications are outlined, and car storage is thereby placed within the larger context of America's automobile dependence. Part 1 treats the initial public and private responses to downtown parking needs in cities. The inadequacies of curbside parking and its further reduction through municipal regulation led to the rise of commercial off-street parking lots and garages and, indeed, to the rise of a commercial parking industry. These are stories told in chapters 1 and 2, respectively. Chapter 3 concerns the rise of public parking, at first in competition with, and then as a complement to, commercial parking interests. Part 2 treats the urban developmental implications of parking, linking auto storage to other kinds of land use. Chapter 4 outlines the rise of the open parking lot. Chapters 5 and 6 consider the evolution of the parking garage as a distinctive architectural form. Chapter 7 relates parking to downtown redevelopment.

In part 3, attention shifts from downtown parking, for the most part inserted into city space through the demolition of urban infrastructure once pedestrian-oriented, to parking in outlying urban areas, for the most part built to accommodate motorists from the very beginning. Chapter 8 focuses on outlying shopping districts and suburban shopping centers, dealing in the process with automobile-oriented commercial strips. Chapter 9 considers institutional parking *at*, for example, hospitals, universities, and airports. The conclusion offers synthesis by relating parking as a historical process to contemporary urban design issues. Considered are the larger and, perhaps, more basic issues of individual self-expression and community orientation in America as they have related to parking.

Our concern is to focus intellectually on a kind of behavior (parking) and kinds of derived landscape features (especially parking lots and garages) little considered previously by students of landscape. Few scholars, except those narrowly focused on such specific topics as traffic management and parking deck design, have dealt with parking at the book scale. Few of those authors have sought to put parking into broad historical and geographical contexts. In dealing with auto use, most students of landscape emphasize what might be thought of as motoring's ultimate destinations. It is not the parking lot, but the structure of the shopping center that attracts attention. It is not the parking deck, but the soaring tower of the skyscraper that is noted. Even the city street is so assessed. It is not curbside parking, but the stream of traffic flow that is emphasized. Parking has remained in the background. Over recent generations, landscape in America has been substantially remade through accommodation to the automobile. The story has been told with focus on the history of automobile technology, the history of street and highway improvement, and even the history of specialized automobile-oriented buildings, such as gas stations, motels, and roadside restaurants. It is time, we feel, to enlarge the story with focus on parking. It is time to give parking a role in the foreground.

Parking's relative obscurity as a commercial enterprise or public service has directed the authors to rely especially on the experience and insights of owners, designers, and public officials concerned with parking. For the invaluable material or experience shared, we are indebted to the following people and sources: Charles A. Bassett and Wally Park, Los Angeles; Patricia Cantley and International Parking Design, Sherman Oaks, California; Central Parking Corporation, Nashville; City of Detroit Planning and Development Department; Josef Diamond, Debora Davenport and Diamond Parking, Inc., Seattle; Therese Encarnacion and Car Barn Airport Parking, Los Angeles; Michael Federman and the City of Danville (Illinois) Department of Development Services; Barry Green and Ace Parking Management, Inc., San Diego; Perry Griffith, Robert Ketring, and Denison, Inc., Indianapolis; John Haggerty and PRG Parking, St. Louis; Jim Konecny, Ron Himes, Garry Saffran, and the Pro Media Health System, Toledo, Ohio; Steve Jenco and the City of Joliet (Illinois) Department of Public Works; Sally E. Merar and Standard Parking, Chicago; Gary B. Pohrer, Terrie Weaver, and Hobbs and Black, Ann Arbor, Michigan; JoAnn Whelan and Alco Parking, Pittsburgh; and Sonya Wright, Municipal Parking Department, Detroit.

For their help and guidance in accessing archival materials or providing material from their personal collections we are indebted to the following: Audrey Arlington and the City of Beverly Hills Planning and Community Development Department; Martin Aurand and the Carnegie Mellon University Architectural Archives, Pittsburgh; David Becker and the City and County of Denver Planning and Development Office; Brian Butko; Laura Corwin and the National Automotive History Collection, Detroit Public Library; Karen De Seve and the Eastern Washington Historical Society, Spokane; Judy Endelman, Melissa J. Haddock, Linda Scolarus, Leo Landis, and the Henry Ford Museum and Greenfield Village, Dearborn; the Getty, Los Angeles; Laura Graedel and the Museum of Science and Industry, Chicago; Esley Hamilton and the St. Louis County Department of Parks and Recreation; Nini Harris and the Carondolet Historical Society, St. Louis; Michael Jackson of the Illinois Historic Preservation Agency; Jennie Johnson and the Map and Geography Library, University of Illinois at Urbana-Champaign; Jim Johnston; Indiana Historical Society, Indianapolis; Susan Kammen and Western Michigan University, Kalamazoo; Kansas State Historical Society, Topeka; George J. Kelly and the San Francisco History Center, San Francisco Public Library; Carole S. Mazzotta, Media Center, Kaufmann's Department Stores, Pittsburgh; H. Carl Walker, Andrew W. Miller, and Carl Walker, Inc., Kalamazoo; Nancy O'Neill and the Santa Monica (California) Public Library; Anthony Rubano; Claudette Stager and the Tennessee Historical Commission, Nashville; Asa L. Rubenstein and the New York Public Library; Al Tannler and the Pittsburgh Historic Landmarks Foundation; Anne Taylor and the Arizona Historical Society, Tucson; Mary Turner and the Illinois Association of Museums, Springfield; Tim Utter and the Hatcher Graduate Library, University of

Michigan; and Sweson Yang and the City of Indianapolis Department of Metropolitan Development.

Several people furnished significant technical support. For cartography we are indebted to Jane Domier and for typing various stages of the manuscript we are indebted to Barbara Bonnell, both of the Department of Geography, University of Illinois at Urbana-Champaign. Mary Ann Pohl of the Illinois Historical Library obtained invaluable interlibrary loans and verified bibliographical citations.

George F. Thompson, president of the Center for American Places, has consistently encouraged our research into the manifold ways that the nation's passion for automobility has affected the landscape. His understanding has made possible the publication of this book by the University of Virginia Press. We respect and enjoy our relationship with him.

Wives Cynthia Jakle and Tracey Sculle have more than listened to the book's conceptualization and have carried on during our long absences for fieldwork together and writing alone. Their research and alertness to important resources also have helped make this book.

LOTS OF PARKING

INTRODUCTION

They paved paradise
And put up a parking lot.

—JONI MITCHELL, *Big Yellow Taxi* (1969)

And it appears that they did so almost everywhere—those makers of the American scene. They paved over farm fields to create shopping centers surrounded by acres of asphalt. They replaced woods and forests with sprawling subdivisions, the houses dominated by driveways and attached garages. They disemboweled American towns and cities with pavement. The parking lot, augmented by the parking garage, joined the widened street and the city freeway to produce a very new urban geography, a human ecology dedicated to automobile use. But it was not only the car in motion but, as well, the car at rest that wrought revolutionary impact. Space for storage is as essential to car use as space for movement. Parking remains a critical preoccupation in the nation's making and remaking of landscape and place.

Some quick calculations establish the magnitude of the parked car's intrusion. There are 8,760 hours in a year, and if one assumes that the average mileage driven per car per year is 10,000 miles, and that the average car moves overall at an average speed of 25 miles per hour, then the total travel time accumulated each year is something on the order of 400 hours. That leaves 8,360 hours per year when the typical automobile is merely parked. Let us assume that the average size of parking space is 150 square feet, ignoring for the moment that an equal amount of space is required for maneuvering in and out. At recent count, there were some 101 million households in the United States with an average 1.7 motor vehicles per household.[1] Therefore, car storage, calculated only for home needs, consumed some 688,000 acres of land, or 1,100 square miles of real estate, an area nearly equal to the size of Rhode Island. Of course, cars in regular use require two spaces—one at home and one at destinations away from home.

Needed is parking space at work, where one shops, where one plays, and, indeed, wherever automobile trips terminate. Today, space devoted to parking in the United States is easily as large, by total extent, as that of several New England states combined.

The automobile has become indispensable to modern life in America, like electricity and running water. The motor car promised, and continues to promise, degrees of freedom and outright convenience in travel not offered by other forms of transportation. It has enabled and sustained preference for suburban living. American cities, where the vast majority of Americans now live, sprawl over vast territories with space for parking an essential element. With cities built to low population densities reflecting the automobile's needs, alternative forms of transportation, such as mass transit, are today difficult to rationalize. By the 1980s, autos accounted for over a trillion vehicle miles yearly. The journey-to-work, as one kind of trip taking, was fully dominated by auto travel, with mass transit serving only 6 percent of all commuters.[2] Between 1980 and 1990, the total number of commuters increased in the United States by over 18 million, but the number cars used in commuting increased by over 22 million. In 1990, there were some 115 million commuters, all but 15 million of whom used private vehicles. During the 1980s, the number of cars in America increased at a faster rate than the population.[3]

Cars also dominate the journey-to-shop. Retailing in America has been totally reconfigured around automobile convenience. Commerce sprawls outward from city centers in elongated commercial strips, and roadside margins are patterned repetitiously—with driveways, giant signs, parking lots, and sign-like or sign-bedecked buildings beckoning at intervals the motorist as consumer. By 1970 there were some 13,000 shopping malls in the United States, each set in a large parking lot. By 1997, there were nearly 43,000 malls, over 5,000 of them designated as large regional centers.[4] So also do cars dominate trips to church, to the doctor, to government offices. Most leisure-time travel is car-dependent, including that of vacation holidays. In all categories of movement, the motorcar is the transport mode of choice in America, and the problem of where to park is a universal constant.

The parking problem, and the nation's proclivity to turn vast amounts of real estate to its solving, came to the fore in the years immediately after World War I. The inexpensive motor car, pioneered by the Ford Motor Company and the General Motors Corporation, enabled Americans of even modest means to embrace automobile travel even in the most ordinary routines of life. By 1924, there were some 13.5 million passenger cars and, in addition, some 1.7 million trucks crowding America's streets and highways. In some two decades the automobile industry had grown into a giant, directly employing some 2.8 million workers.[5] City and rural thoroughfares, built for slower horse-powered and pedestrian traffic, were overwhelmed by the demands of high-speed automobile movement. In cities, the parking of cars at street margins reduced street capacities, filling lanes that might otherwise have been used for moving cars. Cars jostling for curb space interrupted traffic flow. The very functioning of downtown districts, where commercial activity concentrated, appeared threatened by the congestion induced, as suggested by the following verse:

> There's a game we all play
> In our town every day,
> From rose-tinted dawn until dark,
> The young and the old,
> The timid and bold —
> 'Tis hunting a place to park.[6]

Where commerce was established out along thoroughfares away from downtown, broad streets were constructed to facilitate curbside parking. Increasingly, merchants provided off-street parking to attract customers. Commercial buildings were moved back from sidewalks and streets, and business premises were increasingly configured to be seen across parking lots through automobile windshields (fig. I.1). Sense of place — both that of specific business locations and that of overall commercial strip configuration — came to carry stronger and stronger parking lot implications. Large signs anchored parking lot approaches at curbside, the signs often more pretentious as attention-getters than the buildings themselves. The car was king, and the architecture of retailing evolved very much in subservience, with structure and open space made to communicate as integral. Parking lots not only set buildings off to be seen, but, of course, they also offered the convenience of leaving one's car seemingly close to, if not actually right at, one's ultimate destination.

Auto-oriented suburbia engendered sprawling subdivisions, and the attached garage and the expanded driveway were made private adjuncts to public rights-of-way. Mandated by federally sponsored mortgage insurance programs, often codified in local zoning ordinances and building codes, the spread-out suburbs absolutely required automobile use. When women

FIG. I.1

The automobile-convenient landscape of a suburban commercial strip. San Antonio, 1982.

entered the work force in large numbers, two-car households became a necessity. Women constituted some 30 percent of all workers in 1960 but over 45 percent in 1990.[7] Women tended to be more reliant on automobiles than men since in most families the wife/mother remained primarily responsible for household logistics. Women made more linked trips than men — for example, between home, a place of work, a child-care center, or a grocery store, and home again.[8] As retailing decentralized in full embrace of auto travel, so also did other urban functions. Office, warehousing, and industrial activities found new locations, sometimes clustering in "edge city" business complexes but, as often as not, scattering to "green field" sites widely separated.

Automobile dependence drove reconfiguration of older, traditional urban landscapes. Center cities required reconfiguring to make them competitive with suburbia. Indeed, central business districts were remade substantially in the new suburban image. Off-street parking became essential for those business and governmental functions that chose to stay downtown. Decentralization produced substantial structural redundance, especially marginal to downtowns, with vacant or underutilized older buildings ripe for demolition. At first incrementally, with individual structures removed, and then with entire blocks leveled, the parking lot came to downtown. At the very centers of big city downtowns, parking garages appeared.

FIG. I.2
Parking lot "erosion" of downtown. Detroit, 1963.

But, overall, many central business districts came to be reduced to simplistic formula—tall skyscraper buildings set in parking lot surrounds in total mockery of traditional urbanity (fig. I.2).

DEFINING TERMS

As automobile use increased and the nation's geography, especially its urban landscapes, came more to reflect the needs of motoring, appropriate descriptive vocabulary quickly developed. What, for example, to call places where cars were stored? Indeed, what to call the very act of storing a car? To the fore came terms descriptive of both the act and the place. The word "rank" was early popularized, derived from the "ranking" of horse-drawn carriages awaiting hire and thus standing arrayed at curbside. Other precedence was offered by the term "park," among other meanings a reference to the placing of gun carriages parallel to one another in both battle and parade formations.[9] The "parking" of artillery was something fresh in the minds of veterans returning from World War I. The word traces its origins to the medieval Latin word *parricus,* meaning an enclosure.[10] *Webster's New International Dictionary of the English Language* (2nd ed., 1949) establishes the verb "to park" as meaning "to enclose." But, in early twentieth-century America it could, and did, also mean "to stop and keep standing," the meaning applied to car storage.

Various categories of parking activity took notice as the new profession of traffic engineering emerged in the 1920s.[11] "Standing" came to describe vehicles with drivers present that were stopped to unload or load passengers or goods, a transfer operative from vehicle to sidewalk or vice versa. "Live parking" referred to a standing vehicle not engaged in any transfer, so its driver was therefore capable of yielding curb space upon demand. "Dead parking" referred to the outright storage of a car with its driver engaged elsewhere in activity fully divorced from a vehicle. "Double-parking" referred to two ranks of vehicles positioned along a curb. In addition, the term "cruising" came to describe cars or trucks being driven in search of parking space. During business hours, a sizeable percentage of vehicles in any downtown were in motion, having reached their general destination but not yet parked. Cruising was seen to be a kind of "mobile parking."[12]

"To park" quickly came to mean the leaving of a "dead" vehicle at a curb parallel with the street (at first called "line parking" and then "parallel parking") or at an angle with the curb ("angle parking"). As cars came to be stored increasingly off-street, use of these terms was extended accordingly. But what to call those off-street areas? Before World War II, a variety of terms applied: parking ground, parking station, parking terminal, parking field, and, of course, parking lot. The term "ground" had widespread application in American English. It meant a surface or a portion of an area dedicated to a particular use and, therefore, set apart, often surrounded by a fence or a wall. The word "station" implied a place where vehicles were brought to a halt and, thereby, set to standing. Implied was a situation or location where vehicles took up stationary position, such as a train stopped at a railroad depot. The word "terminal," also borrowed from railroading, implied connection with receipt of or delivery of people or freight. It implied a place for terminating a trip. "Field" referred to open or cleared space, such as a farm field carved from a forest, an apt analogy for parking lots since most of them, at least in downtowns, were established on the footprints of demolished buildings. The verb "to allot" meant to divide and distribute by lot, to parcel out or apportion. The word "lot" implies a portion of land parceled out from, or divided from, a larger area. In American cities and towns, the term was widely used to distinguish ownership parcels, the properties into which blocks of land within surveyed street grids were themselves divided. The "lot" idea readily applied when properties were cleared of buildings. The term "parking lot" came to signify vacated spaces used for storing cars.

The term "garage" was reserved for auto storage spaces fully enclosed structurally. A parking lot might be surrounded by a fence, but a parking garage had solid walls and a ceiling as well as a floor. The French verb *garer* meant to make safe, to secure or protect. As a noun, the English word "garage" was borrowed directly from the French, as were many other terms associated with motoring, including the very word "automobile." Garages protected cars under full cover. Before automobile bodies were enclosed, open cars required such storage, especially in inclement winter weather. When repair, sales, and other activities began to complement car storage in garages, the term was extended to signify, as well, auto repair shops, dealer showrooms, and other facilities with large automobile-accessible work floors. The narrower use of the word still applies to domestic car parking today, and most houses in the United States have garages. After World War II, commercial garages were designed with open parking floors stacked one atop another, and the term "parking deck" became popularized.

THE ISSUE OF AESTHETICS

By whatever terms the parking of cars was designated, or places for parking identified, the whole issue of storing cars tended to receive little thought from ordinary Americans beyond the immediately practical. There was little consideration for what might be termed parking's visual aesthetics. Parking was seen as merely facilitative. Parking was not expected to contribute to the visual enjoyment of landscape. Parking contributed little to what architectural historian M. Christine Boyer labeled "city tableaux."[13] Boyer argued that the art of great city building was rooted in the creation of "stage set" spectacles to be widely shared as civic gestures. Parking in

America was not something important in making cities imageable or truly memorable. Visually exciting landscapes with temporal depth, as architectural historian James Marston Fitch argued, offered residents and visitors a strong sense of place.[14] Important was historical accumulation of intricate, complex, and often random infrastructure, built environment largely unpredictable and thus exciting to the eye and mind.

Nothing over the past century in America has proven as disruptive of traditional urban landscape as parking. Perhaps nothing has made American cities less memorable. Certainly, widened streets and new city freeways broke up traditional cityscapes and hastened the decline of the pedestrian-orientation of cities. But nothing fragmented urban space more than the parking lot. In the half-century between 1920 and 1970, most traditional big city downtowns substantially unraveled—disemboweled, building by building, by expanses of parking lot asphalt. Again, in the suburbs, buildings were increasingly sited in parking lot surrounds that substantially negated the traditional street. The transition from pedestrian-oriented to automobile-oriented landscape in America proved very disruptive, for the most part accomplished in ad hoc fashion. Americans allowed parking, as a land use, to evolve with little thought of control beyond that offered by market forces. Laissez-faire attitudes prevailed. Past indifference to parking's design opportunities only heightens today the sense of loss that more and more Americans feel as they experience the now pervasive automobile-induced sameness of landscapes. Nothing, for example, is so readily predictable than the typical parking lot, be it suburban or central city.

For many Americans the word "park" holds aesthetic leisure-time implication. Parks are landscaped places sylvan or otherwise picturesque—pleasure grounds to be enjoyed visually. Parks are protected places often enclosed by fences and walls, the connotation that gives linguistic tie to such very different kinds of place as parks and parking lots. The noun "parking" can mean a ground adorned with trees, lawn, or shrubbery, as in a park, and it can mean a landscaped strip down the center of or along the side of a street. What irony! What paradox! Nothing has negated more the park idea in America than automobile parking. Widened streets to accommodate parked cars saw widespread removal of street trees after World War I. As for off-street parking, nothing could be farther from the parkland ideal today than the typical parking lot apron marked off into individual parking spaces, with trees and other landscaping largely absent.

In the nation's central cities parking lots have long stood as stark symbols of ephemerality. The demolition of old buildings and the clearing of entire city blocks were rarely championed as enlightened city making. But rarely was it ever condemned as wasteful of environmental and social resources. Rather, the economic principal of "highest use" was invoked as land use rationale. Redundant buildings with inadequate demand and low profitability were best demolished, it was argued, and the land turned to more profitable use, even that of car parking. Land thereby "cleansed" stood available both for short-run profit taking and long-run recycling. In the latter instance, parking lots came to be considered a kind of land banking. Downtown parking lots were easily overlooked as things unto themselves. They were readily passed off as merely transitory between old and new. Accordingly, parking lots were made out to be a form of progress.

THE RISE OF MACHINE SPACE

Parking lots and parking garages are but pieces of a larger travel puzzle. They represent first-stage arrival in the motorist's termination of a trip. They connect the openness of a street with the enclosure of a building as ultimate destination. With the car conveniently stored, the commuter, the shopper, or the pleasure seeker is free to access a final goal. Parking is part of the infrastructure of auto movement, what planner Victor Gruen dubbed "transportationscape," a fabric comprised of "millions of square miles covered with the tinny surfaces of automobile, the concrete bands of highways, freeways, expressways, parking lots, cloverleaves and their spaghettilike convulsions, all tastefully trimmed with traffic signs, billboards and dangling wires of power and communication lines."[15] Gruen, perhaps more than any other writer of the 1950s and 1960s, was an advocate of parking lot solutions for urban problems. As a planning consultant, his ideas drove the actual configuring of scores of large shopping centers and the partial redesigning of several city downtowns. Today, the nation's transportationscape comprises 38 million acres of roads, streets, and parking lots.[16]

In 1988, the United States averaged 82 feet of roadway per capita, compared to approximately half that figure for the nations of Western Europe.[17] The automobile had greatly accelerated what geographer Ronald Horvath termed the rise of "machine space," area devoted to machines and their operation.[18] In America, it was primarily "auto territoriality," in the words of landscape historian John B. Jackson, or what we might simply call "auto space."[19] Auto space stands to anathematize the pedestrian. There the pedestrian treads only with great care. In auto space vehicles enjoy priority, so conflicts between cars and pedestrians are almost always resolved in favor of cars. Today, roadways and parking facilities consume over 30 percent of the developed land in most American cities and in excess of 75 percent of the land in many big city downtowns.[20]

Los Angeles came of age as a metropolis very much dependent on the automobile, a dependence that continues today. The city was a pioneer, not just embracing the motor car but developing early freeways and the prototypes of commercial buildings fully accommodating to customers who arrived by car — such as gas stations, motels, and drive-in restaurants. Drive-in architecture, prominent early in suburban Los Angeles, spread nationwide very quickly. But pioneering auto impact was also felt in downtown Los Angeles, with the automobile's accommodation fully evident in re-engineered streets and the demolition of buildings for large parking lots. By 1960, some 28 percent of the land in downtown Los Angeles was dedicated to streets and another 38 percent to off-street parking.[21] In other words, auto space, as machine space, consumed over two-thirds of the city's central business district.

Detroit became the acknowledged "Motor City," the focus of the nation's automobile industry. By 1972, some 74 percent of the city's downtown was devoted to automobile movement and storage (fig. I.3). The Detroit City Plan Commission's 1972 planning report summarized the car's intrusion: "The automobile has an insatiable appetite for space. It needs about 300 square feet when stored in its home quarters; 300 square feet when stored at its place of destination; and 600 square feet on its way. It further needs about 200 square feet for those places where it is sold, repaired and serviced. Thus an automobile needs 1400 square feet of living space. That is equal to the living space of a family unit." Auto use in Detroit was seen as not only wasteful of space but as disruptive. In advocating a revival of mass transit in the city, the report emphasized the "aesthetic costs" of automobility. The city's residents, it asserted, suffered from an "assault" upon their "senses and sensibilities." With nearly complete automobile-orientation, Detroit had suffered "a loss of human scale." Too much of the city was "a massive and oppressive conglomeration of boulevards, freeways, parking lots, filling stations, drive-ins, ramps, and interchanges." The "isolated spaces left over for human activities," the report's authors argued, seemed "discontinuous and somehow uninviting." The city's built environment lacked "uniting and cohesion."[22]

Auto space in and around big city downtowns appeared all the more negative for the disruption and loss engendered by demolition. Downtown

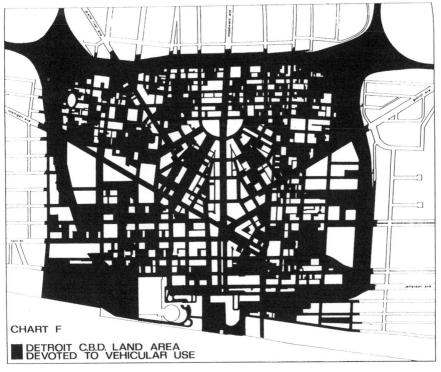

CHART F

DETROIT C.B.D. LAND AREA
DEVOTED TO VEHICULAR USE

FIG. I.3

Diagram of downtown Detroit showing area devoted to automobiles, 1972. More land
was dedicated to automobiles, either moving or parked, than to any other use. "Auto
space" is shown in black. *Source:* Detroit City Plan Commission, *Urban Transportation
and the Detroit Bus System* (Detroit: 1972), chart F.

Detroit appeared eviscerated (fig. I.2). Parking lots not only took up enormous quantities of real estate but, for the most part, looked wrenched from
an earlier urban order, with disorder readily discernable in relic structures
still extant. In general, all automobile-dominated downtowns, not just Detroit's, appeared disrupted to some degree. In place of solid cityscape of traditional pedestrian-orientation stood the vacuous interruptions of parking
lot emptiness. Only in cities with healthy mass transit (in New York City,
Chicago, Boston, and San Francisco, for example) did something of the
pedestrian-oriented city substantially survive in downtowns.

Urbanist Jane Jacobs was one of the first to attack the parking lot as an
anti-urban form. Parking lots in city centers resulted from widespread demolition, she noted. It was as if it had been necessary to tear down the city in

order to save it. Jacobs saw in urban parking lots what she called "the curse of border vacuums." Parking lots formed borders, she wrote, and borders in cities usually made for destructive neighbors. She defined a border as "a single massive or stretched-out use of territory." Parking lots were barriers across which pedestrians moved with difficulty. Even as destinations for motorists, they were overly ordinary and, in their single use, deadening to adjacent streets. "Borders can thus tend to form vacuums of use adjoining them. Or to put it another way, by oversimplifying the use of the city at one place, on a large scale, they tend to simplify the use which people give to the adjoining territory too, and this simplification of use — meaning fewer users, with fewer different purposes and destinations at hand — feeds upon itself." A kind of "unbuilding," or running-down process, was set in motion. Thus parking lots were "instruments of city destruction" that could "disembowel" a city. "City character is blurred," Jacobs continued, "until every place becomes more like every other place, all adding up to Noplace."[23]

THE SCHOLARLY RECORD

Against the weight of accumulated indifference and nascent criticism, it is no wonder that few scholars, beyond traffic engineers and other planning specialists, vigorously engaged parking as a topic, let alone as a topic with broad social and environmental implication. Most of the scholarly writing on parking appears in engineering journals and trade magazines and offers pragmatic advice on solving parking problems based either on systematic research or some other practical experience.[24] Rapidly increasing street congestion, especially in big cities, prompted traffic regulation. The first rules for automobiles were put into effect in New York City in 1903, and the city's police were charged with oversight. As traffic management became increasingly technical, with long-term planning essential, engineering and planning skills came to the fore. Separate municipal traffic departments were established in cities across the nation. But most traffic engineers actually found themselves lodged in, and dominating, city planning departments.

Organizations, such as the Institute of Traffic Engineers, were created to facilitate communication from city to city and from state to state once state highway departments were mandated. Instructional programs were established at many universities including Yale, Rutgers, and the University of Michigan.[25] Private research groups, such as the Eno Foundation for Transportation, became important publishers, along with government agencies, of reports and articles on parking. Books appeared, such as Geoffrey Baker and Bruno Funaro's *Parking*, a review of parking lot and parking garage design published in 1958.[26] Nonetheless, few authors working within the problem-solving tradition assessed the role of parking as a variable in overall landscape design. An exception is Mark C. Childs, whose recent book *Parking Spaces* treats the aesthetic as well as the functional implications of parking in the development and redevelopment of American cities.[27]

Other scholars have given little emphasis to parking of and by itself. Parking was treated as but one element of the commercial strip in Christopher Tunnard and Boris Pushkarev's *Man-Made America: Chaos or Control?*, an assessment of environmental change in post–World War II America.[28] Architectural critics Peter Blake, in *God's Own Junkyard*, and Ian Nairn, in *The American Landscape: A Critical View*, skeptically assessed the changes wrought along American's roadsides, including that of parking lot reorientation.[29] John B. Jackson, on the other hand, found functional value, if not aesthetic merit, in such emergent automobile-oriented places.[30] Fuller appreciation came with the now classic *Learning from Las Vegas*, written by Robert Venturi, Denise Scott Brown, and Steven Izennour.[31] To them, the strip was not totally disordered in a breakdown of traditional landscape. The parking lot, the giant sign, and related programmatic architecture did combine to offer visual order, at least to rapidly moving motorists. But to geographer Edward Relph, every strip looked and communicated essentially the same. He decried the commonplaceness (what he called the "placelessness") of new automobile-oriented landscapes, placing the roadside's monotonous homogeneity fully at the doorstep of planners, engineers, and architects caught in the myopia of single-purpose problem solving.[32]

So also has parking been treated tangentially by scholars writing the history of roadside architecture. Our own consideration of gas stations, motels, and drive-in restaurants as place-types in the American highway experience focused more on structures and less on the open spaces of driveway and parking lot surrounds.[33] As the eye is drawn to architectural substance, so also is the mind drawn. Writers tend to see the American roadside as architecture rather than as architecture and space together.[34] Architectural historian Richard Longstreth, while focusing on building form, did consider parking space in two recent books concerned primarily with Los Angeles, one a history of shopping centers and the other a history of drive-in restaurants and supermarkets.[35] The history of the commercial parking garage remains largely unexplored; assessment of the lowly domestic garage has only recently begun.[36]

Parking we argue, is more than a mere adjunct of architecture. Of course, parking lots and parking garages enable the accessing of buildings as people shift from movement by car to movement afoot. But they are also landscape expressions with intrinsic physicality and functionality of their own. They stand with clear spatial and temporal dimension. They are usually clearly bounded, with their boundaries requiring appropriate entrance and exit behaviors. They open and close, functioning cyclically day to day and week to week over set durations of time. They are deliberately constructed, furnished, and signed in ways facilitative to narrow ranges of activity, and their programming is conducive to repeated ongoing human behavior. The parking lot, as a ubiquitous form, has proven no mere temporary aberration. Suburban landscapes built around parking facilities are fully intended to be permanent. In most big city downtowns, numerous are the parking lots well over 70 years of age. The life expectancy of the typical lot may well equal, if not exceed, the life expectancy of the average newborn American male or female.

Landscape reflects the accumulated and integrated actions of individuals and social groups governed by cultural traditions that are shaped substantially by economic forces. The city, as physical form, is defined by three fundamental morphological elements: buildings as structures, the interstices of open space between buildings, and streets as paths for movement.[37] Parking, it should be emphasized, figures directly in all three. Garages structure the parking function as enclosed space. Parking lots separate buildings and, like garages, access or service them in facilitating travel. Curbside parking, for its part, contests the street as traffic artery. Parking could not long remain just an afterthought in city making. Parking was fundamental to how modern cities functioned and how they were experienced.

Automobiles not only provide essential transportation, but as machines for rapid movement, they symbolize modernity. Landscapes without automobiles are quintessentially "anti-modern" in the thinking of most Americans today. In American cities, much of the street-life (or the excitement of public space) derives from the presence of moving and parked cars. There is, whether critics of the American scene are wont to recognize it or not, an

automobile "aesthetic" that offers architects and planners (especially transportation planners) extraordinary opportunity. Streets largely without automobile traffic, and totally without parked cars, are read by most Americans
as empty and uninteresting, and, accordingly, as uninviting. The value of
roadside places, such as gasoline stations, motels, and fast-food restaurants,
is judged today as much by what goes on in their parking lots as by what
goes on inside. Is the lot full? What kinds of vehicles are parked there? Is
access easy? Unfortunately, the inability to imaginatively embrace the car,
especially the parked car, has resulted in substantial planning failure in the
United States.

It is easy to conceptualize parking as a category of concern largely separate from all else. It is easy, given the current compartmentalizing of knowledge, to focus on aspects of parking demand and capacity, the overwhelming preoccupation of traffic planners. It requires, perhaps, more subtlety of
mind to consider how parking impacts the human habitat as landscape. It
requires more subtlety, perhaps, to consider parking's full place-making implications. How does parking contribute to the overall experiencing of
landscape as that container of human life organized as meaningful place?
Places defined at different scales nest in landscape, providing meaningful social contexts through which behavior can be anticipated and directed.
By practiced "reading" of the built environment, life's satisfactions can be
more readily obtained, and life's dissatisfactions more readily avoided.[38]

Places have symbolic meaning as well as physical substance. Places nest
in landscape as "to whom it may concern" messages waiting to be read variously by potential users.[39] Place meaning is a matter of belief, attitude, and
intentionality. Thus a parking lot, as a place, can potentially symbolize
a wide range of meaning, although in any society degrees of consensus
reached through repeated sharing of experience come readily to the fore.
Understanding what automobile parking means requires consideration of
differing points of view. There is, of course, the orientation of the traffic engineer whose job is to anticipate parking behavior by tying intended program to carefully considered physical design. But there are, as well, the ori-
entations of the entrepreneur (who seeks profit or other benefit), the
politician (who, in pursuing the art of the possible, manipulates the legal
environment for parking), the manager or employee (who actually runs a
parking operation day to day), and, of course, the user (who, as resident,
customer, or member of a workforce, actually parks a car in a given place).
As well there is the citizen as taxpayer since, in the final analysis, much of

the social cost of parking in America is borne through taxation, with the government functioning as the nation's transportation problem solver of last resort.

As automobile owners, most of the readers of this book are already, to varying degrees, experts on parking. As authors, we do not pretend to bring to the topic special insight other than a willingness to synthesize and assess in essay form what previously has been written about parking in America. We are scholars — a geographer and a historian — smitten with an interest in the automobile's impact on America's landscapes and places. However, we are also creatures of our American roots, no more and no less than other Americans. Parking pervades our lives to the extent that we too are substantially dependent on our automobiles for everyday mobility. What we do offer, however, is a new approach — a clear focus on parking as a commonplace of everyday life.

PART

1

PARKING AS
MODERN CONVENIENCE

Americans are a hurried people seemingly always on the move. They are a practical people dedicated to doing things efficiently and with minimal cost. They like to think themselves resistant to undue authority: to be flexible in mind and action in the pursuit of personal satisfaction. They crave success, especially of the materialistic kind. Prized are life's conveniences. All of these things (and more) the automobile reinforces. Indeed, for most Americans today automobiles not only enable but also symbolize much of the above.

Perhaps, nothing is more important to car-owning Americans than the sense of convenience that automobility implies. In travel, the motorist determines the destination, sets the route, and chooses the time. There is no dependency on a corporate timetable: be it of a transit company, a railroad, or an airline. Travel can be fully personalized by car in terms of destinations bundled into trips, travel companions chosen, and even cargo carried. Besides the car, all that is needed is adequacy of street and highway and, of course, adequacy of parking.

It is parking most of all that makes auto use convenient. Without places to park, driving remains most inconvenient. Cocooned in their vehicles, motorists move rapidly to destinations. But where to store the cocoon upon arrival? That was the problem crucial to keeping American cities functional once widespread car use came to the United States in the years just before World War I. Would parking in public streets at curbside suffice? What role should off-street parking play? Would off-street parking be privately owned as a kind of commercial enterprise? Or would it be publicly owned as a kind of public utility? Just how would automobile convenience be sustained?

PARKING
AT CURBSIDE

The automobile came unobtrusively. Americans hardly suspected that the primitive "horseless carriages" that appeared around the beginning of the new twentieth century would not only change substantially how people traveled but, by altering travel habits, would also change fundamentally America's geography. In 1900, automobiles on the nation's streets and highways numbered in the thousands. Motorcars were little more than sporting devices, machines for the amusement of the well-to-do, who could afford the costs of purchase and maintenance. By 1920, however, there were some 8 million automobiles registered in the United States, and 10 years later some 23 million.[1] It was assumed initially that motor-powered vehicles would merely replace horse-drawn vehicles. As with carriages and wagons, it was assumed that barns and livery stables would suffice for overnight auto and truck storage, and that motor vehicles in use during the day would be accommodated at curbside whenever and wherever need arose. With the coming of mass-produced cars for the middling classes, however, old ways of thinking and doing quickly became obsolete.

At first, it appeared that motorized transport would reduce the total number of vehicles on the nation's streets and highways. Weren't trucks bigger and more efficient than horse-drawn wagons and capable of doing more work accordingly? Confidently, one observer predicted as late as 1912: "Traffic speeds will increase as the number of motors increases, and also as the number of horses decreases. Each motor truck replaces several horse-drawn rigs, so the total number of vehicles on the streets may reasonably be expected to decrease, even allowing for the natural increase in the amount of business done."[2] What was not anticipated, of course, was the rapid embrace of the motorcar by a spectrum of Americans who had never before owned a horse, let alone a carriage. Unforeseen was the traffic-slowing congestion that widespread automobile ownership soon created.

In big city and small town downtowns alike, traffic congested, a function of vehicle numbers, their competition with pedestrians, and a general lack of curb space for parking. In the small farm town of Tabor, Iowa, the local newspaper editorialized in 1917: "Leave your car at home Saturday night, you who live in Tabor or live close in, especially. It is very difficult for people coming in from the country or surrounding towns a little late on Saturday afternoon, to find a place to park their cars."[3] Car ownership soared in the agrarian Midwest, with commercial farmers, as a class, among the very early adopters of the new automobiles. So also did auto ownership soar in the Midwest's metropolises. In 1924, there were 242,322 motor vehicles registered in Detroit, or an average of 2,850 motor vehicles to the square mile.[4] In Chicago, traffic counts showed that every weekday on downtown streets there were about 175,000 motor vehicles, 10,000 streetcars, and nearly a million pedestrians.[5] Every morning, wrote traffic specialist Miller McClintock in 1927, some 850,000 residents of Chicago, or approximately 25 percent of the entire population of the city, left their homes and journeyed an average of 4.5 miles to the Loop, or business district, an area less than one mile square.[6]

After 1920, Iowa main streets might have their problems on market night, but downtown in every big city traffic congestion reached emergency proportions every workday. Postcard publishers delighted in depicting business streets clogged with traffic cities were made to look exciting and vital in the press of the downtown activity pictured. In Los Angeles, cars parked at the curb constricted the street as traffic way, a compound of vehicles and pedestrians mixing in the public right of way (fig. 1.1). It was one thing to marvel at the big city crowd, but it was quite another to manage the congestion that commuting and other kinds of daily travel placed on central business districts. In 1910, there were approximately 16,000 automobiles registered in Los Angeles County, but by 1918 there were some 110,000. Over the next 5 years the number increased 300 percent to about 430,000, one car for every 3.6 Angelenos.[7]

Cars and people might mix on city streets, but they did so problematically. Accident statistics were disturbing. Between 1916 and 1920, for example, some 5,700 people were injured in motor vehicle accidents in Newark, New Jersey, alone; 362 people died. On average, therefore, 4 people were injured every day, with one death occurring every 16 days.[8] Traffic

FIG. 1.1

Postcard view of Broadway Street in Los Angeles, 1917. The city's principal shopping street was serviced by streetcars around which automobiles maneuvered; street capacity was reduced by other cars parked at curbside. Here was a scene exciting to the eye, a place worth picturing for the urban energy implicit. But jammed-up traffic also meant lost time for drivers and, by implication, the dysfunction of wasted energy.

congestion not only spelled inconvenience and frustration for motorists and pedestrians alike but carried serious life and death implications as well.

Highest traffic densities invariably occurred at city centers, where commuters and shoppers, among others, focused in daily cycles of ebb and flow. By the mid-1930s, literally every American municipality of any size had mapped the flow of traffic both through vehicle counts and surveys of motorists coming and going downtown. In Detroit in 1936, it was found that more motorists came from the more affluent neighborhoods northwest of downtown rather than from the blue-collar, largely German and Polish

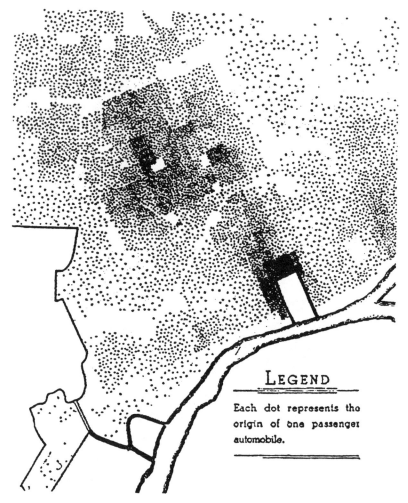

FIG. 1.2

Points of origin of automobiles entering downtown Detroit, 1936. Each dot represents the origin of one passenger automobile. Through surveys, traffic engineers sought to better understand the "where and when" of auto movement so they could plan street improvements and anticipate parking needs. *Source: Street Traffic, City of Detroit, 1936–1937* (Lansing: Michigan State Highway Department, 1937).

areas to the northeast (fig. 1.2). Detroit was laid out on flat terrain, but even where steep hills and narrow valleys channeled traffic flow, as in Pittsburgh, the overall pattern of vehicular movement was very much the same from city to city (fig. 1.3). On maps, major thoroughfares stood out as heavy black lines focused on central business districts. Two "rush hour" periods stood

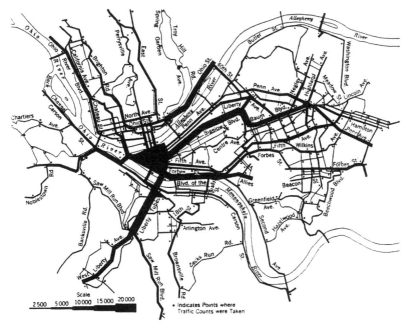

FIG. 1.3

Traffic flow patterns in Pittsburgh, 1933. The typical American city had but one large commercial district to which and from which traffic moved in diurnal cycles. *Source:* Lewis W. McIntyre, "The Scientific Approach to Traffic Problems," *Civil Engineering* 6 (Sept. 1936): 577.

out everywhere on workdays. The lesser traffic peak was early in the morning when people left home to travel rather slowly downtown, and the more intense period was late in the afternoon when they hurriedly returned home.

Of course, not everyone arrived at and departed from big city business districts by car. Indeed, in cities with a mix of subways, elevated transit, or commuter railroad lines, as well as streetcars, there was less automobile dependence. In Chicago in 1920, only 18 percent of those entering the Loop area each workday did so by car.[9] But in cities with less well developed transit or with heightened auto mania, such as Los Angeles and Detroit, upwards of 40 percent of the daily downtown traffic was car-oriented. Ultimately everyone who arrived in the downtown became a pedestrian, as people completed their travel on foot (fig. 1.4). Within downtown districts, the flow of foot traffic was also found to display clear geographical and temporal regularity. Where tall office buildings and large department stores clustered, the highest pedestrian densities were invariably found.

FIG. 1.4

Broadway Street in Los Angeles, circa 1920. Whether arriving by car or by streetcar, commuters in America's big city downtowns ultimately became pedestrians, accessing offices or stores on foot. As streets were widened to better accommodate cars, sidewalks were narrowed, crowding people. Displaced were vendors and many other activities long traditional to the public right-of-way.

Skyscrapers, with their large scale, generated substantial ebb and flow. Where numerous skyscrapers clustered, as in New York City's financial district, it was clear that relatively few office workers could commute by automobile, as only limited curbside parking was available. Planner Raymond Unwin calculated that the day population of the Woolworth Building (for over a decade the world's tallest structure), if spread along both sides of Broadway on sidewalks 20 feet wide, would extend for one and one-quarter miles. Assuming that only one-tenth of those workers drove to work, their parked cars would completely fill Broadway for nearly a mile.[10]

TRAFFIC REGULATION AND STREET IMPROVEMENT

Municipal governments were forced to take action as automobiles and trucks congested downtown streets. Formulated similarly, from city to city, were laws regulating motorized traffic. Until the beginning of the twentieth century, police in most cities gave little attention to controlling traffic except to monitor parades or other special events or react to fires and other emergencies. In 1903, policemen mounted on horseback were assigned to traffic duty on Manhattan's busiest streets, their attention directed to the street intersections that regularly snarled. Standard hand and whistle signaling was quickly adopted, with police officers mounted on stands for visibility. In 1913, permanent towers were erected in New York City, Detroit, and several other cities equipped with semaphores and colored lights to signal "stop and go." Such "crow's nests" were quickly superceded, however, by automatically timed signal lights first introduced in Cleveland in 1914.[11] Standardized red, yellow, and green lamps were arrayed either vertically or horizontally on posts erected at street corners or hung from cables over street intersections. Their sequencing, from intersection to intersection, fostered a steady traffic flow on major thoroughfares.

Another way to speed traffic was to widen streets. Typically, most downtown city streets were wide enough to accommodate vehicular traffic in two directions, but traffic was often slowed or stopped by streetcars moving at the center of the street. On narrow streets, motorists were further prevented from passing streetcars on the right when cars were parked at curbside. Traffic also stopped when motorists maneuvered in and out of parking spaces. Given that both streetcars and curbside parking both seemingly stood as urban necessities, street widening was commonly promoted as the best means of increasing street capacity.

The widening of a street usually came at the expense of sidewalk space, with the diminished sidewalk, in turn, crowding pedestrians. Occasionally, sidewalks might be "arcaded" or moved inside a building's wall to accommodate street widening (fig. 1.5). More commonly, however, buildings were cut back, with entirely new facades attached along new sidewalks, or buildings were raised up and shifted back on their lots. Then again, and this was especially true of thoroughfares widened beyond central business districts, an array of buildings along one side of a street, block after block, might be demolished to make way for street improvement. Commerce Street in downtown San Antonio was widened from 36 to 50 feet, including 12-foot sidewalks on both sides of the street. Most of the buildings were cut back, but some, such as the 5-story Alamo National Bank, were picked up and moved back some 16 feet.[12] A survey of 233 cities in 1924 revealed that 71 had completed one or more street-widening projects, and 41 had additional projects under way.[13] Municipalities exercised rights of eminent domain in taking private land to accommodate street widening.

Even where overall street widths remained the same, curb cutbacks at intersections were commonly made. Sharp corners, where curbs literally met at right angles, were cut back into broad curving arcs to facilitate mo-

FIG. 1.5

Scheme for improving the Chicago Loop. Both arcaded and raised sidewalks are included in this suggestive diagram. With various proposals, few of them financially feasible, planners sought to excite interest in downtown improvement calculated to better integrate the automobile into the traditional walking city. *Source:* "Raised Sidewalks and Traffic Separation Urged for Chicago," *American City* 35 (Sept. 1926): 335.

torists glancing down cross streets and turning at intersections.[14] So also did the one-way street come into popularity. Detroit's first one-way street coupling was installed in 1939 to relieve the press of north-south traffic that even a widened Woodward Avenue could not accommodate. One-way traffic was found to increase street capacity upwards of 30 percent, with substantial increase in speed of movement as well. By 1954, Detroit had over 60 miles of one-way streets.[15] One-way designation reduced accidents it was found. But more signage was required compared to regular streets. And motorists usually ended up traveling farther to reach destinations since additional circling of blocks was often required. Merchants were disadvantaged when traffic moved only in one direction in front of their stores, essentially denying them access to motorists in one of two rush hours.

More dramatic was the cutting of new streets. In Detroit immediately north of downtown, an east-west downtown bypass was constructed on a swath of cleared land one block wide. High Street, once 80 feet wide, became Vernor Highway, 120 to 150 feet in width. Almost every city entertained grand thoroughfare plans conceptualized as part of a local "City Beautiful" initiative. Produced in Chicago, Cleveland, Buffalo, and other cities were extensive downtown civic centers featuring large parks served by broad new thoroughfares.[16] In Indianapolis, it was the Veteran's Plaza area. Later, freeway or expressway construction made a dramatic impact. Freeways, radiating from or encircling central business districts, came to the fore after World War II, although the idea originated and was widely publicized as early as the 1920s in many cities.[17] The Arroyo Seco Freeway in Los Angeles opened in 1939. In Detroit, Vernor Highway, across the top of downtown, was replaced by the Fisher Expressway in the 1960s.

CURBSIDE PARKING AND THE PUBLIC STREET

Initially, motorists were free to park their vehicles very much at random along the margins of city streets. When they were relatively few in number, parked cars and trucks fit in readily, but when vehicles accumulated in great numbers, they were clearly problematical. Certainly, parked cars reduced a street's carrying capacity, thus congesting traffic. But, as well, curbside parking increased traffic volumes in its own right when motorists in large numbers cruised on downtown streets in search of empty curbside spaces. Rather than spend substantial sums of money in widening existing streets, or in building new streets or freeways, traffic circulation could be improved merely by eliminating parked cars from curbside. And through banned parking, street cleaning would be facilitated, and during the winter months in northern areas, snow removal would be made easier. But, most important of all, banning curbside parking would encourage investors to more rapidly develop private off-street parking facilities.[18]

Surveys confirmed that where curbside parking was prohibited, street carrying capacities increased upwards of 45 percent. A 40-foot street without parking was equivalent, as a rule of thumb, to a 68-foot street with parallel parking.[19] But banning or otherwise regulating curbside parking raised the important issue of just what a public street should be. Should streets be uni-functional, developed merely as traffic arteries? Or should multiple activities, including parking, be encouraged? Traditionally, city streets facilitated movement from place to place, but they also served as temporary repositories for activities brought out-of-doors from the private spaces of adjacent buildings. Retailers, for example, often displayed and sold goods from in front of stores. Business streets served as a kind of extended market place where vendors sold from pushcarts and wagons and off of motor trucks. In residential areas, streets were readily expropriated by children for play and by adults for neighborhood events and other socializing. Well into the twentieth century, most urban localities were blessed by a rich and diverse street life.

America's preoccupation with automobiles substantially changed the view of the street. "As the arteries are to the human system," argued A. T. Erwin in *The American City* in 1911, "so are the streets to the physical well being of a city." "The street provides the means of circulation," he continued, "and any factor which checks or impedes its flow is a serious menace to the public good."[20] The *Municipal Journal* provided a broad checklist to remind readers that streets served various purposes. Streets accommodated wheel and foot traffic certainly. However, they also provided space for mass transit and for other communication and public utility technologies: telegraph and telephone lines, water and gas mains, sewers, and, in big city downtowns especially, steam-heating pipes. Streets were lined by fire hydrants, fire alarm boxes, letter boxes, trash containers, street lights, and sundry other furnishings that enabled city life.[21] The issue of what streets were good for, however, was resolved in the courts. At first, litigation raged over use of municipal police powers in regulating traffic. In Massachusetts, the court ruled: "The primary purpose of a street is for passage and travel, and . . . unauthorized and illegal obstruction to free use come within the legal notion of a nuisance."[22]

Translated into auto use, the right to move a car was superior to the right to park a car on the public way, and when or where parking caused a net loss to the public good there should be limitation.[23] Put another way: "Unlimited parking may properly be allowed at all times in all business districts were it does not cost the traveling public more than it saves those who park, nor interfere with the expeditious movement and safety of street traffic, and with reasonable access of vehicles to the curb."[24] The city street became increasingly utilitarian, and the functionality of through movement was made essential. Statistics were compiled to reinforce that view. A Detroit survey showed that an average of 3,380 lineal feet was available for parking cars per frontage mile of typical street. Allowing 20 feet per car, a total of only 165 cars could be "dead parked" along each side of a mile-long thoroughfare. Those cars, however, filled potential traffic lanes capable of sustaining a free flow of upwards of 4,000 cars per hour.[25] The street as traffic artery thus became, according to one observer, "a thing unto itself, an independent design type."[26] The right to mobility became a preoccupation, and the street's other uses dropped largely from sight and mind.

REGULATING CURBSIDE PARKING

Municipal authorities recognized early that parked cars could obstruct access to fire hydrants, thus seriously hampering the fighting of fires. Almost universally, parking at hydrants was made illegal. Cars parked close to intersections could obstruct views cross streets. Thus parking within 15 to 20 feet of corners was likewise banned nearly everywhere. Safety zones associated with boarding of streetcars, loading zones at the entrances to hotels, theaters, and other important points of foot traffic generation, and construction zones, where equipment and materials regularly moved, were also among the categories of curbside space prohibited to parking. It was obvious that parking should be banned at alley and driveway entrances and in front of garage doors and loading platforms.[27] To drive a car was not a right, but a privilege. So also was parking on city streets. Such privileges were subject to the powers of municipal regulation, and even municipal prohibition.

Where traffic frequently congested, the simplest and most readily enforced means of eliminating parked cars was a total parking ban. Indianapolis was one of the first cities to do so on selected downtown streets. Most cities banned parking only for selected hours of the day or week. The decision by Los Angeles officials to ban curbside parking in that city's downtown core during business hours and to limit parking to only one hour in the peripheries of the business district, brought a firestorm of protest not only from motorists, but from retailers and other business people. Indeed, a marked decline in banking and retail trade was observed after the program took effect in 1921. It was quickly discontinued.[28] A revised system was tried in 1924 with parking eliminated on 4 north-south and 6 east-west streets, with 30-minute parking elsewhere during working hours.[29] In 1927, there was 63,844 feet of regulated curb space for the parking of some 3,547 cars in downtown Los Angeles, but by 1930 that total had been reduced to 52,442 feet for only 2,913 cars.[30]

Some cities, such as Boston, sought to restrict the number of parkers as well as the number of curbside parking spaces. In Boston, motorists were required to purchase and display a metal license plate tag when parking downtown. Chicago similarly charged a "wheel-tax" for the privilege of parking on any city street.[31] Chicago adopted a downtown parking plan in

1928 that prohibited parking from 7 A.M. to 6:30 P.M. throughout the down-town everyday except Sundays and legal holidays, and on Saturdays after 3 P.M.[32] Parking rules changed constantly as the political makeup of city councils changed. Pressures for and against curbside parking were brought by merchant organizations, automobile clubs, and other interest groups. Most cities sought to keep parking regulations simple with blanket rules zonal in coverage.

Fully related to the problem of cars parked at curbside was the loading and unloading of trucks. As with downtown streets, back alleys also tended to fill with parked cars, blocking access to freight platforms. Many alleys were overly narrow or otherwise unsuitable for large trucks, so deliveries were necessarily handled at curbside out front. There, in some cities, load-ing and unloading zones were designated during certain hours. In Bos-ton, the delivery of coal, ice, and any commodity packed in barrels or kegs was prohibited throughout downtown between the hours of 9 A.M. and 5 P.M. Drivers at all times were prohibited from backing into curbs, thus projecting their trucks into traffic lanes.[33] In many cities, however, delivery trucks were allowed special privileges at curbside upon payment of special license fees.

The "jitney" was another problem of the 1920s, starting with Los Ange-les and Kansas City. The jitney bus was an ordinary private car, sometimes enlarged, used by its owner to carry passengers for a fee, a fee usually lower than that charged by transit companies. Anyone with enough wherewithal to purchase a used car could enter the business. As rush-hour traffic con-gested on major thoroughfares, slowing streetcars to a snail's pace, more and more transit riders diverted to jitneys, which promised faster as well as cheaper transport. Jitneys, therefore, substantially undermined the profit-ability of mass transit in numerous cities. Even though they were made il-legal, the estimated number of jitneys operating in Detroit in 1926 stood at some 700.[34] They were small in number, in comparison to the 250,000 pri-vately registered motorcars in the Detroit area, but the jitneys' flitting in and out of traffic to pick up and drop off passengers came to constitute a se-rious traffic hazard and substantially slowed the traffic flow. Most cities, in legalizing taxicabs, reserved sections of curbside downtown for taxi stands, just as had been done earlier with stands for horse-drawn cabs. Taxis were strictly limited in number, and their operators were charged license fees. Taxi service, therefore, was not competitive price-wise with mass transit and did not undermine the streetcar's viability in most places.

A bewildering assortment of parking configurations resulted when motorists freely wedged their vehicles together at curbside. Some cars might be left parked parallel to a curb, others at varying angles to it, and still others double-parked. Overall a jumble of vehicles could result. Widely advocated by 1930 was something called "automatic auto parking."[35] The idea was simple. Spaces were to be permanently marked off with painted lines indicative as to where and how cars were to be arranged. Slots would be carefully spaced to ease the motorist's maneuvering in and out. No longer would the excesses of negative territorial instinct be tolerated, specifically the ad hoc and highly individualistic expropriating of the public right-of-way for car storage.

How to sign such designated parking space? In Portland, Maine, city officials had the curbs painted with different color combinations signifying different restrictions. "Where no parking is allowed, the curbs are painted black and white; where cars may be parked fifteen minutes, the horizontal and vertical faces of the curbs are painted white; and where one-hour parking is permitted, they are painted orange-yellow," detailed one observer.[36] Signboards posted at major approaches to Portland's downtown alerted drivers to this coded system. By the 1930s, however, curbs painted yellow or painted red came to signify no parking in most cities. At the same time, standardized signs were adopted that communicated regulations in simple language. Wording such as "No Parking," "Police Order," or "Two-Hour Limit" communicated with force.

By 1940, parking signs were highly standardized, by mandate of many state highway departments. At the threshold of World War II, upwards of 80 percent of all traffic signs in American cities were parking-related.[37] Today, a single standardized system is almost universally in use (fig. 1.6). Parking signs, or individual signs arrayed together, provide the following information arrayed from top to bottom: 1) the nature of the restriction or prohibition imposed, 2) the time of day that it is applicable, 3) the days of the week in which it applies, and 4) other relevant information. Like almost everything else in traffic control, parking signs were standardized as professional organizations, such as the American Association of State Highway Officials, and governmental bureaucracies, such as the U.S. Bureau of Public Roads, exerted influence.

PARALLEL VERSUS ANGLE PARKING

The positioning of vehicles parallel to the curb, in end-to-end rank or array, interfered less with traffic flow. In cities where all downtown streets

FIG. 1.6

Signs typical of parking regulation today.

were narrow, there was no other alternative. Where downtown streets were broad, angle parking, with cars slanted in at the curbs, could be maintained even as traffic levels began to build. In Indianapolis, police regulations required that cars be parked at a 45-degree angle.[38] Curbside capacity, of course, varied with the angle imposed. In a space where only 4 cars could be parked parallel to a curb, 5 could be parked at a 30-degree angle, 7 at 45 degrees, and 10 at 90 degrees. Illustrated are the space requirements relative to parking 4 cars at various angles (fig. 1.7). A street 54 feet wide arranged for angle parking provided only 2 lanes for moving cars whereas the same street arranged for parallel parking provided 4 lanes. Difficulty arose when motorists backed out of angled spaces into oncoming traffic, increasing opportunity for accident.

It was easy to park when the driver simply slanted his or her car forward to the curb. Parallel parking, on the other hand, required a tricky backing maneuver that had to be diligently practiced to be perfected. Getting out of the parking space and into traffic again, however, was easy and involved

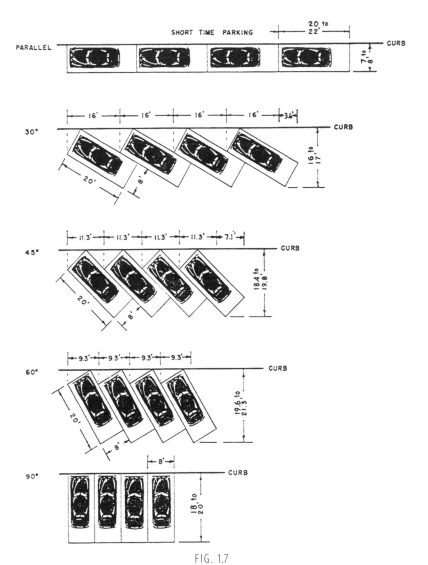

FIG. 1.7

Parking angle and curbside parking capacity. Diagrams show varying amounts of length and width required for parking four cars at different angles to the curb. *Source:* Adapted from J. Ross McKeever, *Shopping Centers Re-Studied: Emerging Patterns and Practical Experiences*, Technical Bulletin no. 30 (Washington, DC: Urban Land Institute, 1957), 39.

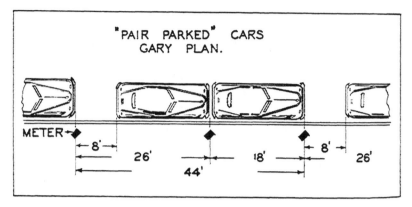

FIG. 1.8

"Pair-parking" or "tandem parking" in Gary, Indiana, 1949. Different parking arrangements were explored to find the parking maneuver that least interfered with traffic flow. *Source:* "Cars 'Pair-Parked' in Gary," *American City* 64 (May 1949): 170.

full visibility.[39] As parallel parking accommodated fewer cars, it substantially opened up streets to view, making them, in relative terms, look vacuous and making the downtown appear a place more for passing through. On the other hand, angle parking made downtown streets look crowded and made the downtown appear more a place for terminating trips.

When parallel parking replaced angle parking, traffic did speed up. In Wichita, average speeds on effected streets increased from 11.8 miles per hour to 16.1 miles per hour between 7 A.M. and 7 P.M. on weekdays. Street carrying capacities increased from 8,800 to 9,500 vehicles per day.[40] Accident rates fell. In Kansas City, an average of five accidents per block per year was reduced to only one accident.[41] Various studies nationwide found accident rates falling from between 12 to 63 percent.[42] Angle parking, however, could be made safer. Many cities required motorists to back into angled spaces. With visibility in pulling out maintained, there were fewer mishaps. Seattle, for example, continues the practice today.

In order to accommodate more cars in a parallel parking configuration, "pair-parking" or "tandem parking" was introduced in the 1940s. Parking spaces were paired with spaces left between the pairs to facilitate maneuvering in and out (fig. 1.8). Where streets were exceptionally wide, a third car might be allowed to double-park, centered on the two paired vehicles at the curb. Center-street parking was another scheme widely adopted where wide streets permitted. In most places with center-street parking, parking at curbside was prohibited, and traffic lanes thus were placed at a

FIG. 1.9

Postcard view of Detroit's Cadillac Square (now Kennedy Square), circa 1925. Public open space was readily usurped for automobile parking in many of the nation's cities. Depicted here is Detroit's symbolic center. City hall and the city's largest hotel anchor the scene in the background.

street's margins rather than located down its center. Such an arrangement proved hazardous because motorists and their passengers were required to cross moving traffic when leaving and returning to their parked cars.

Center-street parking worked best in cities with broad public squares or plazas. Detroit readily converted its Cadillac Square into a giant parking lot to accommodate some 300 automobiles arrayed in two ranks two blocks long (fig. 1.9). Parking in the square began about 1910 when police, impounded cars illegally parked elsewhere in downtown and removed them to that location. All across the United States, especially in county seat towns with courthouse squares, public space was systematically diverted to parking, thus eroding traditional open space in favor of auto storage.

It was a challenge, one observer wrote, to learn "the gentle art of squeezing one's machine in between the tail lights of the car ahead and the headlights of the car behind, without smashing either, without coming as close as fifteen feet to the hydrant, without rubbing the rubber off the right rear tire, and without spending all the allotted twenty minutes in merely completing the maneuver."[43] Women, thought to be less skilled with cars, were stereotyped as preferring outlying shopping districts where angled parking, both on-street and off-street, prevailed. Articles in women's magazines, and even how-to-do-it manuals for women drivers, were published offering advice.[44] Other than the crumpled fender, nothing irritated drivers more than the hooked bumper. After World War II, bumpers were fully integrated with car bodies. Previously, they extended out and away. As the bumpers of different cars were set at different heights, cars readily hooked on to one other, and untangling them often required jacking up one of the vehicles. A hooked bumper was an occasion for neighborly cooperation when strangers stopped to bounce a car on its springs, hoping the offending car would dislodge, thus avoiding use of a jack.

PARKING METERS

Parking regulations were successful only if they were diligently enforced. Motorists with illegally parked cars needed to be ticketed, and on occasion their cars hauled away. Heavy fines usually proved necessary before chronic abusers took parking regulations seriously. Yet violating parking ordinances hardly constituted a serious misdemeanor, and numerous were the humorists who trivialized parking enforcement in newspapers and magazines (fig. 1.10). Very quickly the motorcycle policeman came to the fore not only to monitor speeding and other traffic infractions but to monitor parking also. It was much too costly to employ foot patrolmen to adequately oversee downtown parking. But motorized officers could move quickly and cover considerable ground in short order. Especially useful were the three-wheeled "servi-cars" developed for parking enforcement by Harley-Davidson. With rods tipped with white or yellow chalk, patrolmen cruised at intervals up and down city streets marking tires, in systematic surveillance, to identify those who parked longer than the posted time. What truly revolutionized parking enforcement, however, was the parking meter.

The parking meter made its first appearance in Oklahoma City in 1935 (fig. 1.11). The idea belonged to Carlton C. Magee, editor of the *Oklahoma News* and chairman of the Traffic Committee of the local Chamber of Commerce.[45] A parking survey had established that some 80 percent of the cars parked at curbside in Oklahoma City's downtown belonged to the employees of downtown businesses. Overparking was an endemic problem, and patrolmen, even those equipped with motorcycles, seemed unable to monitor the situation adequately. With little turnover of parking space, downtown retailers were clearly hurting. What was needed, it was argued, was "an efficient, impartial, and thoroughly practical aid to parking regu-

FIG. 1.10

Cartoon lampooning the use of municipal police powers in the enforcement of curbside parking regulations. *Source: Hoosier Motorist* 18 (Jan. 1930): 14.

lation, requiring even less police supervision."[46] Magee approached the Department of Engineering and Management at the nearby Oklahoma Agricultural and Mechanical College (today's Oklahoma State University). A student design contest produced a crude coin-operated mechanism for timing parking.[47] With an improved design, Magee formed the Dual Parking Meter Company to market the idea of metered parking and con-

FIG. 1.11

A parking meter in downtown Oklahoma City, 1935. Parking meters, first introduced in Oklahoma's capital city, were adopted nationwide very rapidly. They greatly facilitated parking enforcement and became an important source of revenue for cities and towns. *Source:* "Parking Meters in Oklahoma City," *American City* 50 (Aug. 1935): 61.

tracted production of the mechanisms to a Tulsa manufacturer. A host of companies soon flooded the market with competing meters. Among the brands marketed in the 1940s were Karpark, Mark-Time, Park-O-Graf, and Red Ball.

City manager O. M. Mosier, outlined for readers of the *American City* Oklahoma City's pioneering use of the new device. One hundred and seventy-four meters were installed on waist-high posts, and parking spaces were marked off in white paint parallel to the curbs of selected downtown streets. When a nickel was inserted and a knob turned, a clockwork mechanism was engaged, and a green flag appeared in a small window. When the timing mechanism ran down, indicating that paid-for time had elapsed, the flag disappeared. In later models, the red flag appeared, which provided a clearer indicator that time had expired. At first, meters were set for either 30- or 60-minute durations depending upon their location, but all could be re-calibrated for as little as 10 minutes or as long as 2 hours.[48] Extensive publicity accompanied meter introduction, especially through newspaper and radio advertising. Both the city government and the chamber of commerce sought to encourage public acceptance and to head off outright opposition. Metering represented a substantial change of public policy in that the public was to be charged for what had previously been free.

Only two days after Oklahoma City's meters went into use, their operation was temporarily enjoined by the Oklahoma District Court. Plaintiffs alleged that the coin-operated devices impaired their right to free use of the streets as specifically provided by state statue. But the court, in dissolving the injunction, ruled that "use" meant "travel" and that parking, which could be prohibited altogether to ensure travel, could be regulated even by charging a fee.[49] In some states, protesters criticized curbside metering as a form of unauthorized taxation. The Alabama Supreme Court agreed, invalidating Birmingham's early use of meters. The state constitution, the court ruled, did not authorize municipal governments to exercise its police powers for taxing purposes.[50] What the courts did not invalidate, state legislation sometimes did. In North Dakota a farmer-dominated legislature passed laws strictly prohibiting parking meters everywhere in the state. In New York, New York City was enjoined from using them.

During 1936, some 26 additional cities adopted parking meters, starting with Dallas, Fort Worth, and El Paso in Texas. By the end of 1938, the number had grown to 85 cities in 26 states, with an estimated total of 24,000 meters installed.[51] By 1942, some 347 municipalities, large and small, were using them, and by 1951, about 2,800 cities and towns.[52] Detroit began experimenting with meters in 1948, despite opposition from automobile interests. New York City was finally allowed to install them in 1951. Parking meters, of course, spread worldwide in subsequent decades — to some 87 countries by 1960.[53] Perhaps the last to adopt them were the cities of the former Soviet Bloc. "There has been a good bit of confusion on the streets of Warsaw this fall," reported the *Chicago Tribune* in 1999. "The advent of parking meters is evoking more animated debate than just about anything, including membership in the European Union."[54]

The parking meter's rapid and eventually universal spread can be understood on at least two grounds. First, they worked. Meters, when linked with diligent enforcement, did regulate parking and, through regulation, did produce parking turnover. On-street parking capacity was thus greatly increased. This was a lesson quickly learned by the nation's downtown merchants, most of whom were vigorously opposed to parking meters initially. Second, parking meters produced a revenue stream, with fines levied on "expired" meters becoming an important source of municipal income in cities everywhere.

Meters installed in downtown Salt Lake City in 1936 were removed the next year due to strong protests. Retailers claimed a loss of business of over 25 percent "while the gadgets were in operation." The term "gypometers" was widely circulated.[55] It was widely believed that a majority of a store's customers parked directly out front at curbside, so anything that potentially diminished such presumed accessibility was to be opposed. Surveys, of course, established otherwise. A parking inventory in Los Angeles established that 68 percent of those parking on downtown streets made no retail purchase whatsoever. Only 16 percent of the total volume of purchases made downtown were made by occupants of cars parked on city streets.[56] Indeed, enforced parking restrictions in Los Angeles actually increased the number of cars entering downtown for shopping purposes.[57]

Parking meters came to be valued for the sense of orderliness they brought to downtown streets. Initially, Oklahoma City's meters were installed only on one side of some streets. "On the unmetered side is confusion," claimed the city manager, "cars jammed together fenders being bent, cars being pushed in front of fire hydrants, and traffic being impeded by those who are trying to back into cramped parking spaces, while shoppers can hardly find parking spaces open." "On the metered side," on the other hand, "is order, sufficient room for every car to be parked and driven out quickly and easily, and there are usually parking spaces open so that shoppers can park within a block of any store or bank."[58] Merchants in the small Texas town of Pampa, who had successfully lobbied to have parking meters removed from selected streets, lobbied to have them put back again two months later. Only merchants on metered streets, it turned out, were enjoying sales increases.[59]

It was the rise of outlying shopping districts that downtown merchants in big cities really needed to fear. There, curb parking tended not to be metered, and stores often provided their customers with off-street parking lots. A nationwide sample of downtown merchants in 1926 established downtown traffic congestion as their most serious difficulty. Congestion was attributed to 1) unenforced curbside parking regulations, 2) lack of off-street parking facilities, 3) narrow streets, and 4) street cars. Business was being diverted to outlying areas, and downtown merchants knew it. Many were actually participating themselves by opening outlying branches. "They go where they can park," concluded one merchant.[60] Not only was it difficult for shoppers, who were increasingly car-oriented, to journey downtown and shop, but downtown stores found it increasingly difficult, and costly also, to deliver to outlying residential areas, although most big city department stores offered home delivery through the 1950s. As one observer commented in 1938: "The public is sadly inconvenienced by the immobile automobile, but the existence of great stores is actually threatened by it." Lack of parking downtown, he continued, "daily becomes more acute and depressing. On its solution depends the shape—and perhaps even the fate—of the city of the future."[61]

Towns and cities hard hit by the Great Depression saw revenues dwindle in the face of rapidly declining property valuations and rapidly shrinking property tax collections. In 1931, real and personal property in Oklahoma City was assessed at $169,774,658, but three years later the assessment was only $119,142,466, a decline of 28 percent.[62] With parking meters, however, a new source of municipal revenue was found. Not only did the nickels paid in by parkers accumulate, but so did the fines imposed for overparking. New meters paid for their installation usually within a year and earned equivalent sums year after year. Cincinnati, for example, applied three-quarters of the meter money collected to pay off the cost of meter purchase, retiring the debt on 735 meters in only 13 months. The city's 104 two-hour meters each produced about 70 cents per week, or a total of $3,785 for the year. By 1944, American cities were generating some $10 million annually from parking meters. By 1955, the figure had jumped to $76 million.[63]

Parking violation revenues grew to be substantial. Chicago, for example, issued some 4 million parking tickets in 1998, generating some $175 million.[64] The collecting of fines in recent years was greatly aided by computerization and threat of "booting." Computers brought memory to the system. Unpaid violations, once posted, could result in a locking up of tires, with cars made immovable by the "Denver boot." Municipal parking bureaus grew large. To the American scene came a new law enforcement type—the meter maid. Women, who were paid less than the male police officers, assumed most of the street-side parking enforcement duties, bringing cost savings to parking surveillance accordingly. Also to reduce costs, most cities undertook their own meter repairs. In San Francisco, 11 meter repairmen were required for the city's 9,500 meters in 1947. Meters were regularly checked at a rate of some 800 a day, with most repairs made on the street.[65]

CONVENIENCE

Finding a curbside space downtown was one thing. Finding a space close enough to one's destination was quite another. Parking in the same block was usually deemed convenient by drivers. But what about the next block? Or the block beyond? Convenience was something "pychological" — something based not on real distance so much as on cognitive distance. The acceptable walk was always a relative thing, a function of geographical context, time available, specific purpose at hand, and the nature of one's destination viewed in terms of what one intended to do there. Surveys from city to city confirmed as much (table 1.1). The larger the business district, the farther motorists were willing to walk once they parked. Employees commuting to work were willing to walk farther than shoppers, and motorists intending to stay for long periods were willing to walk longer distances than those staying for only short periods. In downtown St. Louis it was found that motorists who parked for less than 15 minutes walked, on average, only 218 feet. Those parking for over 3 hours walked, on average, 713 feet (fig. 1.12).

The streetcar and the motorbus offered transportation unburdened by need to park. Indeed, transit riders tended not to walk undue distances at all, at least in the downtown. Transit convenience was further enhanced by the package delivery services of downtown stores. Shoppers could come and go without the cost or worry of parking, and without the need of toting

TABLE 1.1
Distances parkers are willing to walk, based on city size

Population	Average Distance Walked to Shopping Place
under 25,000	234 feet
25,000 to 50,000	295 feet
50,000 to 100,000	391 feet
100,000 to 250,000	539 feet

SOURCE: "Park and Walk," *Downtown Idea Exchange* 19 (May 15, 1972); reprinted from U.S. Bureau of Public Roads, *Parking Guide for Cities* (Washington, DC, 1956).

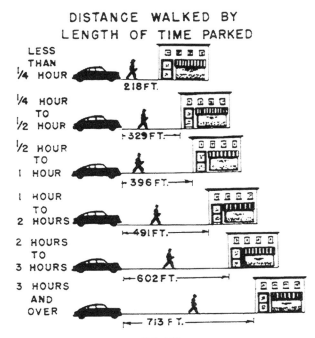

FIG. 1.12

Relationship between length of time parked and distance walked. *Source: A Comprehensive Parking Survey of the St. Louis, Missouri Central Business District* ([Jefferson City, MO]: 1951), 42.

home purchases. An adult male dressed in business suit and overcoat could stand comfortably in a space 5 square feet. But, as Geoffrey Baker and Bruno Funaro argued, dress that same individual in a Ford, Chevrolet, or Plymouth, and a road space of a least 150 square feet was necessary, if only to stand still in a traffic jam. When a pedestrian "puts on his car," they observed, he or she increases bulk by about thirty times.[66] Apart from the inconvenient need to park it, the automobile was, and remains, an incredibly inefficient mover of people space-wise. Assume that the typical car entering a big city town contained 1.75 persons. Thus a single traffic lane could handle in one hour some 1,575 people. In contrast, that same lane, at least under light traffic conditions, could accommodate upwards of 13,500 streetcar passengers.[67]

As automobiles filled city streets, the time-efficiency of streetcars declined precipitously. Motorists readily saw streetcars as a prime, if not the prime, cause of congestion. Streetcars moved on fixed tracks, stopping frequently to pick up and discharge passengers usually in, of all places, mid-street. Transit advocates, on the other hand, saw the reverse relationship. Eliminate curbside parking or, better still, reduce the number of motor vehicles, and everyone, motorists and transit riders alike, would move rapidly. Government could reduce the number of cars coming downtown by requiring drivers to display costly parking permits, or the costs of parking could be raised substantially. Then transit's potential, as a rapid mover of people, would be regained.

Instead, it was the streetcar that declined and, in most cities, disappeared altogether. By the end of 1936, over 600 miles of streetcar track had been removed from city streets nationwide, with the federal government subsidizing the work through the depression-fighting Works Progress Administration.[68] Streetcars were replaced by gasoline-powered buses (or electric trolley buses), which were rationalized as more maneuverable, and thus a better fit with autos and trucks. Buses could shift from lane to lane as needed. They could pickup and drop off riders at curbside, and cars, for their part, could more readily pass a stopped bus. The number of pedestrians in city streets would be vastly reduced. Additionally, nothing so dramatic or drastic as the complete banning of curbside parking would be required.[69] Buses, however, were less comfortable than streetcars. They were noisy. Passengers were easily jostled. Buses belched exhaust fumes into the air. And when traffic congested, as it did in most places anyway, they moved no faster than the streetcars they replaced.

Admittedly, Americans in most cities simply rejected mass transit. They were fed up with corporate mismanagement. Streetcar companies were overcapitalized; accordingly, most of them had delayed the maintenance and upgrading of their equipment. Scheduling was poor, and service often erratic. Incivilities too often played out among strangers. But primarily it was the strong embrace of the automobile that spelled transit's decline. Americans favored the convenience that the motorcar implied. Hypothetically, cars were seen as moving people faster and delivering them more directly to downtown and other destinations. They afforded privacy and avoidance of public insult, at least when in close proximity person to person. And if one were lucky, parking would not be a problem. The automobile appealed to individualized survival instincts. Luck, as in finding that convenient parking space, could be optimistically assumed. Important was the pleasure of automobile ownership and of driving one's own car as a status symbol. Driving was exhilarating, and owning and using a car stood symbolic of success. Freedom of movement by car, and the convenience it implied, symbolized upward social mobility. One's car, and one's sense of persona, easily conflated, especially among those enamored with speed.

If motor vehicles came unobtrusively to the American scene early in the twentieth century, they did not remain unobtrusive for long. As for parking, horse-drawn carriages and wagons might be accommodated along the margins of streets as need arose, but by 1920 automobiles and trucks had simply overwhelmed downtown streets in big cities and the main streets of many small towns as well. Cars stacked up at curbs, frequently two deep. Parked cars retarded traffic, and congestion was only amplified by motorists searching for parking spaces. Drivers maneuvering their cars into and out of parking spaces further compounded the situation. Parked cars reduced access to fire hydrants. They blocked the entrances to buildings. Parked cars reduced transit's effectiveness. Clearly, curbside parking needed to be regulated by municipal authorities. And regulated it was.

What ought public streets be? Should they foster a diverse street life, with cars somehow restricted to the encouragement of pedestrianism and other diverse activities? Or should streets be primarily, if not exclusively, motorized traffic ways? Streets, it was determined, were to be traffic arteries, and all other activities, including curbside parking, were to be subjugated to the needs of moving vehicles. Traffic would be regulated by signs, including electric signals that were specially timed. Streets would be widened and made one-way to sustain greater carrying capacities. Increasingly, parking would be regulated and even restricted. The marking off of individual parking slots made for more efficient use of curbside space. Time limitations, when enforced, fostered turnover of parked cars, thus increasing on-street parking capacity. The parking meter not only mechanized enforcement, reducing its cost substantially, but it produced a solid revenue stream.

As we subsequently discuss, meter revenues could be turned to creating off-street parking lots. With the number of motorcars increasing ever so rapidly decade by decade, cities had no choice but to accommodate parked cars primarily off-street. Sheer numbers simply demanded it. Curbside parking, for all its convenient implications, was simply inadequate, especially in big city downtowns. Parking, angled or parallel, might suffice along small town main streets, but in big cities parking lots would quickly prove absolutely necessary. Curbside parking would continue to be important in most places, but steep prices meant that it would primarily serve the short-term parker. Shoppers would continue to seek curbside spaces as the parking alternative of first choice, with curbsides continuing to imply maximum convenience. Curbside parking would also continue to add a sense of visual interest to downtown streets, the margins of which could appear totally vacuous without it. Americans, in liking their cars, liked to see them close at hand. Curbside parking thus continued to energize American cities both functionally and visually.

COMMERCIAL
PARKING LOTS

Automobile congestion downtown built to critical levels in the nation's largest cities in the years prior to World War I and in virtually every other city, no matter its size, in the years immediately thereafter. As parking at curbside proved inadequate, especially as cities imposed street-side parking bans, motorists were forced to look off-street, opening opportunity for commercial parking operations. Off-street parking took two forms: enclosed storage under a roof and open-air storage out-of-doors, the former ultimately evolving into the parking garage or parking deck and the latter becoming and remaining the ubiquitous parking lot.

At first, indoor car storage involved conversion of livery stables, carriage shops, and other structures originally supportive of horse-drawn transport. Soon other kinds of buildings (theaters, warehouses, and small factories, for example) were also being converted to car storage, given their large size, diminished utility vis-à-vis original function, or convenient location. By 1915, most cities also contained at least a few garages purposefully built for car parking, a topic on which we elaborate in a subsequent chapter. Early storage garages, irrespective of their origin, were used primarily for long-term parking, especially winter storage in cities where open or unenclosed cars precluded year-round use. But as larger and larger storage garages were constructed, short-term parkers also were accommodated. Parking lots, the emphasis of this chapter, appeared initially in some cities as adjunct to other car-related businesses, such as gas stations or body shops. In other cities they first appeared from the beginning as independent, self-standing enterprises.

Downtown parking lots were established in spaces open or clear of structures, specifically on vacant lots or portions of developed lots not actually built upon, such as the front and back yards of houses along residential streets immediately adjacent to downtowns. More commonly, however, old structures, such as houses, were demolished, and their cleared spaces were given over to parking. Indeed, the clearing away of buildings for car storage became, after 1920, the single-most important "urban renewal" activity in America's central cities. As traffic congestion made downtown increasingly inconvenient, retailing, wholesaling, and many other kinds of economic activity began to shift to outlying business locations, reducing demand for rental space in downtown commercial buildings. As structures aged and became both physically and functionally obsolete, low demand and the resultant low rents generally precluded renovation. Many landlords with marginal downtown properties found renting parking space by the hour or day more profitable than renting floor space by the month or year.

THE PARKING BUSINESS

So who created the first parking lot? We are not sure that anyone can say. The parking lot was an idea so logical, given that the demand for parking space was universally so great, that business entrepreneurs in a host of cities must have simultaneously brought the innovation to the fore. A 1914 news item in the *Horseless Age* announced: "Herman R. Schmitt, for the Duquense Parking and Automobile Company, has leased the Henry Phipps property at Cecil and Duquense Ways, facing the Allegheny River, for automobile parking purposes. The location of the lot will assure its popularity among automobile owners. It is within two minutes walk of at least six great office buildings and as many large stores." [1]

For many decades Detroit's Max Goldberg was given credit for creating the nation's first commercial parking lot. Goldberg, operator of a seat cover and cartop upholstery business in downtown Detroit, was said to have begun renting out parking space in a vacant lot adjacent to his business in 1917. [2] True, the General Auto Trimming Company, with Mrs. Anna Goldberg as president, was listed in the 1918 Detroit city directory at the northeast corner of LaFayette and Cass Streets. [3] However, a 1924 photograph of that intersection seems to confirm that the company's operation had actually been on the intersection's southwest corner, across the street from the *Detroit News* (fig. 2.1). Pictured in 1924 was a previously affluent residential zone into which business enterprise had been intruding for a decade or

FIG. 2.1

Parking lot at LaFayette Boulevard and Cass Avenue in downtown Detroit, 1924. Shown is what may have been the city's first commercial parking lot and what was long thought to have been the first parking lot in the United States. *Source*: "An Airplane View of the Addition to the News Plant," *Detroiter* 15 (Jan. 28, 1924): 48.

more. The parking lot in question, surrounded by a tall fence plastered with advertising signs, occupied two properties from which houses had been removed. Born in 1886 in Odessa, Ukraine, Max Goldberg emigrated to Detroit in 1907, becoming part of a growing Jewish community dominated by small shopkeepers, the more ambitious of whom remained ever vigilant of emerging and potentially lucrative business opportunities.

It is ironic that Detroit's first commercial parking lot sprang from a shop selling "California tops." It was not until automobiles were enclosed, first by cloth convertible tops with side curtains and then by solid metal covers with glass windows, that parking a car unprotected out-of-doors became fully practical. After 1910, local fabricators city to city made kits available for "weatherizing" (or "winterizing" as the case might be) open vehicles. But after 1915, first with luxury sedans and coupes and then with lesser models, manufacturers began to offer cars with metal- and glass-enclosed bodies. For the Goldbergs, the Detroit market for cartops reached a sudden plateau, and what had started in an almost offhand manner — car park-

FIG. 2.2

Parking lot at Thirteenth and Arch Streets in downtown Philadelphia, circa 1926. Cleared of buildings, capped with asphalt, and anchored at the corner by an attendant's stand, the typical parking lot in Philadelphia, as in other cities, was utilitarian in the extreme. Here billboards hid some of the scars of demolition left on adjacent buildings. *Source:* Urban Archives, Temple University, Philadelphia.

ing—became their principal occupation. Under the name Service Parking Grounds, Inc., the Goldberg firm had 36 downtown parking lots in 1936, the year of Max's death.[4] Service Parking was not the only parking lot chain in Detroit. Also in 1936, Randolph Parking Grounds operated 12 lots, Larned Parking, 10, Madison Parking, 8, and Public Parking Grounds, 6. However, Service Parking had expanded beyond Detroit to operate parking facilities in Toledo, Chicago, Pittsburgh, and Washington, D.C., becoming one of the nation's first large-scale parking corporations.[5]

By 1920, every large city had dozens of small business entrepreneurs variously experimenting with parking as a profit-making enterprise. Many succeeded in establishing multiple locations, all networked under a single corporate logo. In Philadelphia, W. W. Smith started with a single lot in 1921, rapidly expanding in 5 years to 20 lots and 8 garages.[6] As in Detroit, Philadelphia's downtown parking operations occupied lots cleared of buildings, with corner lots being preferred (fig. 2.2). In Los Angeles, also in 1920, Andrew Pansini started with a leased property where he rented parking space and also ran a shoe-shining operation. In 4 years his business expanded to

24 parking lots and 2 garages; his shoe-shining days were in the past. Operated as the Savoy Auto Park System, the firm was parking upwards of 4,000 cars a day, with Pansini calling himself the "Automobile Parking King."[7] Also in Los Angeles, Walter Briggs hired on as a parking lot attendant to pay his way through the University of Southern California. On graduation, he managed the Coliseum parking for the 1932 Olympic Games, investing his earnings in a leased downtown parking lot. In 1961, his Saf-T-Park Corporation operated at over 100 Los Angeles locations, mainly downtown. As well, the firm was active in San Francisco, Sacramento, Reno, New York City, and Philadelphia.[8]

More common, however, was the small operator who stayed small, or who left the parking business after only a few years. In Detroit, only 3 of the 7 operators listed in *Polk's Directory* for 1923 were listed 3 years later. Of the 30 operators enumerated in 1926, only 7 remained among the 99 listed 10 years later, with all of the survivors being chain operations.[9] One is struck, looking at the names in directory listings year after year, how the operators were of various ethnicities: Arab (Gulbaz Khan), Armenian (Charles Vartanian), Greek (Thomas Azar), Irish (Paty Morhan), Italian (Joseph Gucciardo). Numerous were the Jewish names of central and eastern European origin, such as Abraham Brinkovitz, Mannie Dulberg, Al Feldman, Reuben Kravetz, Charles Soloman. The typical parking lot operator moved from one enterprise to another in search of success. For most, parking proved but a stepping-stone to something else somewhere else.

Despite operator turnover, the industry overall grew very rapidly. There was not a city in the United States that did not witness rapid expansion of its commercial parking. In downtown Birmingham, for example, the number of parking facilities grew from 5 in 1925 to 25 in 1935 to 101 in 1949, with storage capacity increasing from 441 to 3,361 to 9,915 cars accordingly. Whereas the overall space devoted to parking increased from 70,560 to 539,960 to 1,588,020 square feet in the 3 respective years, the number of operators in Birmingham increased only modestly, from 5 to 18 to 40. In sum, parking operations grew more in size than in number, with increased scale of operation dictating success.[10] In 1961, there were over 19,000 downtown off-street parking facilities in the United States, including some 11,700 surface lots and 7,300 garages. Some 90 percent of these facilities were privately owned. In that year, the parking industry employed about 36,000 people.[11] In 1996, the number of surface lots in cities stood at some 16,000, only about half of which were privately owned. However, the vast majority of the publicly owned facilities, the topic of the next chapter, were operated

TABLE 2.1
Breakdown of expenses for a hypothetical commercial parking lot

Expense Item	Percentage of Total Cost
Charge for land	33.9
Salaries	54.7
Insurance	1.0
Taxes	2.4
Maintenance	3.6
Utilities	4.4

SOURCE: Wilbur S. Smith and Charles S. LeCraw Jr., "Parking Lot Operations," *Journal of Property Management* 13 (June 1948): 267.

by private management companies. Through the 1990s, the commercial parking industry generated business in excess of $5 billion annually.[12]

Traffic engineers Wilbur Smith and Charles LeCraw Jr. undertook in 1948 to describe the typical commercial parking lot, basing their observations on a survey of 25 lot operators in selected cities across the country. The typical lot occupied a rectangle of some 25,000 square feet, with about 10 percent of the total devoted to automotive services, especially the sale of gasoline and lubricants. The typical lot could accommodate 112 cars if parked by attendants backing them into slots angled at 90 degrees and 92 cars if self-parked by customers heading them into slots angled at 45 degrees. By backing cars into position, a shorter turning radius was needed, thereby requiring less aisle space. The typical lot was surfaced in asphalt and was lighted for nighttime operation. It was located on leased land and was 12 years old.[13]

From respondent questionnaires, Smith and LeCraw analyzed operating costs (table 2.1). Land owned was valued from 43 cents to $6.09 a square foot, or $3.50 on average. For leased land (three-quarters of the operations), rentals varied from 8 cents to $1.00 per square foot per year, or 43 cents on average. The largest single operating expense, however, was labor: employee salaries varied from 1.1 to 18 cents per car parked, or on average 7.1 cents. Insurance costs ranged upwards of $2,500 annually but were pegged, on average, at 14 cents per car parked. Property taxes ranged upwards of $15,000 annually but averaged 8 cents per car parked. Finally, annual maintenance costs ranged up to $3,200, municipal license fees to $100, and utility costs to $25.[14]

Revenues varied widely. The lowest annual gross income reported was $7,000 a year, or 9 cents per car parked. This lot, located in a small city, charged customers 5 cents for the first 2 hours of parking, and 5 cents for each additional hour thereafter. The highest reported gross income was $131,000, or 93 cents per car parked. This lot, located in a large city, charged 25 cents for the first hour, and 10 cents for each hour thereafter. Calculated net incomes varied from $160 a year to $34,570, or from $2 to $209 per parking space. The average lot produced an annual net income of $53 per parking space, or 7.9 cents per car parked.[15]

Through the 1950s the vast majority of commercial parking lots in big cities involved land leased on a short-term basis, frequently month to month. Lessees paid landlords a percentage of their net, often 50 percent, while assuming all monetary risk in operating the lot. After 1960, management contracts came to predominate, with operators agreeing to manage a landowner's property for a specified fee for a set period, usually one to three years. Typical contracts provided that all gross income, less operating costs and management fees, be paid to the landlord on a periodic basis, usually monthly. When management contracts were in effect, pay rates, equipment purchases, operating hours, and parking fee schedules remained the right and responsibility of the landowner. The operator, in turn, provided only a qualified manager and other trained employees necessary for actual lot operation.[16] Accordingly, successful parking companies came to be management specialists, preoccupied with the hiring and training of personnel and the perfecting of operational procedures.

Parking lot work was socially stratified. Owner-operators and lessees not only set personnel policy but also arranged financing and oversaw marketing, among other entrepreneurial activities, aided, of course, by an office staff as the scale of operation dictated. Within large chains, each lot usually had its own manager who was responsible for tabulating receipts and making related bank deposits as well as supervising personnel, especially through the keeping of time sheets. Employees in "attended" lots included the attendants themselves, who actually parked the cars, and the cashier. In lots with "self-parking" and with automated ticket machines, the manager's role was reduced to emptying machines of their coins and maintaining lot security. Of course, no cashier was needed. The role of the parking lot attendant was not especially prestigious, and customer behavior was often rude or otherwise uncivil.[17] Paid a low hourly wage, forced to wear a depersonalizing uniform, and provided with a minimum of comfort (often in a cramped ticket booth flimsily constructed), the lot of the parking attendant was often an unhappy one.[18] Rapid turnover of personnel plagued the industry.

THE LARGE CHAINS

Franchising was never important in the parking business, unlike other automobile-related industries, such as automobile sales and repairing, or highway-oriented industries servicing motorists, such as gasoline retailing, lodging, and fast food. Franchising helped companies in those industries to expand quickly through the creation of chains or networks of look-alike stores. For parking companies, however, there were other ways of expanding. Successful players in the parking business aggressively pursued leases and management contracts as well as purchasing their own real estate. They expanded from city to city by acquiring or merging with other firms. There was nothing truly distinctive about how parking firms conducted business. Every company parked cars very much the same way, adopting the same new technologies as they were introduced. There were, wrote one observer, "no special ingredients or complex trade secrets that would give one company distinct advantage over another."[19]

In other industries, franchisers ideally offered franchisees important advancement along the learning curve of a business. They provided brand identity that, supported by various marketing strategies, promised patronage. Franchisees, on the other hand, offered franchisers important access to investment capital through their ability to tap local funding of sources. They brought proprietary interest to managing stores, dedicated management being essential to chain success. At work in the petroleum, motel, and restaurant industries, largely through franchising, was place-product-packaging.[20] Architectural design, signage, color schemes, interior decor, product line, level of service, and other variables were coordinated in the networking of look-alike facilities to achieve, through the defining of trade territories, better market penetration. Place-product-packaging engendered brand loyalty. Each new gas station or motel or fast-food restaurant presented a corporate face readily identifiable.

But parking lots were parking lots. For the most part, they existed not so much from building something new as by demolishing something old. Beyond signage, few of the accouterments of place-product-packaging readily applied. Parking lots did not involve architecture. There was no opportunity to manipulate interior decor. Product line was straightforward car storage. Level of service was, given the high costs of land and labor, almost always minimal. Parking was not the kind of commodity around which clear brand identities and brand loyalties readily developed. Motorists parked where convenient and affordable. However, other business activity "bundled" with parking at a given site was often branded — for example, where a gas station occupied one corner of a parking lot. In the 1960s, car and truck rental became an important adjunct to parking. The Budget Rent-A-Car System of Chicago expanded nationwide by establishing franchise offices at parking lot and parking garage locations in city to city.

Of course, the discerning motorist might come to recognize parking company logos as they repeated from location to location. Numerous firms came to operate nationwide, and several had foreign operations as well. Brief histories of selected firms illustrate their growth and national success.

Louis Diamond's first parking lot, combined with an oil-changing business, opened in Seattle in 1922. In the 1950s, the partnership of Lycette, Diamond and Sylvester innovated the "park-by-number" self-park system that allowed revenue collection without the expense of on-site parking lot attendants. In 1999, Diamond Parking Service operated at some 850 locations in 9 states, including California, Oregon, and Washington.[21]

David Meyers began his business career in 1923 by leasing a used car lot in downtown Newark for parking during the Christmas season. In the 1930s, he was joined by several brothers who previously had been in the wholesale produce business. In 1960, the Meyers Brothers Parking System operated some 25 lots and 4 garages in Newark's downtown as well as garages across the Hudson River in Manhattan, including facilities at such locations as the Pan American Building, the Seagram Building, and the Airlines Terminal Building. The firm also operated parking garages in London, with its architectural department offering design services to clients worldwide. In 1964, with 250 locations, the company was sold to Hertz, the car rental firm, which was controlled by the Radio Corporation of America (RCA). The chain was reduced to 104 locations, mainly in New York City and Boston, and was ultimately sold to Central Parking of Nashville, making it one of that firm's earliest acquisitions of the 1990s.[22]

The Allright Parking System originated in Houston in 1926. Under the direction of founder Durell Carothers, the chain grew to 461 parking facilities (in 17 U.S. cities and 1 Canadian city) in 1957. Long an affiliation of linked ownerships (at one point 29 corporations, 25 partnerships, and one proprietorship) the chain operated parking facilities in various cities and regions under a shared logo (fig. 2.3). Consolidated in 1962, the firm went public, with control falling in 1982 to the Hang Lung Company of Hong Kong, a development firm interested as much in Allright's real estate holdings as its parking business. However, in 1996, with downtown redevelopment in the United States at a standstill and the value of the firm's real estate vastly diminished, the company was sold to an investment syndicate

FIG. 2.3

An Allright Parking Corporation parking sign in downtown Columbus, Ohio, 1999.

comprising several investment firms and a cadre of long-time company employees. In 1998, the company, with 2,275 locations, was sold again, also to Nashville's Central Parking Corporation.[23]

Myron Warshauer's Standard Parking Corporation began in 1929 at his Standard Oil gas station in the Chicago Loop. Success in parking led to a range of family business ventures, eventually including Midas Car Care Service Centers operated in conjunction with company-owned parking garages. In 1998, when purchased by the Airport Parking Company of America (APCOA), Standard Parking operated at some 380 locations in 29 cities.[24] The Kinney Service Corporation was organized as a public company in 1962, combining the assets of a diversity of business holdings variously committed to car parking, car rental or leasing, building maintenance, and funeral services. The oldest of its parking operations dated from 1932. In 1967, the chain operated at 96 locations in 7 states. In 1997, when it too became a Central Parking holding, Kinney operated some 400 parking facilities nationwide. It was the largest operator in New York City.[25]

APCOA, founded by Alva T. Bonda and Howard M. Metzenbaum (later a U.S. senator from Ohio) in 1949, began with the parking concession for Cleveland's Hopkins Airport. By 1960, the firm was managing parking facilities at airports or downtown locations in 39 cities across 24 states. The firm had 258 locations in 83 cities (across 39 states, Puerto Rico, Canada, and Mexico) when it was sold in 1968 to the International Telephone and Telegraph Company (ITT). Sold in 1977 to an investor group, the chain was sold yet again in 1981 to Delaware North Companies, a diversified holding company. A separate but related company spread the APCOA logo across Europe, with some 140 lots and garages operating in 1985 in various cities from Vienna to London. In 1989, the North American and European chains were merged, only to be divided again 3 years later and the European operation spun off. In 1998, APCOA managed some 700 parking facilities; its owner, Holberg Industries, was headquartered in Greenwich, Connecticut. Following purchase of Standard Parking in 1998, the new APCOA/Standard chain involved 1,100 locations in 45 cities across the United States and Canada.[26]

Central Parking System, the parking industry's "ultimate survivor," originated in 1959 when Monroe J. Carell Sr. and Roy Dennis opened a small parking lot in downtown Nashville. However, one might consider that the firm's roots extended much further back in that Meyer Lachman, one of the company's longtime executives, began as an associate of Max Goldberg in Detroit. Central Parking's rise to the top of the industry followed purchase of the Kinney and Allright chains. In 2000, Central parking operated 4,454 parking facilities containing some 1.6 million parking spaces. Of those operations, 2,025 were under management contracts, 2,190 were under leases, and 239 were owned outright either independently or through joint ventures. Central Parking operated in 39 states, the District of Columbia, Puerto Rico, Canada, Mexico, Germany, and Malaysia, among other countries. The firm's largest lot, with some 12,000 spaces, was located at Miami's International Airport.[27] Adopted as early as the 1960s was an aggressive "take-away" strategy whereby, as described by one trade journal, the firm began to "woo lots away" from other current operators by promising landowners higher returns.[28] But merger and consolidation were the route most forcibly taken.

Los Angeles–based AMPCO System Parking was founded as a subsidiary of the American Building Maintenance Corporation in 1968. It remains independent. By 1999, its operations were spread across 1,466 locations in 24 states. The company became the nation's largest airport parking concessionaire when APCOA chose to emphasize institutional and downtown parking.[29]

Two other chains were founded in the 1960s: Parking Company of America (PCA) and Imperial Parking (Impark). Headquartered in Albuquerque, PCA operated at some 100 locations in 16 U.S. cities in the late 1990s. Impark was headquartered in Vancouver and operated at some 1,400 locations all across Canada and the United States, mainly in Minneapolis, Milwaukee, Buffalo, Richmond, and Columbus.[30]

The mania for merger, which propelled firms such as Nashville's Central Parking and Cleveland's APCOA to the top of the parking industry at the beginning of the new century, was stimulated substantially by changes in the nation's real estate investment market. The early 1980s was a period of extensive office building development in big city downtowns, and the cumulative value of surface parking lots in North America reached over $12 billion. In major metropolises, such as New York City, Chicago, and Toronto, parking lots were valued as building sites at from $500 to $1,000 per square foot. Observed one journalist: a 40,000-square-foot parking lot that had zoning for an 800,000-square-foot office complex might be valued at $40 per square foot of gross buildable area, resulting in a land value of $32 million, or $800 per square foot. However, with the rapid falling off of building activity in the late 1980s, the value of the nation's parking lots fell dramatically, to an estimated low of $5 billion in 1996.[31] In most cities, financing for parking lot acquisition virtually disappeared because expectations for resale were so very low.

When in the late 1990s building activity in big city downtowns began to revive, investors, especially those with real estate investment trusts, moved to position themselves in urban real estate markets, bidding up land values and thus property rents. Concluded one Houston real estate broker in 1998: "During the past 24 months, it has been very difficult to acquire urban properties in major markets that can be held as investments . . . [and] temporarily used as parking lots as a way to generate profit." Thus did Allright Parking, faced with soaring rents on leased lots and less and less lucrative management contracts, agree to a $585 million buyout by Central Parking. Financial analysts agreed that not only was Central Parking more aggressive in its competition for leases and contracts from locality to locality, but it was also more innovative in its management of lots. Lower operating costs en-

TABLE 2.2
Chain-operated parking spaces in downtown Indianapolis, 1989*

Company	Number of Spaces	Number of Facilities Controlled
Park Kwik	4,712	25
Denison	3,589	4
System	1,283	3
APCOA	790	4
Auto Park	499	5
Allright	388	6
Other	8,876	27
Total	20,137	74

* By members of the Parking Association of Indianapolis.
SOURCE: Member address list and map (Indianapolis: Parking Association
of Indianapolis, 1989).

abled the company to turn the money-losing operations of acquired chains
into profit makers. "Central is a well run company that finds innovative
ways to raise revenue and cut costs."[32]

The impact of the large chains varied from city to city. Various national
chains did dominate some big city markets, especially the cities where they
originated and from which, given their dominance, they were well positioned to expand. For example, Allright dominated its headquarters city of
Houston early on, as did Central Parking in Nashville, Standard Parking in
Chicago, and APCOA in Cleveland. Nonetheless, it is important to emphasize that in most cities local chains, which stubbornly resisted takeover
and were not inclined to expand to other places, were important, if not
more important, than the national operators. Significant also in these cities were operators of but one or two parking facilities. This was especially
true where parking facilities were built in conjunction with large downtown office buildings. Indianapolis was, and is, such a case in point.

In Indianapolis in 1989, several national chains, a regional chain, several
local chains, and numerous single- and two-facility operations were represented in a balance of vested parking interest (table 2.2 and fig. 2.4). In
the square mile centered on Monument Circle, there were 74 parking facilities with 20,137 individual parking spaces. Fifty-six percent of those
spaces were controlled by chains (operators with 3 or more facilities). The
national chains, APCOA and Allright, operated at 4 and 6 locations, respectively, with 790 and 388 spaces. System Parking operated at 3 locations with

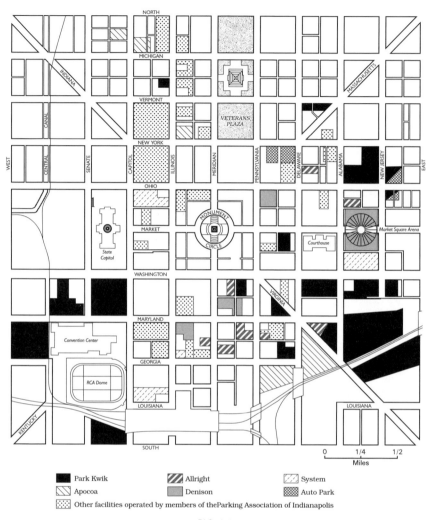

FIG. 2.4

Parking chain operations in downtown Indianapolis, 1989. *Source:* Member address list and map (Indianapolis: Parking Association of Indianapolis, 1989).

1,283 spaces. In comparison, locally based Denison operated 4 garages with 3,589 spaces. Locally based Park-Kwik, primarily a surface lot operator, was spread across 25 locations with 4,712 spaces. Among the Indianapolis-headquartered insurance and banking companies that operated parking in conjunction with their office towers were American United Life, Blue Cross/Blue Shield, and the Indiana National Bank.

PARKING AS LAND USE DOWNTOWN

Even before World War II, traffic congestion, and the lack of parking close to stores downtown, contributed to declining retail sales in most central business districts nationwide. As outlying business districts grew in importance after the war, and especially as large suburban shopping centers opened after 1950, retail activity first leveled off and then began to spiral downward in most downtown areas. Banks, professional offices, service providers of all sorts, and even corporate administrative functions joined in the exodus outward. With declining business activity came declining property values. In Baltimore, for example, property values downtown fell some $60 million, or 34 percent, between 1931 and 1946, reducing the city's tax yield by some $1.8 million per year.[33] The same was true of Boston. Reported Newsweek: "As far back as 1941, Maurice J. Tobin, then mayor of Boston, blamed traffic and parking congestion for a deterioration in property values of $465 million in ten years. Since most cities obtain about 25 percent of their income from property taxes on their central areas, the loss has made itself felt directly in municipal income."[34] Traffic congestion and the lack of parking in downtown Detroit cost property owners dearly. In 1944, there was an estimated shortage of some 2,000 parking spaces. Reported Traffic Engineering: "This is given as one reason for the location of business centers on the city's periphery, which reduced assessed values in the downtown section from $3 billion in 1931 to $2 billion in 1944."[35]

Paradoxically, solving the parking problem with off-street parking only intensified the decline of downtown property values and the fall of municipal revenue, inducing a spiraling downward of both. Most cities reduced tax assessments on aging and underutilized structures while maintaining relatively high assessments on land. The sustaining of high downtown land values reflected traditional thinking regarding the desirability of central location. Such taxing policy only encouraged more rapid and more extensive tearing down of unprofitable (and even marginally profitable) buildings for parking, reducing further overall property values and municipal revenues. With tax revenues down, cities were less able to upgrade streets, regulate traffic flow, improve mass transit, and otherwise work to make their downtown areas more functional in the face of accelerating automobile ownership and use.[36]

Demolition downtown became a growth industry in virtually every American city. At first, and indeed for decades, property owners in most cities persisted in viewing the clearing of buildings for parking as a kind of short-term expedience. Most landlords thought of parking as only a temporary land use that, although not paying a proper return on the alleged capital value of their land, would carry them without loss until such time as a "higher" or a more profitable use of land was possible. In other words, parking became part of the speculative stances whereby properties were held in anticipation of future development. After all, hadn't cities always expanded at their centers? And didn't the open parking lot stand sanitized for such development?

Whereas a parking operation became the quintessential stopgap use for cleared land, very few landlords sought to operate parking facilities themselves, preferring instead to lease their properties or put their properties under management contract to parking professionals. Short-term leases were preferred since one never knew when redevelopment might be possible. It could be next month or next year, and landlords needed flexibility to react. With demand for parking space constantly growing, and with parking lot operators aggressively competing for leases and management contracts, landlords also sought to play one operator against another in extracting the highest possible revenues, a strategy that also called for short-term flexibility. Produced in downtowns everywhere, especially around business district margins, was a ragged-looking landscape of ad hoc transition. Buildings disappeared in seemingly random fashion to be replaced by asphalted lots. Downtowns were fragmented, and traditional urban infrastructure was dissected piecemeal without a coordinated plan and with little thought to appearance. Indeed, the presumption that parking would be only temporary did preclude improvement even of the most superficial cosmetic kind. Parking lots, therefore, usually had a depressing effect on surrounding property values.[37] Noise, dirt, and the many other negative effects of car parking spilled over onto adjacent properties, often inducing disinvestment and additional clearance there. Parking lot–induced blight spread street by street like a contagion. Gaps appeared and multiplied, and the fragmentation of traditional city space spread in an epidemic of piecemeal clearance.

Once established, most downtown parking lots proved anything but temporary. Although fewer people were coming downtown to work and to shop, with business activity diminished accordingly, there were in most cities more automobiles than ever arriving downtown daily. Between 1928 and 1938, there was an 11 percent drop in the number of people entering downtown Philadelphia each day, but a 52 percent increase in the number of automobiles.[38] In Detroit, the people coming to the center each day dropped by 30 percent between 1925 and 1936, but the number of cars increased 6 percent.[39] In the 1930s it dawned on more than a few observers that down-

FIG. 2.5

Postcard view of Detroit's downtown, circa 1920. Depicted is a compact downtown, similar to centers in many big cities in the early 1920s, with car parking available largely at curbside along downtown streets.

town districts were declining relative to outlying business areas. More importantly, that fact, coupled with the impact of economic depression, suggested a reduced prospect even for long-term downtown redevelopment. Parking might well remain the "highest and best use" for cleared downtown real estate for a very long time.

Land use change in downtown Detroit illustrates this point. In 1920, Detroit was a metropolis of some 1.2 million people, a "boomtown" riding a wave of rapid expansion driven by an extraordinary increase in automobile manufacture. The city's downtown, relatively small for a city of Detroit's size but clearly reflective of the city's predominantly industrial economy, occupied an area of some two square miles oriented to the axis of Woodward Avenue northward from the Detroit River. Detroit's downtown was compact, a pedestrian and streetcar area anchored at its core by a cluster of skyscrapers surrounding city hall at Cadillac Square (fig. 2.5). In 1922, very little land was devoted to off-street parking (fig. 2.6). There were 28 garages scattered around the downtown edge, many of them converted livery stables or other older buildings given to auto storage as well as a few purpose-built garages. The 18 existing surface lots were more intrusive, with some lots located close to the very center of the downtown near the city's largest department stores.

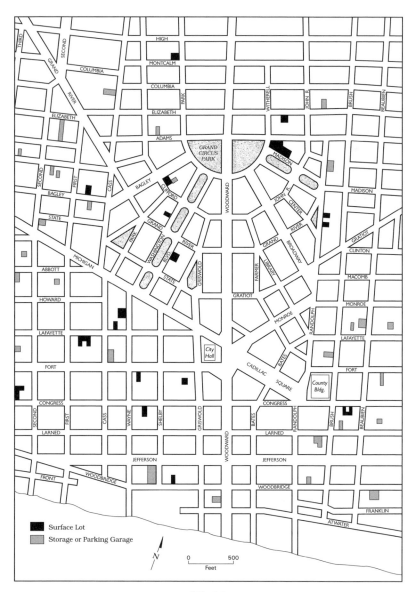

FIG. 2.6

Area devoted to off-street parking in downtown Detroit, 1922. *Source: Insurance Maps of Detroit, Michigan*, vols. 1–3 (New York: Sanborn Map Co., 1921), vol. 4 (New York: Sanborn Map Co., 1922).

Between 1920 and 1936, building demolition for parking lot development in Detroit became endemic. The graph shows the number of buildings, along with their assessed total valuation, that were torn down each of
these years for parking lots (fig. 2.7). The map of garages and surface lots in
1936 (fig. 2.8) stands in striking contrast to that of 1922 (fig. 2.6). Parking lots
surrounded the business district, especially in blocks where housing dominated before. Parking intruded, as well, into blocks densely built with warehouses and wholesale houses along the riverfront. Statistics collected
through the 1920s and 1930s substantiated the change. In 1927, Detroit had
110 "privately owned parking lots" in the "downtown area" with a capacity
for 7,720 cars; by 1933 the number had increased to 265 lots capable of holding 17,251 cars. In 1936, in what was designated in another study as the "concentrated retail area," there were 182 "open parking lots" with space for
23,425 cars. Still another source put the total lot capacity throughout Detroit's central business district in 1936 at 31,724 cars.[40] Whatever the count,
and however downtown was defined, a substantial proportion of the city's
traditional center-city fabric had been erased for parking. Strange new juxtapositions were to be found. Tall buildings stood cheek by jowl with lowly
parking lots in a strange new urban disjuncture of structural mass and open
vacancy (fig. 2.9).

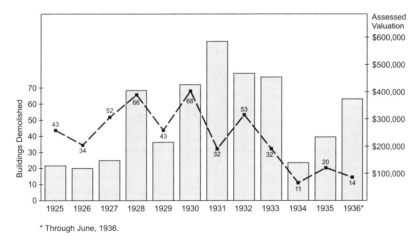

* Through June, 1936.

FIG. 2.7

Demolition for parking lots in downtown Detroit, 1925 to 1936. *Source:* Orin F. Nolting
and Paul Oppermann, *The Parking Problem in Central Business Districts* (Chicago: Public Administration Service, 1938), 2.

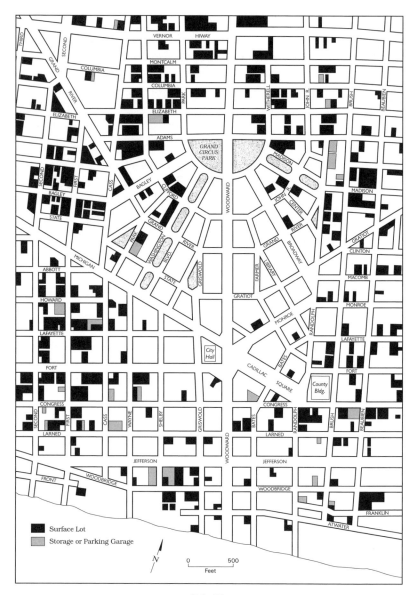

FIG. 2.8
Area devoted to parking in downtown Detroit, 1936. *Source: Street Traffic, City of Detroit, 1936–1937* (Lansing: Michigan State Highway Department, 1937), 163.

FIG. 2.9

Bagley at Clifford Street in downtown Detroit, circa 1930. The new Michigan Theater Building (the theater portion today has been gutted for a parking garage) is viewed across a new parking lot, the corner of which is anchored by an attendant's shack. Such juxtapositions became common in big city downtowns.

Detroit was by no means alone. In Los Angeles, only 5 parking lots existed in a 102-square-block area downtown in 1915, but 40 could be counted in 1920, and over 100 in 1925.[41] In Chicago, the number of people commuting to the Loop each workday decreased by over 7 percent from 1926 to 1938, but the number of automobiles increased by over 52 percent, and this despite the city's excellent mass transit and commuter-railroad facilities. Approximately 15 percent of the city's downtown area was devoted to parking in 1938, with garages and lots holding upwards of 27,000 cars.[42] In Buffalo, 44 buildings, assessed at some $347,600, were demolished for parking lots between 1935 and 1937, bringing the number of lots downtown to 90.

Only 5 new buildings, with assessed valuation of $97,000, were constructed in the same period. Wrote Buffalo planner Walter Behrendt: "It is certainly not by accident that most of the vacant lots used for parking purposes are located around the main shopping center, along the two streets paralleling Main Street. All along both Franklin and Ellicott Streets, over a great number of blocks, the building line is just punched with holes—a condition presenting a very disorderly and unsightly aspect."[43]

New York City, even better endowed than Chicago with mass transit and commuter railroad service, also felt the impact of parking lot fragmentation. In mid-Manhattan, parking lots and garages proliferated, especially on the West Side. They concentrated along both riverfronts northward from the Financial District at Manhattan's southernmost tip. Remaining very optimistic, city boosters saw only progress, progress defined along very traditional lines of thinking based on the assumption that a parking lot was but a temporary aberration in the recycling of city space. "It should be regarded as a healthy sign," claimed Joseph Platzker, secretary of the East Side Chamber of Commerce, "[when] any large community that takes definite steps to either improve or wipe out its antiquated structures." Cleared lots on the Lower East Side covered an area of some 200,000 square feet in 1934 and 646,000 square feet 2 years later. Already 6 "temporary but large parking lots" covered some 75,500 square feet of space, welcome additions, Platzker argued, for their revenue-generating implications. Another million square feet "now covered with closed and boarded-up buildings" would also have to be leveled, he argued. Wasn't the parking lot, he asked, a sign of an impending building boom? Wouldn't it be possible to construct over 100 new buildings?[44]

MERCHANT PARKING ASSOCIATIONS

Although vast amounts of downtown real estate were converted to parking in downtown districts through the 1930s, much of it was peripheral, being beyond easy walking distance of downtown stores. Parking space that was close to stores often filled with the cars of office workers and store clerks rather than the cars of shoppers. In many cities merchant associations organized to promote downtown business generally and retail trade specifically, especially through increased parking. In Milwaukee, it was the East Side Association whose members were entitled to buy parking stamps for distribution to customers. Each stamp, when attached to a customer's parking check, entitled its holder to an hour's free parking at a number of co-operating lots, with lot operators being reimbursed, in turn, by the association. "With neighborhood stores in Milwaukee constantly advertising unlimited parking privileges," announced a news release, "the downtown merchant has been obligated to find some means of preventing his business from going to the outlying sections of the city."[45] Milwaukee's downtown department stores had already established "parking stations" for customers. The association's action was an attempt to extend parking convenience to downtown shoppers generally.

In Los Angeles, Robinson's Department Store opened a parking lot adjacent to its remodeled downtown location. The May Company operated a garage but also contracted with nearby lot operators in subsidizing customer parking. Bullock's did likewise. But in 1941, the Downtown Business Men's Association moved to establish an integrated parking system that would serve the whole of downtown. With the Arroyo Seco Freeway nearing completion, and a vast increase in the number of customers arriving by car anticipated, the organization moved to subsidize a system of downtown parking locations. Through use of validated claim checks, patrons of a wide variety of participating stores would be extended courtesy parking, as in Milwaukee. The initiative was only part of a "seven-point plan" that, in addition, called for improvements to mass transit, promotion of a civic center, the clearing away of blighted buildings, storefront "modernization," street and sidewalk improvements, sign control, and enhanced downtown publicity.[46]

By far the most influential of the postwar cooperative parking plans was launched at Allentown, Pennsylvania. Under the name "Park and Shop," it spread nationwide. Donald P. Miller, general manager of the Call-Chronicle Newspapers, promoted the idea through the Allentown Chamber of Commerce. His plan picked up where similar plans left off, especially with regard to financing. A corporation was to be formed in order to establish parking lots downtown. Stock issued was to be purchased by retailers according to their scale of operation. Once land was purchased and buildings cleared for parking, lots would be leased to private operators. On making purchases above some minimal amount at a cooperating store, patrons would be reimbursed for parking charges, and operators would later be reimbursed by the corporation. What brought the idea to the fore in Allentown was the announcement by Sears, Roebuck and Company that it intended to move from downtown to a new suburban shopping center. The

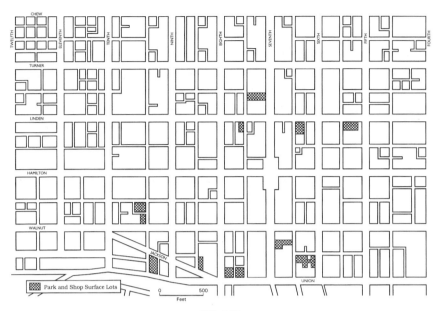

FIG. 2.10

Park and Shop parking lots in Allentown, Pennsylvania, 1949. *Source:* Adapted from Charles S. LeCraw Jr., "Allentown Saves Its Shopping Area," *Traffic Quarterly* 3 (Jan. 1949): 69.

fear spread quickly among downtown business interests that other retailers would follow.

Park and Shop, Inc. was launched in 1947 by 30 cooperating merchants, including the city's several locally owned downtown department stores. Stock quotas imposed on members ranged from $300 to $50,000, based on size of store as measured by sales volume and square footage. Three tracts of land were purchased and turned into parking lots with overall capacity for some 300 cars.[47] Simultaneously, the city installed parking meters on many downtown streets, and all curbside parking was banned on Hamilton Street, the principal shopping street. Two years later Park and Shop was operating 7 lots with space for 660 cars (fig. 2.10). All lots were located within 1,000 feet (300 steps) of the city's principal intersection, Hamilton and Seventh Streets, a fact emphasized in Park and Shop's promotional literature. Lot operators paid an annual rent equivalent to 10 percent of the corporation's purchase price of the land. Parking cost 25 cents an hour, with the customers of affiliated merchants eligible, upon presentation of an appropriately stamped parking ticket, to park free for the first hour. Monthly, operators presented the corporation with the validated tickets accumulated and were reimbursed 80 cents on every dollar. In the first year of operation, some 14,000 parking tickets were validated.[48]

Allentown was a diversified manufacturing city (producing cement, trucks, electrical machinery, and electronics, among other products) that was densely built on a low ridge north from the Little Lehigh River. By 1964, however, parking had substantially intruded into the city's downtown, reducing building densities there significantly (fig. 2.11). There were 85 parking lots, including those of Park and Shop, spread across blocks immediately north and south of Hamilton Street, with several of them breaking the continuity of building lines fronting Hamilton Street itself. In Allentown, major streets were twice the width of minor streets, and the two kinds of thoroughfare alternated with one another in the city's street grid. With the arrival of parking, minor streets downtown came to function more as back alleys, and it was off these alleys that most of the city's parking lots were first located. In 1966, 120 merchants were enrolled in the Park and Shop scheme, or some 90 percent of the retailers downtown. The system provided about 3,700 parking spaces, or 75 percent of the total downtown off-

FIG. 2.11

Area devoted to parking in downtown Allentown, Pennsylvania, 1964. *Source: Insurance Map of Allentown, Pennsylvania Including Part of Whitehall Township,* vol. 1 (New York: Sanborn Map Co., 1958; revised to 1964).

FIG. 2.12

Cities affiliated with Park and Shop, 1962. *Source:* "Park and Shop vs. Meters," *Parking,* fall 1962, 23–29.

street parking available. Some 1.4 million parking tickets were validated that year.[49]

The Park and Shop name did not originate in Allentown. In 1928, a development and property management firm used the term "Park-and-Shop" to promote a new neighborhood shopping center, one of the first in Washington, D.C., to have off-street parking placed in front of stores. In St. Louis in 1939, a "Park-N-Shop" plan was launched when some 70 retailers subsidized a shuttle bus service between a garage, located at the periphery of downtown, and the core of the retail district. Nonetheless, it was the Allentown system, or some variation of it, that spread to other cities under the Park and Shop logo. In 1962, there were 115 cities with affiliated programs (fig. 2.12). Most of the participating cities were of modest size (fewer than 75,000 people), but a dozen or so very large cities were involved, including Baltimore, Denver, Detroit, Kansas City, New Orleans, St. Louis, San Diego, Seattle, and Washington, D.C.[50] The largest operation was in the nation's capital. In 1966, 200 merchants, or 24 percent of the retailers in downtown Washington participated. The program controlled some 98 percent of all off-street parking downtown, utilizing 143 lots and garages with 38,000 spaces.[51]

CONCLUSION

As traffic congestion built up in city business districts nationwide, municipal governments turned to regulating curbside parking, which reduced substantially the amount of curbside space available and thus hastened development of off-street parking. This encouraged a private parking industry configured first around surface lots and then, as we detail in a subsequent chapter, parking garages. The parking lot was foremost, serving the needs of landlords left holding antiquated and otherwise obsolete buildings. Once cleared of buildings, open lots that were turned into parking lots met both short-term and long-term landlord needs. In the short run, parking lots covered taxes and other property expenses and sometimes even returned a small profit. In holding on to property, landlords might, in the long run, benefit substantially from property redevelopment. Firms that specialized in parking lot management competed vigorously to control the parking trade.

Parking lots came to be viewed as a kind of temporary land use, a form of "land banking" against the future. A property cleared of buildings and hard-surfaced as a parking lot stood sanitized, immediately ready for redevelopment. Thought of as merely a transitional land use, most downtown parking lots remained strictly utilitarian, with little if any money spent on amenities. Indeed, the economics of downtown parking allowed for little but the strictly functional.

For merchants determined to maintain central business district investments in the face of accelerating retail decentralization, the provisioning of downtown with improved customer parking became an absolute must. So it was that merchants in Allentown, Pennsylvania, and other cities developed Park and Shop and other similar cooperative parking programs. But what shoppers really wanted was parking very close to if not right at store entrances, the kind of convenience that suburban shopping centers offered. Called for downtown were new close-in lots, and even parking garages, located adjacent to where shoppers ultimately wanted to be. Such development, however, was rarely commercially feasible. It was beyond the ability of private interests to deliver. Needed, it was increasingly argued, was government intervention. Local government should no longer restrict its role in parking to just regulating curbside space. Local government needed to get into the parking business. With downtown property values and municipal tax revenues at stake, municipal governments had a vested interest, if not an obligation, to do so.

MUNICIPAL
PARKING LOTS

It was argued almost from the beginning of the automobile age that city governments would have to be proactive in developing parking downtown. After World War I, literally every American city came to regulate curbside parking at their centers, and in the process, downtown streets became fully defined as arteries for traffic flow. Curbside parking, when not eliminated as a traffic hindrance, was carefully rationed, with turnover of parking space calculated to increase the number of motorists served. But just before, and then just after, World War II, the argument developed that municipalities needed to do much more. They needed to enter the parking business, not so much to supply parking per se, but to supply parking where it was truly needed. Appropriately located close to stores, rather than at a distance, municipal parking would re-energize retailing and thus be fully supportive of central business district stability, if not growth.

Too many commercial parking lots were located at the peripheries of downtown, too far away from stores and offices for easy walking. Peripheral parking lots little aided downtown stores in their competition with suburban retailers, many of whom offered customers at-the-door free parking. In virtually every city, building demolition for parking lot development had substantially reduced city tax rolls, deflating municipal tax revenues accordingly. But it could get much worse. Municipal governments, therefore, had a vested interest in seeing that downtowns remained viable, if not expansive. Private interests might finance peripheral lots, but government subsidy was necessary for truly close-in parking, given that land costs remained high in downtown cores. Center-core parking, and certainly free or even low-cost parking located there, absolutely required municipal subsidy.

GOVERNMENT INTERVENTION

There was clear precedence for government intervention in downtown parking matters. Most cities actively, and even aggressively, regulated the commercial parking industry. Commercial parking was not without its negative implications, for there were many operating abuses. Potential was great for negative spillover onto neighboring properties, and onto public sidewalks and streets as well. Noise, litter, and, of course, the movement of cars deflated the quality of parking lot surrounds. Through the 1920s, enabling legislation and court tests established the right of cities to license (and therefore tax) parking lot and parking garage operators and also to establish ordinances governing their conduct of business. In 1929, for example, the Minnesota Supreme Court upheld the right of the City of Minneapolis to impose $10 annual license fees on "open-air motor vehicle parking places" that operated for hire and accommodated ten or more vehicles. Said places were also subject to city supervision.[1]

Commercial parking lot abuses documented in Philadelphia included using sidewalks to maneuver cars in and out of lots, thus jeopardizing pedestrian safety, and backing cars out into streets, thus disrupting traffic. Many operators parked cars on sidewalks as well. Other "irresponsible practices" included refusal to pay for damages to cars, moving cars from lot to lot without owner consent, posting confusing rates, and frequently changing posted rates, even hour to hour. The 1941 Philadelphia Parking Lot Ordinance required that parking operations be licensed and a full description of each lot or garage be made a matter of public record. License fees varied according to size of operation. Barriers (brick or concrete walls or wire fencing on metal posts) were required around the perimeters of lots larger than 2,500 square feet, with their height to reflect the material used. No driveways were to be over 30 feet wide, and their number was restricted according to the length of street frontage. Signs bearing the operator's and the property owner's names and the parking rates applicable were to be clearly posted at all entrances. Prices posted at 8 A.M. each day were to apply unchanged for 24 hours. Lots used after dark had to be floodlit.[2]

The Philadelphia ordinance further required signed customer consent before cars could be moved from lot to lot, and a record of all parked cars had to be kept according to license plate number. Operators were required to post bond against instances of car damage. It was made illegal for lot operators to park cars on public sidewalks. Philadelphia's Department of Public Safety was charged with determining the maximum car capacity for each operation. In addition, license applicants had to secure approval from the Zoning Commission, the Bureau of Highways, the Building Inspector's Office, the Fire Marshall's Office, and the Electrical Bureau. In 1941, there were over 3,000 commercial parking lots and garages in Philadelphia, which was a challenge to the law's implementation. But operators who failed to obtain license approval were liable to a penalty of $50 per day, placing the onus of approval squarely on their shoulders.[3] Problems remained. A 1942 assessment of parking in downtown Philadelphia concluded that aesthetics, or lack thereof, remained problematical. "Many of the parking lots have become eyesores because of unsightly makeshift shelters provided for attendants, the erection of unsightly fences and barriers, and the exposed walls [of adjacent buildings] with broken plaster and dirty wall paper showing after razing of buildings for parking lot purposes."[4]

In general, the courts determined that cities had the right to grant or, conversely, to withhold licenses in regulating commercial parking. Such was a rightful execution, they held, of city police power used in promoting the public health, safety, morals, and general welfare. License fees could be charged to cover administrative costs and to either encourage or discourage parking activity as might be a municipality's intent. It was generally left unresolved as to whether parking rates charged by operators could be regulated. Was parking a public utility? Was there a service being rendered the general public? In the words of one commentator, was parking of such a nature and importance as "to constitute . . . a common necessity or general convenience, the provision of which [could not] with safety be left to the unrestrained enterprise of private individuals?"[5] Parking was not, he concluded, "a common necessity or general convenience." For example, in New York City in 1940, there was but one car for every two families, and thus some 80 percent of those entering Midtown Manhattan each day did so by means other than private cars.[6] Parking was not a universal need. Most cities, including New York City, required only that operators post rates, and the setting of rates was left squarely to the marketplace.[7]

Zoning ordinances also provided precedent for municipal regulation. Beginning in the mid-1920s, zoning ordinances were adopted as a means of promoting stability in land use, and hence stability, if not growth of, property value. Zoning was validated in the courts as a means of preventing development harmful to public health and welfare. The implications for traffic control were many. By controlling the height, bulk, and areal extent of new buildings, population densities could be set within acceptable ranges, and the traffic generating implications of new buildings assigned indirectly. With specific parking requirements mandated, however, street congestion could be directly targeted. Columbus, Ohio became the first city to require off-street parking, the city's 1923 zoning ordinance mandating that new apartment buildings be so provided.[8]

By 1949, some 185 American cities had adopted parking requirements for various land uses, including apartment houses, hotels, boarding houses, hospitals, theaters, office buildings, and factories. So also was single-family housing targeted. The 1947 Detroit zoning ordinance required one off-street parking space per house. Three parking spaces were required for every 4 units in apartment buildings and 2 parking spaces for every 3 guest rooms (or 1 for every 6 beds) in rooming or boarding houses. For transient hotels 1 parking space was required for every 6 guest rooms and for hospitals 1 space for every 4 beds. For large theaters 1 space was required for every 6 seats and for small theaters 1 space for every 4 seats. There were no parking requirements for stores with less than 2,000 square feet of retail space. But 2 spaces, plus 1 space for each multiple of 333 square feet above 2,000 square feet, were required for larger stores. Department stores (defined as having more than 20,000 square feet of retail space) were to have 56 off-street parking spaces plus 1 space for each additional 250 square feet of sales floor. Factories were to have 1 parking space for every 5 employees. All commercial buildings were expected to have off-street loading and unloading facilities. Surprisingly, the Detroit ordinance did not require that office buildings be provided with off-street parking.[9]

Parking lots and parking garages, as categories of commercial land use, were specifically targeted in most zoning ordinances. At issue was not what these facilities ought to be like. That was covered by licensing laws. Instead, concern focused on where parking facilities ought or ought not be located. As Frank B. Williams wrote in the *American City* in 1934: "The business of conducting open-air garages or parking spaces for profit is a recent innovation in city life. However desirable these parking spaces may be in a congested business district in helping to relieve street traffic, they should not be permitted to invade residential districts and depreciate the value of residential property."[10] Of course, blighted residential streets adjacent to downtowns, especially where business already had intruded, could be, and usually were, zoned for commercial use, so parking was an acceptable land use. As a practice, mandatory off-street parking spread from large to small cities down the urban hierarchy. In 1948, Athens, Tennessee, adopted an off-street parking code and provided residents with a stylized diagram to explain code requirements. The diagram was published in the *American City* with the following caption: "An ordinance of this type will go a long way toward minimizing congestion on the streets as a community grows." [11] Required parking as an aspect of land use control became widely accepted as a preventive approach for achieving planned and orderly development. [12]

PUBLIC PARKING

Although the private parking industry claimed otherwise, commercial parking operations seldom kept pace with demand, especially in big city downtowns. And cities had little assurance that privately owned parking facilities, especially lots, would be permanent. Indeed, most commercial lots were rationalized as merely temporary. Parking, public ownership advocates argued, had reached the public utility stage. Downtown redevelopment hinged on long-term parking accessibility that only municipal government could guarantee. [13] The search for justification, whereby municipalities might play an active role in parking, began in earnest. Perhaps governments could extend tax exemptions to private developers, thus subsidizing downtown parking? In most states, however, such privilege extended only to not-for-profit institutions, especially religious and charitable organizations. In some states, such as New York, quasi-governmental corporations called "authorities" were empowered to build parkways, bridges, and tunnels with tax exemption. Might parking also qualify? Or perhaps governments should own parking facilities outright? Many cities were already in the parking business, as they operated pay parking lots at public beaches or next to civic auditoriums, for example. [14]

But could municipal government rightfully compete with private enterprise? Perhaps private and public interests could divide responsibility for downtown parking in some legitimate way? Gordon Whitnall argued that there were two distinct types of parking: "static" and "dynamic." Static parking involved cars of downtown employees (and their employers) stored throughout a workday. Dynamic parking, on the other hand, was of a shorter, "in-and-out" variety—shoppers, for example, coming and going to stores. It was dynamic parking close at hand that was in short supply in central business districts. Might commercial interests provide parking of the static variety and municipalities provide the more dynamic kind? [15]

As early as 1912, Chicago's mayor proposed setting aside a portion of the city's lakefront for automobile parking, an idea initially rejected. But not all new ideas came from big cities. In 1916, the owner of a Freehold, New Jersey, livery stable bequeathed his community over an acre of land adjacent to downtown, providing, as well, an endowment with which to maintain a parking lot.[16] In 1918, the City of Piqua, Ohio, bought land for a car park.[17] By 1942, approximately 1 of 5 cities of more than 10,000 population operated at least one downtown parking lot for public use. In about half of those cities land had been specifically purchased or leased for public parking purposes.[18] The vast majority of the lots provided were free to motorists; indeed, only 8 cities charged a parking fee.[19] Completed questionnaires in the 1946 *Municipal Year Book* survey established that 280 out of 836 cities, or one-third, operated off-street public parking. In 1961, 775 out of the 1,090 cities responding did so, or about 71 percent.[20] In 1972, over 6,000 communities were involved with public parking, with the estimated value of the land and structures so committed amounting to some $5 billion. More importantly, some 67 percent of the total supply of off-street parking downtown in American cities was municipally owned. Indeed, only one city of over 100,000 people did not have a public parking facility.[21]

Before municipalities could legally venture into public parking, state enabling legislation was usually required. Although California's 1903 Street Opening Act implied that cities in the state could own and operate parking facilities, it was, in fact, the 1941 Automobile Parking District Act that specifically spelled out local government prerogatives.[22] By 1941, 7 states had specifically empowered cities to own and operate off-street parking lots and garages for public use; in addition, 3 states had expressly authorized the collecting of fees in conjunction. The Iowa law authorized municipalities to acquire real estate (by purchase, lease, or condemnation) for public parking purposes and to pay the cost thereof either from the general fund or from a special parking lot tax fund. In addition, Iowa city councils were empowered to collect "just and equitable charges" that could be used in operating and maintaining public parking facilities. Indeed, revenues from established facilities could be used to create new facilities. However, Iowa municipalities were expressly forbidden to sell gasoline, oil, or other motor vehicle supplies in conjunction with parking operations.[23]

Many municipalities moved into public parking for the simple reason that they already owned or leased land that was suitable for car storage. In Memphis, the public levee along the Mississippi River stood largely empty and available for downtown parking (fig. 3.1). Dayton rededicated a portion of the abandoned Miami and Ohio Canal near its central business district. Chicago ultimately committed a section of Grant Park on the lakefront. Oklahoma City gave a portion of its new Civic Center Park. Schenectady, New York, used leftover real estate acquired through the widening of downtown streets. During the economic depression of the 1930s, many

FIG. 3.1

Public parking on the Memphis waterfront, 1964. Many municipalities first established public parking on land that was already city owned.

cities took downtown real estate acquired through tax delinquency proceedings and converted it to parking.[24] Cities continue today to commit otherwise unused publicly owned land to parking, such as space beneath elevated freeways.

Many cities launched parking programs by simply leasing privately owned land already converted to parking, often making it available to the public free of charge. Avoided were the legal uncertainties of property ownership and revenue generation. Where allowed, some cities condemned land through powers of eminent domain, but mainly cities competed in the open market for available property. Brought to the fore were various means of financing. Projects could be paid for by direct assessment through a general tax levy or through special assessment against benefited property only. Projects could be paid for by notes financed in the private sector, with interest and amortization charges met as with bonds. Most common, perhaps, was use of a bond issue with interest and amortization charges carried in a number of ways: by a general tax levy, by assessment against benefited property, by surplus funds, by proceeds from parking meters and other motor vehicle imposts, or by fees charged for use of the very parking spaces created.[25]

Kalamazoo, Michigan, opened its first downtown municipal lot in 1939. Called "The Shoppers Parking Lot," the 390-car facility was financed through a special assessment tax prorated on individual real estate parcels according to their proximity to the lot, with 3 zones of differing potential benefit being identified.[26] In 1953, Silver Springs, Maryland, in suburban Washington, D.C., approved a special taxing area downtown. A 40-cent annual ad valorem tax on each $100 of assessed value on commercial property and a 20-cent tax on unimproved land were established, proceeds from which would finance municipal parking. The Montgomery County Board authorized an $800,000 bond issue and a certification of indebtedness not to exceed 6 years in order to further fund the town's parking program. At the same time, the board also authorized monies for the purchase and installation of parking meters for both downtown streets and public lots, the revenues from which were to be used in paying off bond obligations.[27]

Use of either taxable or nontaxable municipal bonds underwrote most public parking through the 1970s. General obligation bonds, backed by a municipality's "full faith and credit," were usually of low risk and, accordingly, involved low interest rates. A specific debt coverage ratio was not required. In contrast, special parking revenue bonds normally did require a minimum debt coverage ratio—the ratio of net parking revenues divided by debt service load, normally set at 1.5. Higher in risk, revenue bonds brought higher interest rates. Revenue bonds were usually placed on the general market, but they also could be targeted to a specific, prearranged market—for example, a city's downtown merchants. Local revenue bonds made financing possible for longer periods of time and at lower interest rates with lower debt coverage ratios.[28]

In addition, public parking could also be financed in the private sector through conventional mortgages obtained from insurance companies, pension funds, savings and loan associations, and commercial banks. Conversely, municipal governments could play the banker. They could loan money to private entrepreneurs to develop parking. In the early 1950s, the City of Baltimore loaned private operators up to 85 percent of the monies necessary for constructing several new parking garages; the operators, in turn, contributed the land. City government then leased and operated the facilities. By the end of 1952 Baltimore had 15 public garages with some 2,000 parking spaces.[29]

Public-private venturing became very popular after 1970, based on a variety of funding and operating commitments, including, for example, sale and lease-back agreements.[30] With significant increase in federal monies coming to cities through the early 1980s—through Revenue Sharing, Urban Development Action Grant, Community Block Grant, and other programs—public-private partnerships stimulated substantial downtown redevelopment, most of it with public parking implications. Tax increment financing was especially important, and part of the increased tax revenue generated by new development within a taxing district was committed to the underwriting of public parking.

Many cities established local parking authorities. Created through state enabling legislation with governing boards often appointed by the governor, authorities were quasi-autonomous bodies charged with performing specific functions in solving specific public problems. They operated like local governments with prescribed police powers including the ability to tax and issue bonds. However, they existed to be "nonpolitical": that is, to remain beyond the pettiness of obstructionist politics that so often makes municipal government slow in reacting to and solving urban problems. The nation's leading parking expert was a strong advocate of parking authorities. Miller McClintock, director of the Bureau of Municipal Research at Harvard University, founded the university's Bureau for Street Traffic Research, a research institute that eventually moved to Yale University. As a consultant, he conducted substantive downtown traffic and parking studies for Los Angeles, San Francisco, Kansas City, Chicago, and Washington, D.C.[31]

Parking authorities were established in many American cities with San Francisco, Baltimore, Pittsburgh, and Richmond among the earliest. The first one authorized in 1947 in New York State, at White Plains in Westchester County, just to the north of New York City, had the power to acquire land by purchase, lease, or condemnation; construct and operate off-street parking facilities; and lease or rent those facilities to private concessionaires. It could issue bonds up to $2 million and pledge parking revenues for their redemption. In addition, the authority was authorized to operate the city's curbside parking program in order to divert parking meter revenues to the financing of parking lots and parking garages.[32] But when Buffalo petitioned the New York legislature in 1952 for similar powers, the city was turned down on the grounds that existing authorities, such as the one at White Plains, had "too frequently been used to avoid the tax limits set up by the state constitution."[33]

Buffalo then set up a parking board designed to encourage and facilitate private parking initiatives and then returned to the state legislature. This time city officials met with more success, obtaining permission to waive taxes for 15 years on new parking structures as inducement to private investment. In addition, the city, through its parking board, used its powers of condemnation and its high credit rating (and thus its command of low-interest rates), to float bond issues for land acquisition. Once assembled, tracts of land were then conveyed to a purpose-formed merchant group that, with its own financing, undertook the construction of, and the operation of, several parking garages. The garages were operated on a nonprofit basis, with net income over operating expenses going to the city to cover bond obligations.[34] Such parking boards were usually made up of city bureau chiefs and influential business people, among other community leaders, and operated under the direct control of local governments.

Many public parking programs were administered as part of regular departmental or agency programs, such as a city's department of public works or department of transportation, or even the police department. Not infrequently, however, a separate parking agency, with its own director and staff, managed both on-street and off-street public parking. In some localities, bureaucratic hybrids were created. The State of Wisconsin, for example, encouraged formation of parking utilities. A utility operated as any other municipal agency, but with a separate corporate charter as an autonomous legal entity. It had the power to make contracts and exercise full responsibility over public parking, but it was dependent on city government for revenue. Ultimately, Buffalo, New York, was allowed to restructure its parking program as a utility.[35]

LOCATING PUBLIC PARKING

Support for municipal parking lay in the public's continuing perception that downtown commercial lots tended not to be convenient. And yet, as city governments moved to convert riverfronts, parks, and other publicly owned land to parking, many municipal facilities, early on at least, also tended to be peripheral and inconvenient. At first, few cities were willing to buy, clear, and convert land to parking at the very heart of downtown. Many cities planned such lots but never got beyond the planning stage. Only garages could truly promise close-in parking. But, as would prove the norm from city to city, the financing of new parking garages was necessarily linked to new building construction. If parking garages were not integrated into or connected with new office buildings, for example, they were necessarily located close by in order to enjoy a level of anticipated parking demand necessary for financing. The rebuilding of America's central busi-

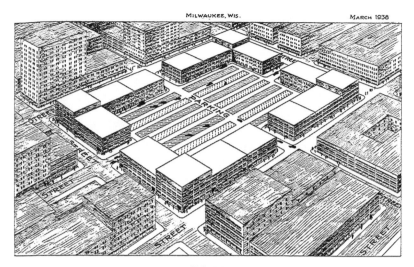

FIG. 3.2

Plan for off-street parking in downtown Milwaukee. *Source:* Orin F. Nolting and Paul Oppermann, *The Parking Problem in Central Business Districts, with Special Reference to Off-Street Parking* (Chicago: Public Administration Service, 1938), 7.

ness districts did not begin in earnest until the late-1960s. And until the boom in office building construction began, "fringe" lots actually dominated municipal parking in most cities.

Planners in Milwaukee proposed the partial clearing of blocks at intervals across the downtown, thereby creating parking lots immediately adjacent to stores (fig. 3.2). The plan was to create a downtown "checkerboarded" with parking "quadrangles." Each lot was to be serviced by a through street in order to facilitate access and "induce private investors to improve surrounding buildings."[36] More practical, however, was a less drastic idea — the capture of open spaces in rear lots and back alleys for parking located in the interiors of business blocks. San Mateo, California, created a linked system of center-of-block parking lots through a special assessment on adjacent properties (fig. 3.3). Of course, such a scheme was practical only in cities where blocks were large and individual building lots were deep. "Main Street" business districts, where the bulk of a town's or a city's retail stores faced onto a single retail street, were usually well suited for such parking. In Quincy, Massachusetts, a low-lying and thus undeveloped area between the main street and the New Haven Railroad to the west was converted into a parking lot for some 560 cars (fig. 3.4). To the east, several blocks were cleared for another parking lot with a 470-car capacity. Both

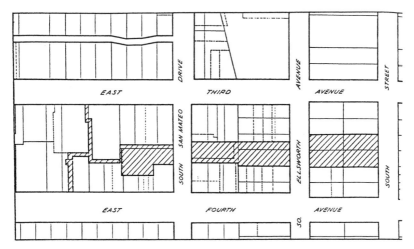

FIG. 3.3

Center-of-block parking in San Mateo, California, 1957. *Source:* Arthur B. Sullivan, "San Mateo Merchants Fight with Parking," *American City* 72 (Aug. 1957): 156.

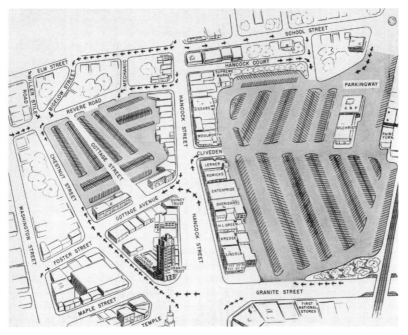

FIG. 3.4

Municipal Parking in Downtown Quincy, Massachusetts, 1955. *Source: Urban Land* 14 (March 1955): 4.

facilities were financed by general obligation bonds retired through parking meter revenues.[37]

Detroit's municipal parking program developed by stages, ultimately to be tied as well to downtown redevelopment. Between 1944 and 1948, parking surveys were conducted by several city agencies. In 1947, the State of Michigan passed a revenue bond act, amended to authorize bond issues for parking facilities. The next year Detroit created a parking "authority," actually a city department empowered only to supervise public parking operations, conduct studies, and make recommendations to the Common Council. The authority did not have, as the name implied, power to finance, buy, condemn, or sell property. Court litigation, which sustained the city's right to own and operate parking facilities, and additional study of the city's traffic and parking problems consumed several more years before the Common Council actually authorized a bond issue, enabling work to commence on several parking lots. In 1954, there were 4 lots with some 1,460 spaces operating.[38] This number paled in comparison to the approximately 29,000 private spaces in and around the city's downtown.[39] By 1966, there were 18 lots and 7 garages owned by the city with a capacity of some 7,525 cars.[40] Detroit's public parking program was not without setbacks. A 1945 proposal to build a 1,000-car garage under Washington Boulevard, which was approved overwhelmingly by voters at a rate of 4 to 1, was defeated in the courts.[41] On the other hand, voters years earlier had decisively defeated a proposed subway system centered on Washington Boulevard downtown.

In many cities, transit was given limited embrace, if only in the cause of municipal parking. Why not establish public lots around the peripheries of downtown and bus shoppers and office workers to destinations at the core? Merchant associations and, indeed, transit companies experimented with such schemes immediately after World War II. In Baltimore in 1946, a 25-cent ticket entitled motorists to all-day parking and bus transportation on shuttle buses running at 5-minute intervals during rush hours. So successful was the scheme that planners urged the city to develop additional lots under public ownership.[42] Perhaps the most successful "fringe" or "perimeter" parking lot in the nation was Chicago's Monroe Street facility in Grant Park on the city's lakefront (fig. 3.5). The lot was huge, accommodating over 3,000 cars. Shuttle buses operated with downtown merchant subsidy, but the lot also seemed within easy walking distance of downtown stores and offices, with the city's skyline looming up abruptly nearby. A similar lot at Soldier Field, some distance to the south, was not successful. Al-

FIG. 3.5

Monroe Street parking lot, Chicago, 1963. Not only does the skyline of the city imply a kind of "closeness," but the lot itself was designed with aisles pointing motorists toward the heart of downtown, a psychological reinforcement of the parking function.

though the lot was provided with shuttle bus service, it was out of sight of the downtown and seemed, therefore, too far away to be convenient.[43]

Chicago's public parking program also grew by stages. In 1946, a parking study was jointly sponsored by the Chicago Association of Commerce and Industry and the State Street Council, two private business groups that then lobbied for public parking. A year later, the Illinois State Legislature passed the Parking Authority Act, an invitation to Chicago and other Illinois cities to embrace municipal parking programs. For several years, however, court litigation delayed action. At issue was whether private operators could manage public facilities, proposed since many cities in the state were reluctant to compete directly with private parking interests. Public parking was actually launched in 1951 when the state legislature authorized the Chicago Park District to build and operate parking lots. Only in 1952 was a municipal bond issue approved for "the acquisition, establishment, maintenance, improvement, extension, and operating of parking facilities" in the Loop and in other business districts throughout the city. Plans for new parking facilities, devised by a Bureau of Parking, were to be approved by the city's traffic engineers, the Chicago Plan Commission, and the Traffic and Public Safety Committee of the City Council before going to the council.[44]

Fringe lots were rationalized in many ways. Parking fees could be set lower than in lots at the heart of downtown, a function of cheaper land costs. Peripheral parking would divert commuters with daylong parking needs, thus opening up space at the heart of downtown for shoppers and others with short-term needs. Accordingly, congestion downtown would be reduced, and buses would be allowed to operate more efficiently, thus remaining a viable alternative to auto use.[45] The Columbus, Ohio, plan located fringe lots at freeway exits near downtown, with shuttle buses to be used for completing downtown commutes. The lots operated with self-parking, but valet service was also available. But as some cities embraced fringe parking, other cities were giving it up. By 1956, experiments in Atlanta, Denver, Pittsburgh, Richmond, and Washington had already shut down.[46] Motorists in these cities, as would eventually be the case in Columbus as well, had difficulty conceptualizing distant lots as part of downtown. There was resistance to riding buses even for short distances. Bus service was too often erratic and always slow. Commuting needed to seem fast and convenient.

PRIVATE VERSUS PUBLIC PARKING

Municipal investment in parking nationwide prompted the American Municipal Association (through its Committee on Parking) to organize in 1954 the International Municipal Parking Congress. The group, which changed its name in 1975 to the Institutional and Municipal Parking Congress, sponsored annual conventions and otherwise functioned to "disseminate ideas and plans on urban parking programs and related traffic engineering."[47] So also did private parking interests organize. In 1951, the National Parking Association (NPA) was launched at a convention in Chicago, establishing its headquarters the next year first in Norfolk and then in Washington, D.C.[48] Previous attempts at trade association organization, such as the International Garage Association, had faltered during the depression of the 1930s. Besides acting as a clearinghouse for parking-related information, the NPA lobbied Congress on behalf of the commercial parking industry. It resisted the spending of public monies on parking at all levels of government in defending private business prerogatives. In 1960, the NPA could report that some 94 percent of all off-street parking in the United States, worth some $4.75 billion, remained in private hands.[49] Although municipal parking represented a very small proportion of the total, its growing popularity, nonetheless, seemingly threatened private parking interests.

FIG. 3.6

Advertisement used in opposing municipal parking in Columbus, Georgia, 1961. *Source:* Harriet S. Kulp, "Parking Authority Defeat in Columbus Referendum," *Parking,* winter 1961, 15.

Diverting curbside meter revenues to meeting off-street parking bond obligations was seen as undermining the money market, as drying up capital that commercial investors might use for commercial lot and garage expansion. Government land assemblage through eminent domain was seen as competition patently unfair, as was government's subsidizing of low parking rates. Privately owned parking facilities, the NPA emphasized, paid taxes. Publicly owned facilities did not. The NPA aided local groups in opposing municipal parking, keeping members informed nationwide as to successes scored (fig. 3.6).

B. M. Stanton was the National Parking Association's founding president. Raised in Birmingham, Alabama, and educated at the University of Michigan, he founded, in 1933, a small chain of 18 gasoline stations located in various Alabama, Virginia, and West Virginia cities. In 1940, he opened a parking lot next to one of his Norfolk gas stations. Provisioned with a tower, from which attendants with megaphones directed motorists where to park, it was one of the nation's first "self-park" lots.[50] Stanton rose to leadership in the NPA when he organized successful opposition to a proposed public parking plan in Norfolk. In later years, he went on to establish a small chain of drive-in restaurants and a car wash. Thus Stanton's entrepreneurial zeal was spread across a host of automobile-oriented enterprises. In 1969, the trade organization he helped found counted some 1,300 members in 43 states, the District of Columbia, Puerto Rico, and 20 foreign countries. As might be expected, the NPA became an important champion of the Allentown Park and Shop idea, helping to spread that idea nationwide as a private alternative to public parking.

At first, commercial parking interests opposed all governmental involvement in off-street parking and, for that matter, any governmental initiative that interfered with private ownership and use of automobiles. Much of the opposition was purely ideological. Some of it was pragmatic. Didn't off-street parking benefit only a few? "That puts it," argued Lyman Wakefield Jr., president of Downtown Parking Inc. of Minneapolis, "in the area of private enterprise, which, being so, makes it properly a free-enterprise function."[51] Public parking also was seen to be inefficient and ineffective and to precipitate categories of loss for communities involved. Some government officials even vigorously criticized municipal parking, as in Boston.

Boston's public parking program was launched in 1946, growing to 8 garages and 7 parking lots by 1962 under the management of first the city's Real Property Department and then its new Commission of Traffic and Parking. Facility development, including land purchase, had cost some $17.5 million. Tax revenues lost amounted to $15.4 million. With parking fees set artificially low, an estimated additional 1,400 motorists had been attracted to downtown each year, costing mass transit an estimated $150,000 loss in revenue annually. Adding in the costs of increased traffic congestion, surrounding property depreciation, and increased street maintenance and comparing that total with the estimated dollar benefit, the chairman of the city's Finance Committee could only conclude that overall costs had far exceeded benefits.[52]

By the 1970s, however, it was clear that the commercial parking industry had little to fear from public parking. Indeed, private interests could benefit. Private operators were more efficient and more effective in managing parking facilities than operatives in municipal bureaucracies. Increasingly, therefore, cities contracted with private operators to manage municipal lots and garages. Thus many of the "special conditions" favorable to municipal parking agencies, previously so vigorously disparaged, actually accrued to private operators.[53] The City of Kalamazoo, a pioneer in municipal parking in the late 1930s, "privatized" its parking system in the late 1980s. The city, which had been subsidizing public parking by some $100,000 annually, extended a management contract to Cleveland-based AMPCO. This placed city-owned lots and garages on a profitable footing both through the cutting of operating costs and through the extension of services.[54] Across the nation private operators aggressively pursued management contracts and leases with public parking agencies as well as with private landlords. By 1977, APCOA, for example, was managing some 140 public parking facilities in a host of cities.[55]

On the other hand, some private parking initiatives faltered, ultimately to be absorbed by municipal programs. Such was the case even in Allentown, Pennsylvania. Park and Shop, the local program that launched nationwide merchant-owned parking cooperatives, sold its assets to the Allentown Parking Authority in 1991. Twelve lots with an assessed value of $3.8 million passed to public ownership, but as previously with Park and Shop, they continued to be operated by private companies (as had the parking authority's other facilities) under management contracts. "Park and Shop," reported the very newspaper whose director a half-century earlier had launched the enterprise, "would wind down its business by liquidating its assets, paying back taxes, and distributing a small dividend to shareholders.[56]

Most businessmen and businesswomen argued that local government had no business competing with private enterprise. Laissez-faire attitudes, roused by perceived threats to private interests, precipitated vigorous opposition to municipal parking, except, of course, when and where private business interests stood to benefit from public largess. Just before World War II, downtown merchants in most cities began to clamor for public intervention to counter what was, by then, clear evidence of the decline of the central business district. Retailers in new outlying shopping districts could offer customers free parking. In addition, most new shopping centers could provide parking immediately at the door. Although redundant downtown buildings were being demolished and converted to commercial parking lots at an accelerating pace, too many of these new lots were peripheral to downtown and of little use to retailers.

Traditionally, cities focused geographically at their centers, a fact reflected in the higher property values there. Most municipalities collected an inordinately high proportion of their revenues from downtown property taxes. Not only would merchants benefit from downtown public parking, but the essential fabric of the city also would be stabilized and municipal revenues protected. Public parking would serve a larger public good as a kind of public utility. Only the commercial lot operators might be excused for thinking otherwise. They clearly could be expected to see government involvement as unfair competition. But precedents for government involvement were well established. Didn't most municipalities license, and thus regulate, commercial parking? Weren't municipal governments inserting off-street parking requirements into zoning codes?

Municipal parking programs were slow in evolving. Not only was there delay in getting state enabling legislation approved, but court litigation had to play out. At first, many cities turned land already publicly owned into parking, creating parking boards or, with state approval, parking authorities. Much of this activity was also oriented beyond downtown cores, offering downtown retailers little immediate relief. What was required, and what came eventually to the fore in most cities, were parking garages located close to downtown stores and offices. Local governments, by and large, did not prove particularly adept at operating parking facilities profitably. By the 1980s, municipalities were turning operations over to commercial interests under lease or management contract agreements. So in the long run, even the private parking industry came to benefit from government involvement in downtown parking, with municipalities becoming just another kind of downtown landlord looking for monetary return on real estate owned.

P A R T

2

PARKING AS
DEVELOPMENTAL STRATEGY

The automobile was not a difficult sell to the American people. At first largely a sporting device for the well-to-do, the car, as a status symbol (as well as a means of travel), spread quickly to the middling classes. There was, of course, no guarantee that the promise of mass automobility would be fulfilled. City streets needed to be upgraded. Rural highways needed to be constructed. In urban places, space needed to be set aside for parking. And not just a little space for parking, but a lot. Nonetheless, so popular did the motorcar become that its accommodation seemed to be almost natural, a fully rational thing to do and to have done. The parking lot, for its role, became a kind of landscape imperative ensuring that the automobile would fully abide in American life.

Ultimately, the automobile, both in motion and at rest, fostered nothing less than a total remaking of American geography, especially the nation's urban geography. It did so by making claim on land use. No store, no office building, no factory, and, indeed, no residence could be sited without automobile convenience being carefully considered. Parking became a spatial adjunct of nearly every enterprise and thus of nearly every developmental scheme, whether large or small or whether located in new suburbs or older central cities. But how should parking be structured? What was the proper role for the parking lot? And what of the parking garage?

Demand for parking brought change to American landscapes, change both anticipated and unanticipated. Largely foreseen were landscapes of low density in new areas: shopping centers and subdivisions made to sprawl outward at city margins, in part through accommodation of parking need. But the "suburbanization" of central business districts was largely unforeseen. Traditional downtowns were eroded incrementally through creation of parking lot voids. Land cleared of old buildings and put under asphalt for the parking of cars stood ready, as well, for more permanent redevelopment. But it was not foreseen just how long redevelopment would be in coming. Most downtown parking lots, thought to be only temporary when created, in fact survived for decades. And it was not foreseen just how heroic the effort would be to fill them up again with something other than cars. As well, it was not understood just how vital parking garages would be in keeping residual activities in central business districts alive.

THE PARKING LOT
AS URBAN VOID

The downtown parking lot was of questionable pedigree. Most parking lots did not reflect acts of creation so much as acts of destruction, developed, as they were, largely through demolition. They resulted from violent action, with infrastructure of the traditional pedestrian city destroyed in accommodating the automobile. Downtown business districts were thinned out, and in the process, the "progress" of city making was redefined. It was not new structure, as built form, that greeted the eye so much as new vacancy, specifically the vacancies of new parking lot voids, fraught with the uncertainties of temporary expedience. Parking lots spoke of short-term, transitory land use. Parking was but a purgatory phase, apologists asserted, between the fully comprehended, solidly built environment of the pre-automobile age and a yet-to-be-fully-disclosed future restructuring of city space recoded specifically to auto use.

Typically, parking lots carried little aesthetic value. They occupied gaps between buildings where once other buildings had been. Parking lots were "messy," architect Robert Weinberg observed in 1937. Merchants, he thought, ought to organize in opposition. Retail districts ought to be protected against their invasion. "It would obviously be harmful to . . . [their] trade," he wrote of New York City retailers, "to have visitors greeted with a nondescript collection of cars on a vacant lot, whose boundaries would be marked at very best by a ramshackle wooden fence; whose pavement, if any, would be fragmentary, and whose condition would be comparable to that of the country fairgrounds the day after the circus had moved away."[1] There was not only the debilitated appearance of the new parking lot, but, as well, there were the spillover effects of lot operation — the noise, dirt, and other hazards that spread beyond.

Many observers saw, and continue to see today, downtown parking lots as negative in both a visual and a functional sense. As Mark Childs observed recently: "The typical design of parking lots as simply mere functional expanse of cheap asphalt and net of white lines is wasteful and destructive." More importantly, he noted: "Parking lots have eaten away cities in the United States like moths devouring a lace wedding gown." Thus what might be vital and delightful in cities was, because of parking lot intrusion, too often unsafe, environmentally unsound, underpopulated, and downright ugly.[2] Unlike other kinds of open space in cities, parking lots did not, by in large, help to weave together an overarching sense of place. Quite to the contrary, they destroyed the traditional fabric of place. Often, in the process, they precluded redevelopment rather than inviting it. "Disorganized motor traffic, overrunning all the spaces between buildings with tumult and mechanical confusion," editorialized the *Architectural Review* in 1941, "cuts us off from the possibility of good architecture."[3]

The new parking lot "aesthetic" grew increasingly dominant in America's central business districts. In the early 1920s, it was the isolated gap in a surround of traditional buildings. By the late 1930s, parking lots were part of an erosional pattern evident block after block in most downtowns. By the early 1950s, whole blocks, especially blocks peripheral to downtowns, were completely cleared. In subsequent decades patterns of parking lot fragmentation could be seen nearly everywhere from big to small cities, and in small towns also. The rise of the parking lot was set in motion by a host of factors. The list is long: mounting traffic congestion downtown, lack of adequate curbside parking, competition from newer outlying business districts, a resulting leveling off and even decline of downtown business activity, accompanying decline of downtown property values, a marginality of redundant downtown building stock, rise of a commercial parking industry, and increasing demand for off-street public parking, among other factors. Parking lots in and around central business districts were intended to save traditional downtowns and thus save the traditional city. Taken to excess, however, their impact was in most instances quite the opposite.

Parking lots helped produce in American central business districts what geographer Edward Relph termed "simple landscape." He wrote: "The simple landscape declares itself openly, presents not problems or surprises, lacks subtlety; there are none of the ambiguities and contradictions and complexities that . . . lend meaning to buildings and man-made environments; there are no deep significances, only a turning to the obvious and a separation of different functions into distinct units." Things are overly orderly in simplified landscapes, for they are laid out in fully predictable ways, and user behavior is fully anticipated. Spaces are not only unifunctional but, accordingly, univalent, with each element having its own significance and identity largely unrelated to any higher unity except through proximity. There is a leveling of experience. "There may be possibilities for sensations, but these are discrete, ephemeral, and unencumbered by catharsis or other emotional upsets and involvements."[4] Simple landscapes, being overwhelmingly of the present, lack significant time depth.

Besides negative visual and place-making implication, the fragmentation of downtown caused by the parking lot also carried negative environmental inference. Expanses of open asphalt impacted hydrology and climate across city space. Runoff from lot surfaces could amplify flooding not only in a downtown but also well downstream from a city's center. Increased intensity of water flow, especially after storms, could alter stream characteristics throughout a basin; stream banks could be undercut and stream beds filled with sediment. Parking lots were a major source of water pollution. Oil, grease, hydrocarbons, and heavy metals, in addition to suspended solids and trash, washed into river basins. Largely unshaded, parking lots became exaggerated heat islands contributing substantially to air pollution, altering precipitation regimes, and exacerbating wind speed. The difference between summer temperatures in urban areas and adjacent rural areas has been increasing in the United States by about 0.67 degrees F (0.37 degrees C) per decade, with cities now 2 to 8 degrees F (1.1 to 4.4 degrees C) hotter than surrounding countrysides.[5] A study in Sacramento established that parked cars produced about 20 percent of the hydrocarbon emissions from vehicles, emissions that inflated air temperature.[6] In addition, the very process of applying asphalt to street and parking lot surfaces was found to add substantially to local smog build up. A study in Dayton linked windswept parking lots at the periphery of downtown with wind turbulence around tall buildings at the city's core.[7]

PARKING LOT DESIGN

What concerned the parking industry was functionality, not visual aesthetics or environmental impact. Quality in parking lot design was primarily a matter of maximizing a lot's auto storage capacity while minimizing its operating and maintenance costs, the ultimate objective being to enhance profit. Just what were the attributes of a "good lot"? In 1945, Henry Evans outlined for the readers of *Traffic Engineering* the following. A good lot was one that offered a minimum of inconvenience, that is, delay and accident hazard to the motorist. Size and shape, grading and surfacing, lot enclosure, marking of parking stalls, positioning of entrances and exits, layout of aisles for car movement, and illumination — these were the important considerations.[8] Parking was an activity that could and should be reduced to a relatively few functions. A parking lot did not need to be anything other than a straightforward container for its function.

Forty-five years later, Robert Weant and Herbert Levinson asserted a somewhat expanded design agenda, but with functionality still dominating. A parking lot needed to be convenient and safe. Therefore, adequate sight distances needed to be maintained at access points and sufficient "reservoir space" maintained within the lot itself. Internal circulation patterns needed to be as obvious as possible. In lots with self-parking, parking spaces needed to be large enough for average drivers to maneuver in and out. But, most important, lot design needed to maximize the number of parking spaces in the least amount of paved space. Lot layout needed to minimize maintenance costs. It needed to minimize operating costs as well, especially labor costs. And it needed to minimize liability potential. Finally, Weant and Levinson argued, parking lots also needed to look nice and be visually compatible with their environs. "Visual amenities" needed to be incorporated not just to enhance lot appearance but to better complement surrounding development.[9]

As parking lots were essentially open spaces hard-surfaced for the storage of cars, the choice of surface material loomed large in parking lot construction. Before 1920, dirt, cinder, and gravel surfaces were not uncommon, but these unstable surfaces were difficult to drain and difficult to maintain. After 1920, harder and thus more durable flooring for parking lots became increasingly requisite. Brick or poured concrete was expensive and pretended a permanence inappropriate to a land use thought to be temporary. Asphalt paving came to the fore as a relatively inexpensive surfacing material that could, when need arose, be removed with relative ease.

Asphaltic material derived as pitch from natural seeps and pools and in solid form from asphalt-impregnated rock and sand. But most of the asphalt actually used in the United States over the past century was a byproduct of petroleum refining. As gasoline production soared to fuel America's motorcars and trucks, so also did asphalt production soar to pave America's streets, highways, and parking lots. Asphalt surfaces were created in a variety of ways. Asphalt could be applied as a diluted spray on a graded dirt surface or as a penetration treatment on a macadam or other rock base. It could be thickly laid down as either a hot or a cold mix, a blend of stone, slag, sand, or gravel called asphalt concrete (and, sometimes, merely "blacktop").[10] The actual asphalt content in asphalt concrete rarely exceeded 5 percent. Often a mineral filler was introduced to eliminate voids between larger aggregates. Of the nearly 1.2 million miles of paved streets and highways in the United States in 1960, over a million were asphalted.[11] By 1999, an estimated 250 billion tons of asphaltic material had been laid on American road surfaces.[12]

In highway construction, asphalt paving was put down in layers, the nature of the layering a function of underlying soil conditions and anticipated loads. Some sort of subbase (crushed stone, slag, or gravel) was laid down as a foundation on top of which another base, usually with the same materials, was overlaid, but loosely bonded with asphalt. On top of this, a well-compacted asphalt concrete surface, two to five inches in thickness, was applied and carefully pitched for drainage. For parking lots, a single application of asphalt concrete might suffice or perhaps a buildup comprising successive layers of gravel or crushed stone permeated with an asphalt spray.[13]

Asphalted parking lots were seen to be less costly than other kinds of paved lot, because the construction was seen as relatively uncomplicated and fast. These lots were not easily damaged by de-icing salts, snow, and ice melting off relatively rapidly. Blacktopped surfaces offered ready contrast for painted white (or yellow) stall and lane markings. However, asphalt surfaces could at times prove problematical. Raveling involved a progressive separation of aggregate particles, beginning on the surface of a pavement and progressing downward. Shrinkage cracks could form, as could potholes. Upheaval, the result of expansion through ice formation, was common, especially in northern cities. Grade depression could develop from excessive weight concentrated on cracks. Nonetheless, it was generally acknowledged that problems such as these were easily overcome. Repairs could be made rapidly and at low cost.[14]

Lot location and size of lot were largely predetermined as a function of property availability. Of course, corner lots were preferred as they were more visible to prospective customers and more convenient, because motorists were able to enter and exit through driveways off two streets rather than only one. Large lots were preferred over small lots if only for design flexibility. When working with unconfined spaces, lot designers enjoyed greater degrees of freedom in laying out stalls and aisles. Lot designers tended to be preoccupied with the following kinds of questions. How large

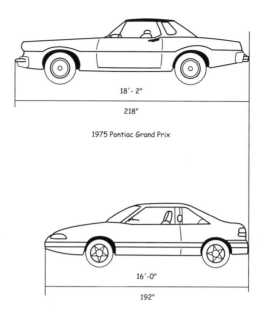

18'- 2"

218"

1975 Pontiac Grand Prix

16'-0"

192"

1988 Pontiac Grand Prix

FIG. 4.1

The Pontiac Grand Prix as downsized between 1975 and 1988. *Source:* Modified from Richard S. Beebe et al., *Recommended Guidelines for Parking Geometrics* ([Washington, DC]: National Parking Association, 1989), 9.

should parking stalls be? How should they be angled? How should they be arranged along aisles? Widespread experimentation, widely reported in trade journals and in design manuals, engendered a relatively narrow array of standardized parking lot arrangements.

Parking lot layout was very much a matter of applied geometry, with relevant calculations involving a number of basic measurements such as automobile sizes. Cars varied widely from compact sports cars and inexpensive coupes to oversized luxury sedans. Average car width and length also varied substantially year to year. Generally speaking, American cars got larger through the 1930s. Vastly scaled down after World War II, they grew in size through the 1960s. They became compact once again with the oil embargoes and related gasoline shortages of the 1970s and with the stricter Environmental Protection Agency (EPA) air pollution mandates of the 1980s (fig. 4.1). There followed widespread popularity of vans and sports utility vehicles (most built on a truck chassis), making the American passenger vehicle larger than ever.

In 1971, the average full-sized car was 80 inches wide and 220 inches long.[15] How much extra clearance space was required in marking off parking stalls? The answer lay in how cars were to be parked. Would they be parked by lot attendants, presumed to be accustomed to precision driving, or would they be self-parked by motorists, presumed to be less skilled in tight-space maneuvering? Minimal clearances of 15 inches (or even less) between cars would suffice for attendant-parked vehicles. As for self-parking, most design consultants distinguished between long-term and short-term parking needs. Charles Boldon and his colleagues at Parking Standards Design Associates recommended a 20-inch clearance to enable long-term parkers to swing doors open and squeeze in and out of cars. More energized short-term parkers, on the other hand, would need at least 24 inches (fig. 4.2). As for stall length, designers advised providing space for at least a minimal 6-inch front bumper clearance.[16]

Fully related was the issue of stall orientation. At what angle, and thus at what turning radius, were cars to be inserted into parking stalls? As with size, turning requirements varied from car to car, with averages changing year to year and decade to decade. Diagramed are the minimal turning requirements for various 1955–56 automobiles (fig. 4.3). For lots with attendants, stalls at right angles to narrow aisles were recommended (fig. 4.4). More cars could be stored than with oblique parking, and wide aisles were not necessary. Attendants were usually instructed to back cars into stalls, which requires less aisle space as a function of tighter turning ratios. But for

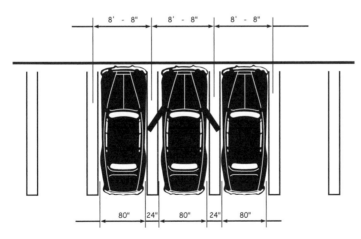

FIG. 4.2

Critical door-opening dimensions acceptable for short-term parking patrons. *Source:* Charles M. Boldon et al., *Parking Standards Study* ([Los Angeles]: Parking Standards Design Associates, 1971), 12.

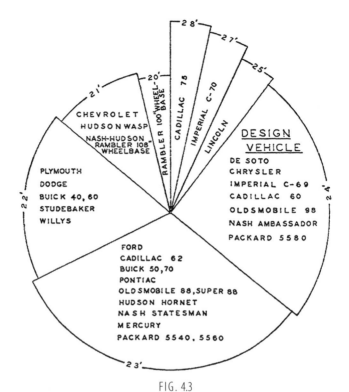

FIG. 4.3

Minimum turning requirements for 1955–56 model cars. Depicted are turning ratios measured on a car's extreme dimensions. *Source:* Edmund R. Ricker, *Traffic Design of Parking Garages* (Saugatuck, CT: Eno Foundation, 1957), 66. Reprinted with permission by the Eno Transportation Foundation, Washington, D.C.

lots with self-parking, stalls needed to be obliquely angled off wide aisles, thereby facilitating customer ease of entry and exit.

Overall size and shape of property greatly influenced stall size and orientation as well as width of aisle. Few parking lot operators would operate lots narrower than 60 feet. A lot 60 feet wide could be subdivided into 240-square-foot stalls when arranged at right angles to service aisles. Such a facility absolutely required attendant parking. Cars moved in both directions up and down a single service aisle and fit into stalls very tightly.[17] A lot 120 feet wide, on the other hand, could accommodate rows of right-angled stalls down both sides and two "island" rows down the center as well. Thus customer self-parking was possible with traffic flowing in a single, predetermined direction around the lot (fig. 4.5). But as the lot designer moved from 90-degree to 60-degree to 45-degree parking, for example, storage capacity declined (fig. 4.6). The arraying of parking stalls and aisles in different patterns, even mixing patterns in a single lot, did help designers increase lot capacity. Among the more popular patterns of stall arrangement were so called single-line, herringbone, and interlocked patterns (fig. 4.7).

Entry and exit zones needed to be carefully articulated, especially in lots with attendant parking. Important were the "reservoir" spaces where cars, vacated by drivers, awaited attendant attention or, conversely, where cars delivered by attendants awaited owner recovery. A small building might be erected, not only to house attendants and the cashier but perhaps also to serve as a waiting room for customers. Car-servicing facilities might be included, such as a gas station located in one corner of the lot. Traffic circulation in service aisles needed to be carefully thought out. In general, one-way traffic was preferred over two-way movement since there was less potential for conflict with vehicles all moving in the same direction. In general, counterclockwise circulation was preferred over clockwise since it followed from the normal pattern of Americans driving on the right.

Since passage of the Americans with Disabilities Act of 1990, special stalls have been required in self-parking lots, configured according to a set formula: 4 spaces out of the first 100 spaces, 2 more out of the next 100, and

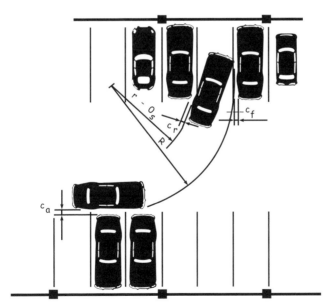

FIG. 4.4
Parking lot organization with right-angle stalls. *Source:* Modified from Charles M. Boldon et al., *Parking Standards Study* ([Los Angeles]: Parking Standards Design Associates, 1971), 12.

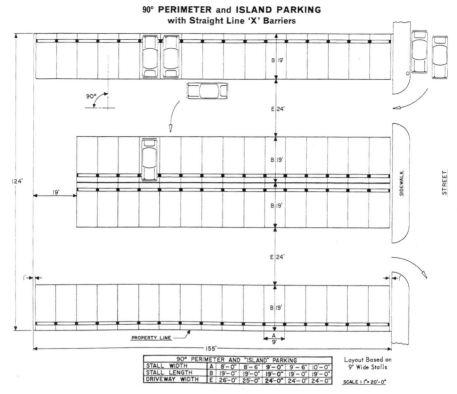

FIG. 4.5

"Perimeter" and "island" parking with stalls at right angles to service aisles. *Source: How to Lay Out a Parking Lot* ([Chicago]: Western Industries, 1960), 6.

so forth. Lots with 500 to 1,000 spaces are required to dedicate 2 percent of the total to disabled parking, whereas those with over 1,000 spaces are required to dedicate 20 stalls plus one additional stall for each additional increment of 100.[18] The act's design guidelines cover the following: stall width (a minimum of 96 inches to accommodate wheelchairs and other equipment), surface slope (not to exceed grades of 1:50 or 2 percent in any direction), signs (centered in front of each stall as well as painted on the stall floor), and location (sites maximally accessible to lot entrances and exits).

Most downtown parking lots were created through demolition, with the smallest lots covering the vacated footprints of single buildings and the largest lots stitched together from vacated adjacent properties. As streets in most cities were networked in strict rectilinear grids, the imposed rectilinearity was reflected in property-line divisions as well, so it was that most parking lots were rectangular in shape. Parking lot boundaries were usually straight, marked out along the straight sides of streets or alleys or the straight walls of residual buildings. Although basically open, parking lots were not without some minimal articulation. They were organized spatially in ways fully reflective of their use: stalls arrayed in patterns, usually rectilinear in nature as well, and aisles oriented to, and thus fully reflective of, encompassing street grids. They were not totally empty, although they could appear so without parked cars. Lot surfaces were, of course, variously striped with painted lines to guide parking behavior. Such was the standard parking lot vision brought to the fore aggressively in city after city.

Parking lots were "furnished." They were provided, in other words, with light infrastructure variously useful to car parking. All parking lots required

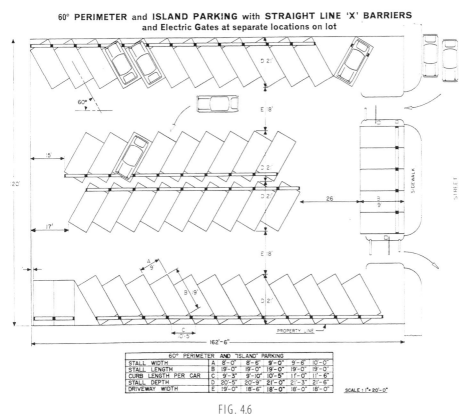

60° PERIMETER and ISLAND PARKING with STRAIGHT LINE 'X' BARRIERS
and Electric Gates at separate locations on lot

60° PERIMETER AND "ISLAND" PARKING					
STALL WIDTH	A	8'-0"	8'-6"	9'-0"	9'-6"	10'-0"
STALL LENGTH	B	19'-0"	19'-0"	19'-0"	19'-0"	19'-0"
CURB LENGTH PER CAR	C	9'-3"	9'-10"	10'-5"	11'-0"	11'-6"
STALL DEPTH	D	20'-5"	20'-9"	21'-0"	21'-3"	21'-6"
DRIVEWAY WIDTH	E	19'-0"	18'-6"	18'-0"	18'-0"	18'-0"

SCALE : 1"= 20'-0"

FIG. 4.6
"Perimeter" and "island" parking with stalls angled at 60 degrees to service aisles.
Source: *How to Lay Out a Parking Lot* ([Chicago5: Western Industries, 1960), 13.

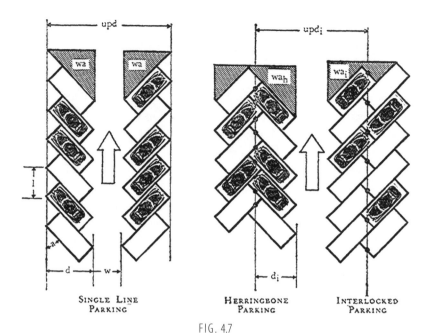

FIG. 4.7

Patterns of parking stall arrangement. *Source:* Modified from Robert H. Burrage and Edward G. Mogren, *Parking* (Saugatuck, CT: Eno Foundation, 1957). Reprinted with permission by the Eno Transportation Foundation, Washington, D.C.

signs, especially at driveway entrances to identify operators, establish operating hours, and set rates. In attended lots, little additional signage was usually necessary because the parking program was fully known to attendants. But in self-parking facilities motorists needed to be carefully directed, with the act of parking clearly choreographed. One-way arrows and arrows pointing to exits, among other sorts of informative messages, were absolutely necessary to lot functionality. Signs also delimited operator liability, privileged certain kinds of customers over others in the allocation of specific parking spaces, and gave warning as to criminality and other hazards. Self-parking required that the parking program be communicated over and over again through a host of embedded reminders, not only verbal in form, as with most signs, but structural as well. Curbing, speed bumps, raised islands, fencing, and landscaping were used as anonymous "to whom it may concern" messages variously directing motorist behavior.

In pay lots with self-parking formats, charges had to be assessed, usually by the hour, and fees had to be collected. After World War II, the drive to cut labor costs inclined lot operators toward automation, bringing to the parking lot scene a host of highly standardized machines. Parking gates and ticket dispensers tied to car counting devices made lots accessible when space was available, turning motorists away when it was not. Customers paid cashiers at drive-up windows on leaving. Other devices allowed pre-payment, and parkers were to display receipts on their dashboards as proof of payment. For municipal lots, parking meters served admirably as money collectors and as time allocators. Lots open at night needed to be lit; the rhythms set up by evenly spaced lamp standards reinforced, more often than not, the other rectilinear cadences of lot organization. Recommended levels of illumination varied from 1.0 to 5.0 foot-candles, depending on lot design and level of use. Low luminance might suffice for private employee lots, but public lots, with heavy traffic and high security concerns, needed to be brilliantly lit.[19]

Lots with limited space, but favorably located and thus under intense demand, could be "enlarged" by employing stacking machines or parking lifts (fig. 4.8). Fabricated of steel and aluminum, car stackers arrived in "knock-down" condition ready to be erected on site as a means of placing two, three, or more cars where only one would otherwise go. Among the brands marketed in the 1960s were Dubl Park, Duo Park, Park Plus, Space Maker, and Space-o-matic, their names fully suggestive of their purpose. Such ma-

FIG. 4.8

Parking lift in downtown New Orleans, 1999. Stacking cars in parking lots increased lot capacity.

chines were related to the so-called automated parking systems built to be permanently installed in multilevel parking garages.

IMPROVING THE GAZE

As more and more buildings were cleared away in America's central business districts, the utilitarian nature and overly utilitarian look of parking lots loomed increasingly problematical. The traditional city was evaporating rapidly before the public's eyes, creating, in most downtowns, off-putting fragmentation that was negative in implication. For the most part, parking lots did not contribute positively to a downtown's look. Usually too many lingering wounds remained from ad hoc demolition, the scarred walls of buildings, for example, standing symbolic of landscapes lost. Even where new buildings rose close at hand, islands of residual infrastructure, tucked around the margins or in the corners of parking lots, too often offered demeaning contrast. Parking lots spoke not of urban strength, but of weakness. They spoke of mere expediency: motorists craving cheap parking convenience, and property owners and lot operators seeking maximum profits.

Another problem with parking lots, especially with the very large lots pieced together around downtown peripheries, was their intrinsic openness. When empty of cars they were particularly vacuous to the eye, but even when they were filled with cars a certain vacuousness remained. Row on row, lot to lot, and block to block, a sea of parked cars flattened to the gaze. Very few Americans thought parking lots picturesque. And when parking lots were celebrated in art, which was rare, it was usually through an artist's heightened sense for the mundane or the ridiculous. Edward Rusha's *Thirty-four Parking Lots in Los Angeles* provided, without accompanying text, photographs of selected parking lots. Most of the images were from above, with the aerial gaze further flattening the massed cars portrayed in the photos.[20]

Limited debate did surface in industry trade journals concerning parking lot appearance. Frequent calls were made for lot beautification. But, for the most part, such advocacy fell on deaf ears. Customers, after all, sought cheap parking convenience and usually little else. The vast majority of Americans were perfectly willing to accept meanness in parking lot surrounds. What mattered was not visual amenity so much as location and price and whether a specific lot did or did not have a vacancy when specific need arose. Ideally, lots should never be full. Lots should function at approximately 85 percent of capacity, it was preached. Lots that were fuller discouraged customer approach, even when spaces were available. Furthermore, operation at full capacity was only a sign that a lot's rates were set too low.[21]

In recent years, psychologists have begun to focus on parking lots, considering them ideal laboratories for studying spatial memory among other human behaviors. How do motorists, having parked their cars in large open lots, ever find them again? How, in other words, do people with a general lack of fixed landmarks orient themselves geographically? Conclusions are yet tentative, but according to one study, returning motorists do not employ so-called minimum effort strategies as common sense suggests. They do not just remember a general direction, for instance, and move in that direction until encountering their car. Rather, before leaving their cars, most motorists mentally rehearse a specific strategy of return. They construct a return scenario from the limited repertoire of location indicators available: for example, the number of aisles away from the entrance or the number of light poles along a given aisle.[22]

Equally interesting is how people select parking spaces. Picking an aisle and then a space in that aisle closest to one's destination is one method: a "satisficing" strategy. Driving aisle to aisle in search of a vacant space absolutely closest to one's destination is another: an "optimizing" strategy. Time and motion studies seem to imply the former preferable to the latter.[23] It is interesting that people in shopping center or mall parking lots are willing to walk farther than those parking downtown. As one merchant concluded: "They can see the stores from most points on the parking area of a center. Downtown, visibility is not as good."[24] In other words, what is out of sight seems farther away, whereas that within view seems closer at hand. Entering the large lot of a shopping center carries implication of arrival (of "being there") even when walking distance remains equal to or even exceeds that experienced downtown.

Interesting also are the territorial behaviors observable in parking lots. A motorist tends to take proprietary interest in his or her space, especially when another motorist is waiting. "The average driver," one study found, spent 32 seconds leaving his or her spot when no one else was jockeying for it, but an additional 7 seconds maintaining possession when another car appeared eager to enter.[25] Other user-perception research has focused on the motorist's sense of security in parking lots. Parking industry trade journals have not only emphasized the need for surveillance, either directly by attendants positioned outside or indirectly by inside personnel using surveil-

FIG. 4.9

Parking lot in downtown Dallas, 1982. Here was the juxtaposition of pretentious modern design, the residual expediency of old buildings, and a parking lot—a sight all too common in big city downtowns after 1950.

lance cameras, but also the need to make lots "look safe." Graffiti should be removed as quickly as possible. Trash should be eliminated and lots otherwise kept clean. Facilities that look disorderly or poorly maintained tend to also be "read" as dangerous.[26]

After World War II, more and more parking lots were landscaped. Few of them were downtown, however; most were located in the suburbs. Architect Leopold Kohr advocated transforming at least a few downtown lots in every city into elegant public squares while still, of course, retaining their parking functions.[27] Basically, there were two approaches to parking lot improvement through beautification. One used the gaze from outside (the view looking in), and the other used the gaze from inside (the view looking out). For the view looking in, one could screen lots using walls, shrubs, trees, or other devices (fig. 4.9). In Kansas City, Missouri, such screening was required by law. "Screening by fencing, walls, planters or shrubbery is required of all street sides and must be at least thirty inches high," a city ordinance read.[28] It was argued that cars could be things of beauty when taken singly, but not when concentrated in large numbers. "The motor car in isolation may be well designed, beautifully finished and pleasing to look upon," asserted civil engineer John Brierley, but "When viewed en masse on a highway or on a parking ground it can be an ugly sight."[29] For the view looking out, walls, shrubs, and trees could also be used to break up expanses of openness, for instance. One could organize lots with different sections built at different levels, each section given separate identity accordingly. When so divided, oppressively large lots could be reduced to a more pleasing scale.[30]

For motorists arriving downtown, the pedestrian experience often began in a parking lot. Once the car door was slammed, downtown became something to be experienced on foot. Possible then was a more intimate visual tie to a city and opportunity as well for highly personalized social interactions—chance conversations, for example, even in the lots themselves. With thoughtful articulation, the parking lot, like the open space of a well-designed public square, could be made to function like an outdoor room more encouraging to social interaction.[31] For pedestrians it was absolutely essential that distances within lots seem comfortable. Sight lines needed to be short. Landmarks, encouraging to movement on foot, needed to be plentiful. For example, aisles could be curved, and sight lines along parking lanes would thus be abbreviated. Additionally, views could be deliberately terminated. Clumps of trees, walls, and even sculpture could be inserted as focal points to help guide pedestrians in and out of lots. Paving material also could be varied to direct pedestrian movement. It was important to tie parking lots visually to their surroundings, if only to give pedestrians walking from parked cars a reinforced sense of destination. Architect E. M. Whitlock challenged the parking lot designer: "One of . . . [the] prerequisites of design is to integrate a parking facility within the community; try to match the surrounding; try to develop a theme; try to give some coherence to the end product."[32]

For all the talk about design enhancement, most parking lots remained fully utilitarian with little to recommend them aesthetically. Nor did attempts to tie the landscaping of parking lots to wise environmental management change many minds. True, landscaping could help maintain "nature's balance." Trees, shrubs, and ground cover served to regulate heat, reduce wind, and absorb run off. Terracing could help regulate drainage. But as long as profit margins remained narrow, owners and operators had little incentive to either beautify their lots or become environmentally sensitive. Surveys established that few motorists were willing to pay extra for special parking lot amenities. "It is clearly evident," reported the editor of *Parking*, in reviewing a 1980 parking survey conducted in New Orleans, "that people who park in off-street facilities strongly oppose any parking tax or the erection of opaque fencing or other barriers around the perimeter of parking lots when these measures would increase the parking rates."[33]

The economics of parking, specifically, and the realities of downtown real estate development, generally, little encouraged parking lot improvement. Indeed, many parking lot operators found that lease and management agreements often precluded aesthetic improvement. "Design" in downtown parking lots played out mainly as enhanced functionality. It played out in the signage, layout, and furnishing of lots only in so far as it served to attract customers and insert them readily into lot routines. Whereas attendant parking continued to characterize close-in downtown locations, where customer demand was high and operators thus were concerned to squeeze maximum patronage from limited space, self-parking lots came to dominate beyond. But in lots with self-parking, at least limited articulation was essential to aid motorists in positioning their cars. Nonetheless, even these lots remained, for the most part, little more than open expanses, vacant sheets of asphalt largely unencumbered, and thus vacuous to the eye.

Americans, both accomplished designers and uninformed lay people, have always tended to conceptualize landscape, especially urban landscape, primarily in terms of form or structure. The gaze, both professional and casual, is easily directed to objects, to things in the built environment. Space (that is, geographical space), to the extent that it is attended at all, is thought of as mere surround or as separation. Things are seen as located in space and thus as related visually across space. Space, in other words, provides mere context. When applied to conceptualizing the built environment, this kind of thinking (or seeing) engenders a kind of myopia. The spatial vacancy of parking lots in America's downtowns, for example, was given, at best, neutral valence. Parking lots stand expedient as sustainers of automobility. They enable us to park where we otherwise might not be able to do so. They also stand ready for redevelopment and thus, in a way, are contextual temporally as well as spatially. They provide context for buildings yet to be.

Preoccupation with objects in geographical space reduces the parking lot to mere urban void. It dismisses design potential. The typical downtown parking lot stands, in most minds, as little more than vacant space. The open lot leaves parking, as an activity and as a profession, without respectful structural expression. It does not provide imagery engendering pride of place, nor does it provide imagery stimulating pride in accomplishment. What brought esteem to the parking industry, as we detail next, was not the off-street parking lot so much as the parking garage. Garages were things of substance, structures that could be seen as "permanent" rather than as temporary in landscape. They spoke not merely of a lost past or of an uncertain future, but of a credible present. Their pedigree was sound and, indeed, usually beyond question in a commercial sense. Their creation was fully meaningful as architectural expression. They resulted from constructive acts. They were things — objects — that could be fully valued as built environment.

5

FROM GENERAL SERVICE GARAGE
TO URBAN PARKING STRUCTURE

Parking garages are urban fixtures to-
day, but, in fact, they are relative newcomers to the urban scene, the complex product of numerous factors interacting over the last century. How did
entrepreneurship, automobile design, construction technology, the automobile boom, downtown commerce, and public demand combine to create the urban parking garage? In this chapter we explain the first half-
century of this new facilitator of life and work in the city.

1890s–1920s

Garages first offered various services of which parking was but one. Habitually claiming low profit margins, garage owners tested the income from
adding various auxiliary services before sorting out those most lucrative at
their particular site.[1] The multipurpose garage — or, in the vernacular of
the early twentieth century, the "service station" — combined mechanical
repairs, battery recharging, washing and waxing, sometimes body repair,
and, almost always, storage. In the profit-making exploration of the various
combinations formulating the automobile service industry through the
early 1920s, several specialized businesses in their own building types began
to emerge — the gasoline station, the auto dealership, the "auto laundry,"
and, this chapter's subject, the parking garage. Thus, the parking garage's
evolution was circuitous, not a linear development of obvious outcome until the 1920s.

Businesspeople were not strongly drawn at first into garage work for the
public. The Electric Vehicle Company, founded in 1897 in New York City,
and the Illinois Electric Transportation Company, founded in 1898 in Chi-

cago, are credited as the nation's first garages. Although both maintained "stations" for the cars they sold, they neither repaired nor stored cars for the public. Private auto clubs housed some of the first big garages, but only for their members, who were largely sportsmen at the time when the car was a plaything of the wealthy. The Massachusetts Automobile Club's 3-story facility with basement opened in 1902 and was one of the best provisioned garages, housing repair shops, wash racks, and storage for 25 cars.[2]

Storage was essential for automobiles throughout the early twentieth century. "Live storage" for automobiles driven daily, what has been called "parking" for most of the century since, and "dead storage" for those cars immobilized during winter was commonly distinguished. In dead storage, autos were raised on jacks to save their deflated tires, their radiators and gasoline tanks were drained, and their batteries were drained and disassembled. That was the most laborious and time-consuming seasonal ritual of early automobile maintenance.[3]

Storage in public garages was eventually taken as a business opportunity and initially earned more income than repair, where the two functions were combined. Automobile dealerships provided some of the first public garages. A 1901 survey of 6 storage-repair garages in New York City included the Winton Motor Carriage Company, where cars were repaired and 33 were stored when the reporter visited.[4] The 6 garages surveyed, "undoubtedly the pioneer garages in America, because then as now New York was the greatest automobile market in America," offered repair, storage, and related services to any motorist who would pay.[5] Yet those too were linked to automobile manufacturers in either renting office space to manufacturers' agents or space for display. Although in New York City the number of garages with storage grew quickly, quadrupling to 24 by 1902, Chicago with 6 was noted simultaneously as considerably lacking. The Banker Brothers, distributor for 9 different automobile manufacturers in New York, Philadelphia, and Pittsburgh by 1903, moved beyond the garage-dealership arrangement in that it operated the first garage chain in those cities.[6]

The Wanamaker Garage in Philadelphia first linked incomes later common in parking, the store and the garage. Wanamaker, one of the nation's first automobile retailers, opened a facility for repairs, accessories, painting, and storage in 1901.

Garages became independent and common in cities of almost every size in the second decade of the twentieth century. Reflecting the elitist presumptions of the several automobilists in New York City who founded the Automobile Club of America in 1899, the club failed to build a clubhouse with a garage until 1907, when public garages were plentiful throughout the city.[7]

The Pittsburgh Motor Service Corporation demonstrated how an early entrepreneur grasped the business potential in the garage's combined services. Paul Azbill, an auto salesman with Carl H. Page and Company in New York City, set out to take advantage of Pittsburgh's early garage trade. Its reputation for bad gasoline and oil sales, a strangely abused revenue source for a trade frequently complaining about low profit margins, may have helped alert Azbill. He purchased a 5-story building in the warehouse district of Pittsburgh's "Triangle," where he could count on the profitable patronage of truck fleets if his services were decent and his marketing aggressive. Storage garages 3 to 5 miles beyond the city's core charged comparatively low rates, $8 per month versus Azbill's $20–$40 per month, because they were located on cheaper land. Azbill bought and provisioned his building for the huge sum of $400,000, advertised to attract three-fourths of his customers, supplied names of drivers on a 15-minute notice to short-handed companies, repaired vehicles, sold gas, oil, and accessories, and stored vehicles on 3 of the 5 floors.[8]

Location was important to the emerging garage industry. Azbill's operation demonstrated how close proximity to his trucking patrons was key despite his high storage prices. Most of the new garages were positioned close to wealthy residential districts whose motorists dominated the early automobile market. The *Horseless Age* specified this vital geographical dimension in several articles attempting to structure the young industry. Not only was Bruening Brothers Garage in Kansas City, Missouri, across the street from "a group of large and fashionable 'inns' or family hotels," but it was within a "high-class" apartment house district and within a mile radius of "three distinct high-class residence neighborhoods." The Atwood Garage was "just at the edge of the better residential section of Toledo," and the Savage Garage in Springfield, Illinois, typifying the small town facility that sold and stored vehicles overnight, was adjacent to one of the town's "choice resident districts."[9]

Indianapolis illustrates the spatial array of garages in a single urban center. The reference here is the first installment of several throughout our discussion of the garage to represent spatial distribution in a single urban location. Mile Square, the commercial heart of Indianapolis consisting of approximately 100 blocks bounded by East, West, North, and South Streets, provides the figurative datum line, and the 1914 Sanborn fire insurance map provides the data (figs. 5.1, 5.2). In 1914, when horses worked along with

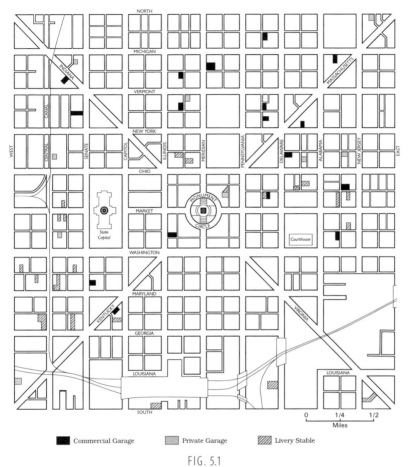

FIG. 5.1

Automobile storage garages and livery stables in downtown Indianapolis, 1914. *Source:* Sanborn Map Company, *Sanborn Insurance Maps of Indianapolis, Indiana* (New York, 1914).

self-powered vehicles, livery stables were located mostly on the south side of Mile Square in the warehouse and railroad district. A few livery stables were interspersed near public automobile storage garages immediately north and east of the city's center, Monument Circle. Private and public storage garages were distributed evenly throughout the northern half of the square, in close proximity to upper-class residential areas. Except for one repair garage in the south half of the square, repair garages and automobile sales and service garages were in the northern residential district. The latter took premier sites concentrated on "automobile row" on North Capitol, where one could shop in 3 blocks at the Ford Motor Company, Cole Mo-

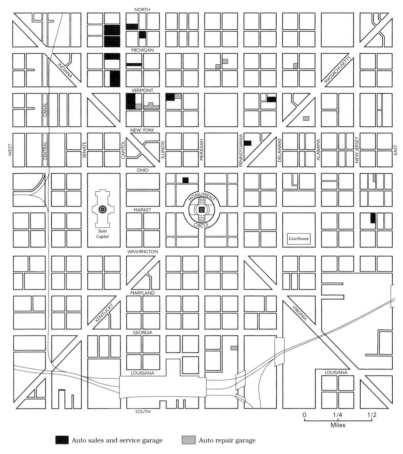

FIG. 5.2

Automobile-oriented businesses in downtown Indianapolis, 1914. *Source:* Sanborn Map Company, *Sanborn Insurance Maps of Indianapolis, Indiana* (New York, 1914).

tor Car Company, Empire Auto Company (including Cadillac and B. F. Goodrich), Stutz Motorcar Company, Gibson Auto Company, Fisher Auto Company, and two unidentified dealers. Except for the automobile dealerships that faced for obvious display and the easiest access on arterial streets or their intersections, garages—especially storage garages—were situated with striking regularity on lots within blocks accessed through alleys dividing whole blocks into quarter blocks.

Here the cheapest real estate close to motorists' destinations was available. A noteworthy case of the square's evolutionary land use is the eastern half of the half block bounded by Delaware and Ohio Streets on the northeast corner. Site of the Columbia Theater (1800 seats, 2 balconies, and entrance east off Delaware) in 1914, the lot would devolve to the Empire Theater before it was retrofitted as the old Empire parking structure in 1927. South across the alley intersection, Keith's Grand Theater would be raised for a parking lot. Garages of various kinds were business opportunities in the kaleidoscopic urban landscape reformed in the automobile's wake, with storage garages entering like poor relatives in the new family of automobile-convenient places.

Garages helped puncture the uniformity of the previously pedestrian urban landscape. Curbs broken and replaced with short inclines at the entrance for motor vehicles signaled the reformation in an elementary way. Cities enacted new fire codes for garages, thought especially incendiary, and with dramatic effect. In the state of New York beginning in 1914 all structures used as a garage, a "building wherein are kept more than three automobiles or motor cars charged with or containing a volatile inflammable liquid for fuel or power," had to be built according to fireproof regulations and located between 20 and 50 feet from other buildings, and those garages existing before December 1, 1914, had to be remodeled. The existing garages had to have the first floor covered in concrete not less than 3 inches thick, ceilings in garages higher than one floor had to be covered with metal lath and "hard plaster" at least three-quarters of an inch thick, stairways and elevator wells had to be enclosed in similar fireproof material, doorways had to be fitted with iron frames and automatic fire doors, exterior windows facing outside structures had to be fitted with wire glass and metal sashes or sealed, and a sprinkler system had to be installed in buildings higher than 2 stories.[10] Safety precautions were dictated to the work being conducted inside. New garages had some of their work prescribed to avoid fires, but their construction and materials resulted in structures fully different than the adapted first-generation buildings. Stout interior pillars of reinforced concrete were necessary for bearing the great loads combining upper floors plus vehicles. The poorest of those poor relatives in the new automobile services seemed antiquated in the rapidly changing consumer culture where investors sought profitable opportunities.

What else did people see outside and inside those new garages? Facades echoed impressive apartments or emporiums, often with extensive first-floor glazing. In buildings that combined an auto dealership and parking garage, the latest cars were displayed for window shoppers. In structures that combined the automobile clubhouse and garage, windows opened on offices, lounges, or work and storage areas (fig. 5.3).[11] Exteriors of common

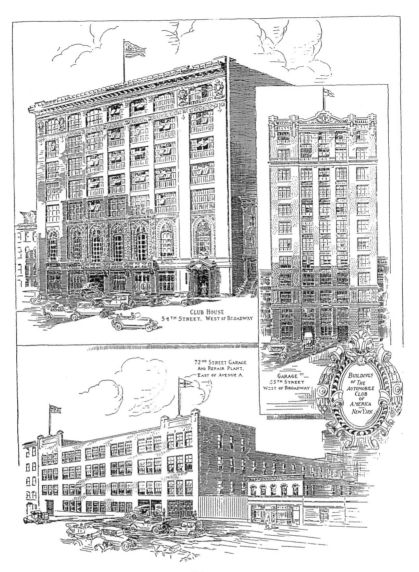

FIG. 5.3

The Automobile Club of America, headquartered in New York, opened three buildings: its Club House (left) in 1908, 55th Street Garage in 1912 (center), and 72nd Street Garage (right) in 1915 to store and repair its members' cars. *Source: The 1920 Associated Tours Guide* (New York: Automobile Club of America, 1920), 2.

brick or building tile usually enclosed the sides and back of the garage unless one of the sides fronted on a busy street, where pretension was implied in decoration or advertising signs. Windows, however, were numerous on all sides to maximize ambient light. Truss-supported roofs, most often on one-story examples, provided the maximum interior workspace unobstructed by posts. Distinctively profiled tangent-of-circle roofs masked by mercantile facades made memorable hybrids akin to boomtown facades.

Interiors were utilitarian. Lathes and other machinery required in early automobile repair were located within easy reach in the repair area, preferably on upper floors of multistoried garages. Storage occupied spaces remote from daily work areas. In 1916, the *Horseless Age* published rare advice on floor plans, including 2- and 3-story garages.[12] Tacit functionalism instead informed most garage arrangements, and it wasn't until the 1920s that designers commonly offered idealized ones.[13]

Growing competition and traffic produced significant changes including provisions for chauffeurs. Chauffeurs were common in early motoring for wealthy car owners, and consequently chauffeurs' recreation rooms were standard in automobile club garages. To thwart the "grafting chauffeur" who charged public garage owners 10 percent of the fee for serviced autos, the New York Transportation Company garage reduced the price of its gasoline so that it was sold virtually without profit when the garage opened in December 1914. Cheap gas and free chauffeur amenities — a billiard room barring the professional gamblers who customarily preyed on chauffeurs, a barber, and a bootblack — were nonetheless extended to draw business. By 1920, before chauffeuring practically disappeared as more people drove their own cars, one motor journalist proposed that garage owners take and deliver stored cars to the customer's house.[14] Garage owners were doubtless eager to forgo the questionable expense of chauffeurs' provisions before 1920.

Entrepreneurs also questioned other services of the multipurpose "service station" concept as it peaked in the years between 1910 and 1920. Engine repair, towing, and maintenance of various systems — suspension, exhaust, and electrical — remained the core services. Other services were added, and their profitability was tested through strong advertising, while others were subtracted — all depending on the individual operator. A checklist of services offered at 5 model garages described in trade publications between 1915 and 1917 reveals they all repaired and stored vehicles, whereas only 3 sold gasoline and just 2 washed them.[15]

Gasoline sales were the most problematic. Garage owners complained that evaporation, leakage, and spillage during the several stages of storage diminished income enormously. In 1915, the 20 million gallons lost through evaporation alone cost New York City retailers $4.8 million, calculated at the wholesale rate of 24 cents per gallon in that city. Garages were encouraged to implement various ways to prevent loss. Customers were often upset with gasoline and oil contaminated from poor storage and lackadaisical refueling. Petroleum refiners and distributors, with their large upstream investments, launched company-owned and -leased gasoline stations between the late teens and the early 1920s to control sales, and many garagemen abandoned gasoline sales without second thoughts.[16]

"Auto laundries" came forward as one way to augment profits. Washing and polishing cars was important early in the twentieth century when paints were highly perishable. Auto laundries sprang up first in the Midwest and West. Indianapolis's experience again illustrates. In 1919 Gus A. Showalter was reported to have opened the S. & S. Auto Laundry in downtown Indianapolis just north of Mile Square. Although he did not make a profit at his first location, he did when he moved to 332–334 North Illinois Street, just north of the city's central business district, where he drew customers from the busy street and had them exit through one of those alleys characteristically quartering business blocks in downtown Indianapolis. It took 10 minutes and cost $1.00 to wash and polish each car, far cheaper than the 4 frustrating hours, expensive supplies, and ruined clothing that Showalter suffered in his car-washing episode one day that inspired his thoughts about a business operated a better way. Auto laundries were spectacular novelties but often depended on their allied services for success. In 1919, in Hollywood, brothers Frank and Walter Muller began the "World's Finest Service Station," which emphasized a $50,000 auto laundry with the strategy of "selling up." When motorists approached for the $1.25 car wash, one of the Mueller brothers shook their hand, bragged about their car, and then sold them a wax, lubrication, brake test, or something else. The *Accessory and Garage Journal* gleefully reported that "invariably the original $1.25 transaction quickly grows into a much larger sale."[17]

Technological improvements, meanwhile, made the storage option more profitable for garages. The latest repair equipment, of course, enhanced mechanical work. Interfloor access, however, became the key question for entrepreneurs seeking better storage operations. Adapted freight elevators at first were routinely installed in garages to raise and lower vehicles between floors. Growing downtown traffic jams led to increased pressure for the adoption of a means for quicker handling of cars from one floor to another. Elevators handled the one-way traffic of morning and evening rush hours too slowly. Ramps proved faster at moving cars during those critical rush hours. Elevators performed effectively only during traffic lulls, even those that permitted one vehicle to be lowered and another raised simultaneously. Elevators soon became relics of the first-generation storage garages and were seldom installed in new construction after the mid-1920s. Ramps conversely became "a sales talking point" for garage operators advertising speedy service via the latest equipment.[18] Here was a kernel of the parking garage industry.

Competition accelerated in the young garage trade, and with it accelerated the role of parking. Entrepreneurs responding in 1916 and 1917 to a *Horseless Age* contest to identify the world's largest garage supplied information for 3 claimants, all with storage. Alongside repairs in garages, storage was ranked a steady income source and was welcomed as a regularly allied service. The Euclid Square Garage in Cleveland operated a 2-story "garage and storage station" for 1,000 cars with plans to accommodate 3,000 more. In the Commodore-Biltmore Company in New York City, the Hotel LaSalle Garage in Chicago, and the Portland Street Garage in Boston, 3 prominently reported repair garages with large storage capacities, investors could find further encouragement for exploring the storage-repair garage. The Cooper Service Garage with a 55-car area beneath the Advertisers Building in Dayton, Ohio, and the Pacific Mutual Building in Los Angeles with 2 underground parking levels and one atop it for visitors hinted at the engineering as well as the business potential in underground parking garages.[19]

1920s–1940s

Parking became a specialized private profit-making enterprise in this period, and the consequences informed questions of parking garage design as well as the emerging alternative of municipal ownership. Increased automobile use stimulated the transition to public parking. Between 1920 and 1929, annual production jumped from 2 million to 5.5 million vehicles, and annual registration jumped from 9 million to 26.5 million vehicles. Downtowns witnessed increased automobile traffic. In Chicago, for example, even though the number of people arriving by all means of transportation decreased 7.45 percent between 1926 and 1938, the number of vehicles increased 31.37 percent.[20]

Spokespeople for public planning agencies and the architectural and construction trades encouraged more careful thought than entrepreneurs had given to garages in the past. Like most new consumer services, customers had to learn to use garages. Their conviction depended on the virtues of the service and advertising to push sales. One of the construction trade magazines effectively characterized the dilemma of the early 1920s:

> Most public garages appear to be just buildings in which automobiles happen to be housed. They are inefficient in the number of cars they can store per hundred square foot of floor area. And they are monstrously inefficient in the way time is wasted in getting cars in and out. People patronize them reluctantly, for who wants to wait fifteen minutes for his car? Consequently the garage — and the business houses nearby — lose business.[21]

Investors henceforth were advised to select locations and oversee facility design with greater precision.[22] Site selection involved calculations of a particular site's cost and traffic volume, for operating a garage anywhere in a busy downtown did not guarantee a lucrative trade. The prevailing wisdom was to buy cheap real estate where, as one adviser frankly stated, "shabby boarding-houses, rickety tenements, and empty warehouses — buildings too old for comfortable habitation or unsafe for the conduct of business" awaited redevelopment.[23] A traffic survey of the location would determine whether the potential parking demand was sufficient for a business, and if it was, how physical arrangements and operations could be attuned for the best profit. In the cycle of urban demolition and redevelopment, the new parking garages significantly helped transform large sections of pre-motorized urban landscapes.

Parking garages became integral members of the new automobile-convenient city. Their complicated risk taking paid investors dividends only to the degree that they contributed to the success of their business neighbors. Some garages were built with the possibility of later additions if the traffic warranted. Garages built for existing high-traffic locations with their high purchase costs required special calculations in order that the high parking rates to recoup costs did not discourage customers. In those cases, underground garages or garages built in office towers, so-called mixed-use buildings, were advised.[24]

Business opportunities for storing automobiles led in several directions. Entrepreneurs with those more technical skills demanded of mechanical and body repair could emphasize them and leave storage as a secondary income source. Storage demands arising from the seasonal need of earlier automobiles virtually disappeared in the 1930s with improved engineering and, especially, with the appearance of Duco enamel. The new enamel, more durable than the earlier oil- and varnish-based paints applied to cars, allowed drivers to park free outside without damaging their cars' finish.[25] Duco enamel and the new garage companies seriously eroded the mechanic's adjunct income from storage. Entrepreneurs seeking increased income through the less specialized services of oil changing, gasoline refueling, and car washing and waxing could add those to the primary role of short-term storage.

Some enterprisers seeking quick return with the least possible investment pushed yet another dimension by renting unprotected lots. The trend is traceable in case law producing essential definitions. In passing judgment the court defined "storage" as a function in which a business assumes responsibility for theft and damages from weather and physical injury, but "parking" did not involve such responsibility.[26]

"Day storage," as parking came to be called in the vernacular, gained considerable attention. In April 1923, championing the large parking garage as the solution to downtown traffic jams, the *Buffalo Motorist* reported a boom in parking garage construction in the city.[27] The Swan Garage characterized the new class of parking garages. It emphasized speed: "it can be speedily cleared of all cars without the annoying delays of waiting elevators." It was complete with the latest heating system, equipment for washing and repairing cars, accessories for sale, telephones on every floor for communication both within and outside the building, a ladies' rest room, and a room to which shoppers could have their purchases sent directly from individual stores before collecting them for the trip home. At a cost of $250,000 for land and building, the Swan Garage was built to house 350 cars.[28] The competing Dickinson Garage System boasted a chain of 3 facilities "in the heart of Buffalo" with a total capacity for 1,500 cars. The Statler Garage adjacent to the Hotel Statler, however, proclaimed itself "Buffalo's Finest Garage" because of its convenient location nearby the prestigious hotel and close proximity to shops, theaters, and businesses. In the harsh depression economy, the Downtown Garage (fig. 5.4), situated for the banking and commercial district, and the Genesse Motoramp Garage, situated for the shopping and theater district, extended free parking to patrons of its automobile services.[29]

Profit mindedness naturally produced the tendency to judge a garage's success by its earnings and resulted in short-term planning pinned to the

FIG. 5.4

The Downtown Garage in Buffalo, 1927. Business district patrons warranted the garage's restrained architectural demeanor and clear visual advertising of its allied lubrication and washing services. *Source: Buffalo Motorist* 20 (May 1927): 10.

highly volatile economy. Parking garages as a result gravitated to locations immediately adjacent to big and steady traffic generators. Hence, garages across from hotels or inside hotels were common (fig. 5.5). Department stores and office buildings attracted some garages, but Los Angeles, an especially automobile-dependent city, illustrates that self-interest could be self-defeating. In the 1920s, parking garages there were small. Big and small owners alike did not plan well for their parking futures. Big store owners believed off-street parking should answer the search for where to park but should lead onto a lot, not into a garage. Small store owners believed they could not effect any change in where their customers parked.[30]

In the brief span of the decade before the Great Depression descended, the grand downtown parking garage reached its zenith in most cities. Likened to hotels for automobiles in the zealous trade publications of the late 1920s because hotel services connoted high quality, the grand downtown parking garages occasionally signaled their pretensions with regal facades. It was for their masterful ensemble of efficiency and aesthetics that they commanded respect among commentators on the new parking industry. The Fisher Building (completed in 1928) in Detroit, which Albert Kahn

FIG. 5.5

The Wellington Hotel's advertising postcards boasted of the convenience of its "'garage-in' hotel" for travelers in Albany, New York. The center inset shows mushroom capitals atop columns typical of garage construction before the 1960s.

designed for the Fisher brothers of auto body fame, ranked first among the garages according to some.[31]

Safe yet speedy access to storage and exit from a garage dictated almost every designer's overriding issue, interfloor travel. Answers again varied according to the peculiarities of each site. In 1929, the *Architectural Record* distinguished nine varieties of planes along which drivers could propel cars between levels. Each was basically a helix or ramp. Elevators assisted in some of those designs by moving vehicles between floors before they were driven into their stall, but elevators were no longer state-of-the-art garage technology. One of several d'Humy patents for "staggered ramps" was most commonly preferred for new construction in the 1920s through the 1930s, and various ramp types were installed even through the 1960s. Fernand E. d'Humy, a prolific patentee of lighting, telegraph, and conveyor devices and dirigibles, patented several arrangements of parking garage floors, each half of which was one-half story above the adjacent floor and joined through low inclines (fig. 5.6). Ramp Buildings Corporation, founded in 1920 and headquartered in New York City, assiduously advertised its garage management for local investors and its d'Humy designs and led the way in trying to control the storage garage market.[32]

What look then did this new building type bring to the landscape? Among casual observers the sepulchral effect inside these strange, often dimly lit labyrinths between wide supporting columns with huge flared or mushroom capitals (fig. 5.5) may well have rivaled the intended rationalism of the layout. Their steel-reinforced concrete members of overlarge proportions echoed the warehouse. Outside, extensive glazing to supplement interior light unmistakably echoed the look of factories or high-rise office buildings, depending upon the landscape with which the garage was required to blend. Articulated column-and-beam frames for heavy inside loads behind brick curtain walls, minimally decorated, if at all, completed frankly industrial appearances on the street side of many. Functionalism, however, gained acceptance with the professionals fashioning garage architecture.[33]

As business acumen intensified the fledgling parking industry, emphasis on efficiency brought mechanical parking devices to the fore. Faster elevators supplanting those for freight originally pressed into garage use nevertheless left attendants with the need to drive cars into storage space once the elevator had raised them to the required floor and start the car's engine before driving them to the elevator for exit. Resulting delays continued to

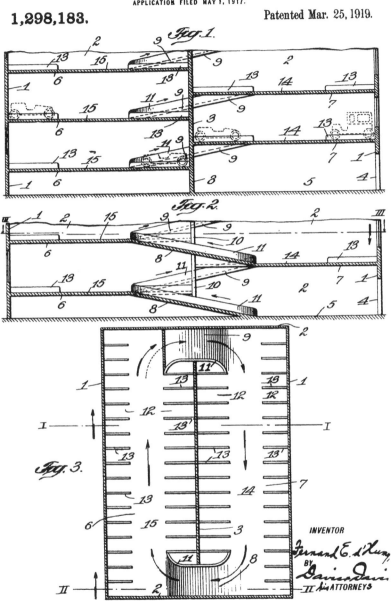

FIG. 5.6

In 1919, Fernand E. d'Humy obtained utility patent 1,298,183, the first of his several parking garage patents.

threaten patronage and consequently dissatisfied garage owners and staff. Thoughts of more fully mechanized parking dawned.[34]

Large prototypes gained publicity as the industry matured. The Kent Automatic Parking Garage first built in 1928 in New York City was the most ambitious of the new mechanical garages. At ground level the driver left the car inside the garage portal, where a device pulled the car toward one of three high-speed elevators traveling one floor per second and loaded the car onto the elevator. An operator lifted the car to a floor with vacancies, which a system of lights signaled, and a device moved the car into storage after reaching the indicated floor. Attendants repositioning cars at the noon rush hour introduced an additional human element, but the Kent Garage remained an essentially mechanical operation. Six were built before the stock market crash a year later ended enthusiasm for more. The Ruth System in the Jeweler's Building built in 1926 in the Chicago Loop was one of the most long remembered. It too used elevators and dollies, requiring no human handling after the car entered at ground level, but it was celebrated because its location at the building's core was convenient for the patrons working in the building. By 1940, when the elevator's inability to accommodate the change in car proportions and a record of chronic mechanical malfunctions accumulated, the Ruth System was forced out of service.[35]

Although mechanical garages remained more curiosities than practical machines in the 1920s and 1930s, they satisfied a cultural streak for mechanical remedies of complex problems. Built almost exclusively at the center of big cities, they were high-rise structures testing the limits of investments in costly downtown lots. The Kent Automatic Garage in New York City towered 28 stories above its 50-foot by 200-foot plot and stored 1,000 cars. Self-operating versions minimizing the number of required staff held out an additional hope of savings to customers and eventually of increased income to owners. Parkers and parking companies could have it both ways, cheap yet profitable and convenient space at the heart of traditional big city business districts. The early technology, however, eventually proved unsatisfactory. Installation costs were high, mechanical and electrical malfunctions were common, and, perhaps most damning, these mechanical garages did not satisfy the demand for speedy service during peak traffic flows. All of Manhattan's mechanical garages, for instance, were bankrupted during the depression. More reliable mechanical garages appeared in the following era of garage design.[36]

FIG. 5.7

Kaufmann's Department Store built this open-deck parking garage, the second in the nation, on Fourth Avenue in Pittsburgh, circa 1937. Architect William Hoover's design became the model for the open-deck garage over the next decade. *Source:* Courtesy of Media Services, Kaufmann's Department Store.

Various alternatives were investigated in the vigorous young parking industry. Downtown real estate was often too costly for profiting from surface lots, while prevailing multifloor garage architecture often resulted in parking fees that were too expensive for profitable customer demand. Depression-era entrepreneurship in pursuit of cheap yet durable designs produced several successful expedients, among them the first steel skeleton garage, built by Jerome Stedelin in St. Louis. In 1933 in Boston, Sam Eliot, manager of several office buildings, constructed the "Cage Garage," the first open-deck garage, the kind lacking envelopes of walls required to protect earlier cars from inclement weather. Open decks also did not need ventilating systems to expel car exhaust and helped diminish construction and maintenance costs (fig. 5.7). Although considered small by later standards, those early open-deck garages clearly demonstrated cost effectiveness, waiting for the coincidence of renewed investment during prosperous times and an end to city ordinances prohibiting them as fire hazards to make the open deck the design of choice and push the once grandly styled curtain-wall garages into extinction.[37]

Department stores introduced roof-top parking in the 1930s, often born of the desire to maximize the use of limited space at existing stores and dispel the deterrent of shopping in traffic-congested downtowns. The 1930s also witnessed planning for big underground parking projects. Chicago's mayor had proposed a garage beneath Grant Park as early as 1913, but the city council quickly defeated it. In the 1930s, the far greater volume of urban traffic forced consideration of underground parking. In 1930, four underground facilities of 4 to 6 levels were envisioned in downtown Detroit to create 3,000–4,500 additional parking spaces and eased the way to the enactment and enforcement of tougher parking regulations. Just 1 of the 4 facilities would have cost $1.5 million. None were built. Costs were too exorbitant for Detroit's depression-ridden voters.[38]

It was San Francisco, just before the wartime moratorium on consumer building, that constructed an underground garage, revolutionary in size but perhaps more important for its interparty cooperation. A few small garages beneath grade had been serving parkers since just before 1920, as noted above. San Francisco's extensive undertaking brought wide public attention to the possibility of parking in center-city underground garages. Whereas the vertical imperative to reduce real estate costs for expensive downtown parcels had almost invariably assumed upward building, the underground garage, of course, directed construction downward. Whereas minimum cost consistent with maximum utility had moved design toward simplicity in the past, underground construction introduced new and costly complexities. And perhaps most important in the future, whereas parking garages had been private initiatives or expedients dedicated to nearby businesses, awareness that individual businesses benefited better from downtown's collective viability coalesced numerous interests — commercial, government, architectural, and engineering — behind San Francisco's novel garage.

After more than a decade of intermittent discussions among business and civic leaders about the need to end San Francisco's traffic glut, the landmark not-for-profit Union Square Garage Corporation faced the task. Miller McClintock, one of the foremost early traffic planners, was hired to determine the storage capacity required of the garage. As a result 4 levels of underground parking were built for 1,700 cars (one of the largest garages at the time) between March 1941 and September 1942.[39]

Services and management gave further luster to the landmark garage. Whereas location and design had first occupied attention at the birth of the parking industry, Union Square demonstrated the significance of effective management. Union Square's entrance fully achieved its designed capability to rival stately hotel lobbies with manager Andrew Pansini's insistence on spotless maintenance and fresh flowers. Not only Pansini's verve but also his faith that the parking trade had not begun to realize its amazing income potential presented one of the industry's pioneers with an opportunity to apply his talents and demonstrate his convictions on a grand scale at the Union Square model.[40] Although many parking "firsts" can be attributed to the first 40 years of the parking garage's history, many with demonstrable influence on successive examples, none surpassed San Francisco's underground garage as an inspiring prototype when flush times resumed in the late 1940s.

What did the spatial array of parking spaces, both lots and garages, reveal about a city with a viable downtown on the eve of World War II? Indianapolis's Sanborn fire insurance map, this time for 1942 in comparison with the one for 1914, provides some answers. In 1942, garages were more numerous, by half again the number, than in 1914; there were 38 garages in 1942, compared to 25 in 1914. Parking lots far surpassed garages, numbering 74. Liveries disappeared with the end of horse-drawn drayage and horse-mounted riders. In 1942, gasoline stations stood adjacent to numerous parking lots and garages, some under the same management. In 1942, lots and garages both were evenly distributed through Mile Square (fig. 5.8), unlike 1914, when garages were concentrated mostly on the north side of the square. With society grown dependent on the automobile, entrepreneurs occupied prime real estate on streets. Few garages were situated off interblock alleys. The downtown parking garage was firmly planted on the Indianapolis landscape.

Parking garages evolved considerably to the midpoint of the twentieth century, but never teleologically. Economic ebbs and flows opened entrepreneurial opportunities as well as closing them with what seemed great suddenness. Automobility's long-term rise, although beset with periodic plateaus or declines in demand, underlay parking demand. The increase in traffic in the nation's downtowns before the redirection to outlying shopping centers in the last half-century encouraged off-street parking most efficiently in multilevel garages. But how best to profit from the costly investment needed to build them? Where exactly to locate them in down-

FIG. 5.8

Automobile parking garages and lots in downtown Indianapolis, 1942. *Source:* Sanborn Map Company, *Sanborn Insurance Maps of Indianapolis Indiana* (New York, 1942).

town areas for maximum tactical advantage vis-à-vis motorists? How to design them for the peculiarities of a particular lot configuration and its traffic patterns? Was it the best use of one's money? Despite the downtown garage's checkered experience, some investors took the risk. The urban garage's form became an ongoing saga.

6

THE MATURING URBAN PARKING STRUCTURE

In this chapter we address the parking garage's development during the last half of the twentieth century. The end of the Great Depression and World War II spurred a voracious appetite for consumer goods and services by the late 1940s. In its wake, parking garages changed from a series of sporadic businesses plagued by numerous bankruptcies and an understandably poor reputation with lending institutions and investors into aggressive contributors to one of the services Americans have come to expect. The automobile, fulcrum for much of the postwar economic upsurge and perhaps the strongest symbol of American luxury, was the object of incredible demand by the early 1950s. At the start of the decade the total motor vehicle production exceeded 8 million for the first time and 9 million by 1955.[1] In 1955, a journalist excited about a mechanical parking garage's solution to one inner-city hotel's parking needs exclaimed: "Next to winning the Peace, America's number one problem seems to be winning the parking problem. . . . It has been growing steadily worse."[2] By 1956, the problem in medium-sized cities began to alarm experts, and within a decade Europeans began to look to America's half-century of experience with the parking garage solution to solve their own similar but more slowly developing urban traffic glut.[3] Unlike the short-lived interest in the parking garage as a new business prospect in the 1920s, motorist and building trades magazines no longer had to frequently reassure prospective businesspeople and counsel them on how to build and manage parking garages. Downtown parking demand swelled and shifted the need to off-street parking in multitiered facilities. The future seemed bright for a long time to come. Opportunistic and enterprising businesspeople responded to the obvious need.

Garage building, maintenance, and operation have since been a tale of largely expanding but always complex horizons. Private and public collaboration became common, as the sides were no longer invariably opposed; indeed, public garage building and operation were steadily accepted as the only practical option in some cases. Demand and opportunity drove experimentation in new materials and structural types and the rise of firms specializing in parking design. By the 1970s, advisers ceased recommending a few best models. Parking garage construction and management became elaborate collaborations of traffic engineers, urban planners, building contractors, and entrepreneurs combining numerous carefully proposed and selected factors rendering each resulting structure unique. Complexity characterized design in a lucrative and mature parking industry through the last half of the twentieth century.

Four general descriptions of state-of-the-art parking garage design published at fairly regular intervals during the period might structure our review. Three are short articles in trade journals: "Garages Grow Up," *Architectural Forum* (1953); "Commercial Parking Garages," *Architectural Record* (1958); and "Urban Parking Garages," *American City* (1970). Charles T. McGavin, a university-educated engineer who emerged with Miller McClintock among the first generation of traffic-planning specialists, advised the anonymous writers of the 1953 article. George Devlin, the National Parking Garages chief designer and a self-taught pioneer in the parking industry since the early 1930s, contributed greatly to the 1958 article. The anonymous authors of the 1970 article synthesized publications of traffic engineers and garage designers. Experts wrote chapters on their specialties in the third edition of a textbook, *Dimensions in Parking* (1993), providing the fourth and latest reference framing this discussion. Historical scholarship is woefully lacking on design in this period.[4] Hence, the sources framing our discussion are tantamount to a survey of exiting practices, given the host of experts writing or advising their writers. We also rely heavily on various parking trade and architectural trade journals and other textbooks throughout the period to afford the details that exemplify assertions drawn from the four main sources.

1940s–1990s
The Common

Planning had been recommended before but was renewed with greater urgency in this latest era. The *Architectural Forum*'s brief narrative history of parking and elaborate table of "operating Costs and Profits" according to the percentage of short-time versus all-day parkers in garages of varying capacity, rate structure, amortized interest, and what gross profit might mean in actual profit perhaps reassured the cautiously optimistic investor. Neither architectural trade magazines, however, wanted their treatments mistaken for encouragement to willing but unspecialized architectural firms, as the *Architectural Record*'s treatment of 1929 left possible. The two 1950s articles advised hiring one of the proliferating professional garage designers.[5] The articles instead constituted a list of issues to check and help frame the client's preliminary ruminations. Despite the recommendation in the 1970 *American City*'s article of computer-assisted design, a complicated procedure that gave further entrée to specialists, complete surrender to experts was not desired.[6] H. Carl Walker, one of the specialists by the 1970s, founded a firm whose staff collaborated in a 1996 textbook that made the salient point about security systems that owners and operators should be the final arbiters, not consultants. The textbook prepared by Walker Parking Consultants/Engineers, Inc., although far surpassing in detail anything previously published, sought to impress readers with the need for careful decision making about the garage as a unique structural type; this was not a self-help manual.[7] Planning was collaborative as well as complicated.

The geographical issue of location remained central in planning. Where exactly to build the garage downtown? Denison, Inc., considering itself the leading owner-operator of parking facilities in Indianapolis, exemplifies an astute member of the parking industry whose founding resulted from the highest virtue of good real estate — location. Pennsylvania, Massachusetts, and Ohio Streets formed a very busy intersection on the northeast edge of downtown Indianapolis when, in 1926, the heirs of Charles Coffin Perry, a prominent member of the city's business establishment, bought the financially fading Denison Hotel on that intersection simply because it was for sale. It was necessary to raze the hotel in 1932, but the family was uncertain how to reinvest in this choice lot. Waiting for a more profitable income from it later, Norman A. Perry and his sister, Ruth Perry Griffith, decided to take at least temporary advantage of the city's burgeoning automobility. Franz W. Fackler, the family's business adviser and an accountant, helped set this course. In 1934, they started Denison Service Parking, named for the former hotel, as a garage for lubrication and washing built in a one-story structure with additional space for rental stores and a gasoline station behind it (fig. 6.1). The store section was constructed in two parts for later reuse by a hotel chain that showed interest in purchasing

FIG. 6.1

In this post–World War II advertising flyer, Denison Service Parking stated: "Park safely in the heart of the business district. Take advantage of our modern one-stop service while you shop." *Source:* Courtesy of Denison, Inc.

the site. Meanwhile, the Griffith family (which bought the property when Norman sold it to his sister Ruth, a Griffith by marriage) earned a good income from their "land banking" strategy; a restaurant, bar, hat store, and fur store in the rented spaces added to the income from the car services. The increased business activity in downtown Indianapolis after World War II and the hotel chain's failure to make an offer for the site induced the Griffith family to further pursue their once tentative parking venture. In 1954, the Denison lot was upgraded to a 7-tier cast-in-place continuous ramp for parking 650 cars, the fifth self-park structure in the nation at the time (fig. 6.2). The back portion of the lot, at first less profitable than the parking lot, became the most profitable, and the Denison operation went on to build or manage other parking facilities in the city.[8]

The answer to where to build a garage beginning in the 1950s, however, was no longer a site wisely chosen within a city, because many sites were traffic saturated. Rather, the task became one of analyzing traffic more minutely than before to determine the most effective design according to its location. Traffic analysis should yield data about parkers' behavior: what attracts them, length of their stay, and their effect on the neighborhood. Information about operation, or the staff and machinery to run the garage, also derived from analysis of the prevailing customers, who were classified as shopper, commuter, or professional. Shoppers were short-term occupants, staying one to three hours. Commuters stayed for their workday, entering and exiting once daily. Professionals were long-term parkers but generally entered and exited several times daily. Professionals usually contracted for assigned parking with the consequence that they were a steady

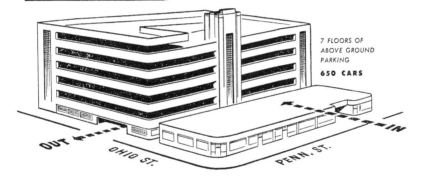

But look what's coming...

DENISON Park-it-yourself GARAGE

7 FLOORS OF ABOVE GROUND PARKING

650 CARS

OUT ← OHIO ST.

PENN. ST. → IN

PARK YOUR OWN CAR ... no waiting, chauffeur service if desired.

NO RAMPS ... gradual sloped floors with only 4% grade make a continuous easy driving spiral.

EXTRA-WIDE DRIVEWAYS and stalls make parking easier for you than on the street.

HIGH SPEED ELEVATORS to speed you from your car to street level.

COMFORTABLE WAITING ROOM and attractive rest rooms for your convenience and use.

WATCH FOR FUTURE DETAILS ABOUT THIS AMAZING NEW

Largest and Finest in the State

PARKING GARAGE

FIG. 6.2

In this 1954 advertising flyer, Denison, Inc. proudly announced that its garage would be opened soon and would provide the very latest advances: self-parking, gradually sloping (not ramped) floors, wide driveways, elevators between the floors of the garage and the street, and a waiting room. *Source:* Courtesy of Denison, Inc.

but often lower source of income. Shoppers provided the "breakage," as parking professionals coined the term for the considerable income derived from the full charge for units of time not fully occupied in the garage.[9]

Emphasis on traffic as the keystone in garage design installed those studying traffic scientifically and advising as authorities on its effects everywhere — traffic engineers — in primary roles on the team creating and evaluating almost every garage. Scientific understanding was their objective because it seemed a widely shared cultural faith that science afforded greater security than any other paradigm. By implication, traditional architects were supplanted as too impressionistic. Like most professionals, traffic engineers were seldom called upon to reveal the procedure of their arcane work for general audiences, although they were anxious to do so when it was expedient. It became expedient in the hectic pace of garage evolution and construction during the immediate post–World War II period. Edmund Ricker, a traffic engineer and staff member of the New Jersey Turnpike Authority, therefore wrote *Traffic Design of Parking Garages* in 1948 and revised it in 1957. Simply titled, it opened to view the complicated variables that traffic engineers manipulated in the effort to control the "increasingly more complex 'downtown parking problem' as construction costs and the use of mass transit decreases, while more and more drivers look for convenient parking for their personal cars." Garages were perceived as extensions of the surrounding street system. Ricker made time-motion studies in 12 garages, observations in 25 garages, and recorded behavior with a movie camera when it was the only way to observe without upsetting normal functions. His careful analysis included the general caution that broad generalizations about design could not be made: "any particular facility must reflect local conditions and values."[10] Site specific planning principles carried over from the prewar period.

The pressure to maximize profit dictated rapidity once customers were on their way in or out of the garage. Arithmetic measures and scientific observation were mobilized to serve "bottom line" entrepreneurs. Each garage's idiosyncratic nature aside, time was tyrant.[11] There was no mistaking the revved-up economy and hectic pace belying the coolly taken decisions behind the newly planned garages.

Occupancy and lot size came next to determine how a garage should be designed. These determinants directed attention inside, making flow and speedy yet safe access more important than the exterior appearance, at least until the late 1960s.

Two inter-floor arrangements were common by the early 1950s. Sloping floors functioned most effectively, but staggered ramps served small lots better because they required less street frontage. D'Humy designs fell from their general prewar favor. With stalls squeezed below the preferred total 18-foot aisle on each level to a 17-foot-6-inch aisle, staggered ramps could barely fit onto a lot with a 105-foot street frontage. Ideal lots, however, were 120 feet by 130 feet in the 1950s. One-way passage along either sloped or staggered ramps was standard because drivers did not like to pass another car even where two-way ramps were built. One-way ramps provided the fastest and safest structures at peak traffic times, marginalizing two-way passage among small garages. Ricker abandoned all subsequent reference to the substandard two-way system once he defined it. He distinguished between "clearway" and adjacent parking ramp types. H. L. Woolfenden, an engineer in Detroit, had coined and patented the term "clearway ramp" to identify ramps with separate paths for vehicles going up and coming down to minimize delays from people parking and unparking. This type was recommended as safer than the adjacent parking type, which maximized storage by permitting parking on the access aisles used for interfloor travel. Temporary blockage — up to a minute — due to parking and unparking could result in losses of always precious time. Garages were judged efficient if they required no longer than one hour to achieve full occupancy or complete vacancy, and minute delays for individual cars were categorically unacceptable.[12]

Each lot's peculiar dimensions determined the ramp type best suited to use. Spiral, continuous and opposed, and modified split-level were highlighted as the types most popular in the 1950s. Efficiency had set limits on profit; several older variations were useful for increasing space — steeper ramp, two-way traffic on a one-way ramp, ramp as parking space, cars parked in aisles, and double-parked cars — but were unacceptable because they slowed service. None of those older variations, except for the ramp as occasional parking space, were advised through the 1960s. The 1993 guide reported that cars parked at 90-degree angles on both sides of the center passing aisle on a helix were most common (fig. 6.3).[13]

A constant in interior design throughout the last 50 years and one distinguishing the era has been the keener attention paid to the look of the garage's interior. Psychological factors generally were absent in advice published earlier but were increasingly recognized beginning in the 1950s when self-park operations became common. *Architectural Forum's* 1953 article observed that "customers balk at driving up a ramp system, however well laid out, beyond a sixth level" and that "there is less resistance to driv-

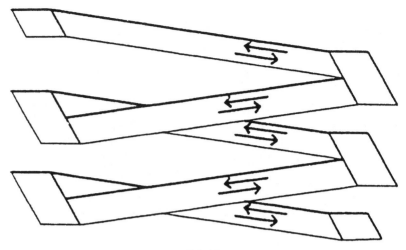

FIG. 6.3

By the 1990s, the single-helix ramp for two-way traffic was the most common. *Source:* H. Carl Walker, "Functional Design of Parking Facilities," in *The Dimensions of Parking,* 3d. ed. (Washington, DC: Urban Land Institute and National Parking Association, 1993), 99.

ing up open-deck ramps than to maneuvering in closed buildings."[14] Both the 1957 and 1990 publications prescribed that length of vision and lighting would stimulate the necessary driver confidence.[15] Garage interiors certainly retained their ominous reputations for darkness in popular culture, but not without designers' efforts to the contrary.

Sloped floors emerged from the 1950s as another preferred design element. General Petroleum Company's garage in Los Angeles was one of the early sloped floor types in the United States, achieving status as a model by 1958. The sloped floor's improved efficiency combined speed and safety in large garages but did not rapidly persuade builders to abandon the older, once preferred staggered ramp variety. Although the 1970 article in the *American City* still discriminated between the best floor types according to site and occupancy, the 1993 textbook noted that the sloping ramp was the most common.[16]

Self-parking contributed further to the design of most parking garages by the end of the twentieth century. Self-parking originated in the West and diffused to the East, as did many aspects of America's growing automobile-convenient landscape. Perhaps the "tradition-bound eastern United States" resisted the innovation.[17] Owners and managers, not customers, seem to have been the first advocates. One regular attendee at the National Parking

Association's annual meetings remembered that no one talked about self-parking until the 1953 meeting, after which everybody seemed to talk about it.[18] Rising labor costs due to rising wages and training expenses, and the unattractive nature of the 9- to 15-hour shifts common in the industry for attendants, made self-parking an alternative for management.[19] Various new construction techniques—long spans between columns, pre-stressed concrete, steel skeleton structures, lower ceiling heights, and lower ramp grades—contributed as well to the adoption of self-parking in the mid-1950s.[20] The primacy of lowered cost to customer and operator alike and customer familiarity with the innovation definitely won out. By 1956 self-parking was increasingly popular despite the initial fear that accidents were more likely and that women were thought reluctant to drive on the new sloped ramps.[21] Valet parking flourished as a variety of attendant parking where high status was implied. For virtually all other parkers, however, self-parking was customary by the 1990s.[22]

Open-deck construction also became popular through the last half of the twentieth century. An experimental expedient of the Great Depression, the open-deck won entrepreneurs' rapid approval in the garage-building boom after World War II because costs were lower—one-third to one-fourth as much as the older, enclosed garage.[23]

Open-deck construction rendered unnecessary some elements that were essential in earlier structures: windows, ventilation, and much artificial lighting.[24] Yet, owners willingly paid the added expense of heated ramps to check the problem peculiar to open-deck garages in northern locations during winter, namely, iced ramps. Garage entrepreneurs complained instead that local building codes discouraged open-deck adoption by requiring useless but costly equipment—ventilation systems, for example—because local code authorities still thought of prewar garages with their firetrap image when they thought of garages. Garage entrepreneurs overcame this impediment, first in Washington, D.C., Los Angeles, and Minneapolis.[25] The National Board of Fire Underwriters' study of fire in parking facilities of all kinds demonstrated the open deck's surprising record of fire safety and concluded that code requirements should be relaxed if the open deck's record could approach the parking lot's safety record.[26] Examples of open-deck construction abounded by the early 1950s.[27]

Changing automobile widths induced another feature common to post–World War II garages, long-span construction. Whereas garages in the previous period could accommodate 3 automobiles side by side between posts, wider automobile bodies rendered those earlier garages obsolete be-

FIG. 6.4

A clear span in the Maryland Parking Garage, Indianapolis, 1950. *Source:* Courtesy of Denison, Inc.; Bass Photo Company.

cause only 2 new automobiles fit between the older post locations.[28] "Clear spans" were called for, by which it was meant longer distances between posts (fig. 6.4). Beginning in the mid-1950s, structures spanning 50–65 feet became common with the use of pre-stressed concrete members, which are discussed further below.[29] So profound was the adjustment to the new auto dimensions that Ricker reasoned he had to rewrite his guide between 1948 and 1957.[30] The *America City* article of 1970 advised hesitantly that "there appears to be some movement toward clear-span facilities."[31] A trend toward small cars following the energy crisis of 1973 ended any doubts. Uncertainty about the impact of constantly changing conditions, a chronic lament in garage design, is demonstrated in the response to downsized cars; by 1980 garage designers were unsure exactly how to lay out stalls. Who knew what those dimensions would be? The constant adaptation to anticipated changes, although of unknown magnitude, made clear-span construction a constant amid flux. The 1993 textbook justified only clear-span design.[32]

Variations notwithstanding, the parking garage most commonly seen in America's downtowns in the last quarter of the twentieth century featured four principle components: open deck, sloped floors, self-parking, and clear-span construction. Those answers to "the parking problem" had focused on the efficiency and economy of its components. Traffic engineers, structural engineers, planners, financiers, entrepreneurs, and managers had identified the four principle components of the common downtown garage, which performed their roles remarkably well, and developed the resulting garage with overall success. But questions about whether the aesthetic whole should be greater than the sum of its structural parts began to be asked in the 1960s. What contribution to urbanism did this ubiquitous new urban form make?

What contribution had it been asked to make? Considerable at first. Popular expectations of buildings generally were of a traditional aesthetic, associating buildings with a look appropriate to their function. This was associative architecture. For example, colleges should conjure faith in deep and long-term learning. Homes should resonate as domestic sanctuaries. Architectural styles often came to be linked with building functions. Collegiate Gothic and various period effects for homes — Tudor Revival, Cotswold cottage, and bungalow — exemplify.[33] Garages, one of the new automobile-convenient building types, began to take on their own look. In the 1920s, when they had been designed to resemble factories, lay tastes appear to have been satisfied. For garages, the associationist aesthetic eroded greatly in the 1940s. Ricker's 1948 guide revealed the supervening role of saving costs and reducing aesthetics to an afterthought. Early-twentieth-century architects designing in the associationist mode had thought of their work as functional, that is, as producing creations appropriate to a circumstance. By midcentury, the hegemonic new functionalism of Le Corbusier's followers was reflected in Ricker's 1957 guide to garage design. To those modernists, function meant how a design worked, not how it looked. While Ricker allowed that a garage's visual appeal "must be thoroughly coordinated," the garage was "to produce the most economical and practical design."[34] The new functionalist aesthetic synchronized with the emphasis on economical cost to command design.[35] Engineering and modernism seized hold of garage design.[36]

The old "closed-wall" garage was relegated to peculiar circumstances where walls were required for structural or aesthetic purposes. In contrast, almost all new designs exemplified the postwar faith in modernism or, consistent with the faith, were expediently stripped to the bare essentials. Most designs, unfortunately, were of the latter kind. Designers believed their work achieved perfection with materials at once enduring and beautiful, but by later standards, those garages came to be scorned as incredibly ugly.[37]

With utilitarianism enthroned, steel frame systems for multilevel parking became the designer's ultimate choice. Having saved 7 to 10 percent of costs by abandoning "fire-protective encasement" for open-deck construction, the steel parking deck promised further savings by replacing the concrete elements — framing, floor slabs, and foundation — that accounted for 55 to 65 percent of costs for new garage construction. In addition to the lower cost of steel, it required other less expensive building materials than the other elements. Assembly too was cheaper because it was "almost automatic," explained an executive of National Garages.[38]

Beginning in the late 1960s, some people opposed the prevailing canons of garage design as environmentalism, historic preservation, and postmodern architecture combined. In 1975, architect Charles M. Boldon recounted the accumulated considerations of recently enacted environmental legislation on future parking garage design: air quality, capacity, and architecture. The Environmental Protection Agency's standards of July 1, 1975, necessitated new standards for interfloor travel, parking angles in stalls, stall width, and entrance design and operation. Different interfloor arrangements on comparable sites could yield a 58 percent difference in fuel consumption "equivalent to three tons of carbon monoxide contamination per year plus 700 lbs. of hydrocarbons per year." Wider bays resulting in large lots for garages were recommended.[39]

The most striking changes were outward. Engineers were rebuked for having derogated their talents and fallen into league with profiteers: "undoubtedly one of architecture's least demanding assignments, it takes little more than a construction bankroll to produce a profitable parking structure," raged one detractor.[40] A critical professor of architecture explained a better garage would be "one hidden or buried, one decorated or marked and screened or draped."[41] In harmony with renewed public emphasis on the visual, some cities periodically gave "face lifts" to old structures of earlier design standards, modestly satisfying the new sensibility without huge public expenditures. Charles M. Boldon's firm, International Parking Design, established in 1969, continued heralding the principle that parking garages be architectural and environmental good neighbors.[42] Formally designated historic areas especially heeded that new caveat. By the late 1980s, some cities firmly regulated parking garage aesthetics throughout their downtown cores and, in a few cases, prohibited their construction altogether.[43]

Smart marketers labored simultaneously to improve function and achieve a genuinely competitive distinction with motorists. For example,

Standard Parking's chief executive officer, Myron Warshauer, patented his "musical reminder system" that played different popular music on every level of its garages to help patrons remember where they parked. Movie posters on each level assisted memory, with the combination permitting Standard's slogan in the early 1990s, "ambiance in parking."[44] Image became a strategy with parking companies as it was already with industries leading the consumer culture.

The design, ownership, and management of the urban garage having become big business, companies ceaselessly developed and used new materials, new construction techniques, new devices, and new services to remain competitive. Parking garages consequently took on many new forms as a result of the many ways those variables could be combined successfully.

In construction, the polarity between initial low cost and durability quickly induced the wide application of several innovations: concrete members cast in place and posttensioned, and members precast and prestressed. Each had relative advantages. Concrete poured into forms on the building site, cast-in-place construction, remained common throughout the last half of the century; its better drainage, lower cost, and better interior visibility (because of fewer beams) were appealing. Concrete members given tensile strength, or posttension construction, became a standard part of cast-in-place frames. Cast-in-place concrete was favored for sites requiring compatibility with an existing structure and locations, such as on the West Coast, that required satisfaction of high seismic building codes. On the other hand, cast-in-place members were more costly to build in colder climates, and qualified contractors were not always available. Since the mid-1950s pre-stressed concrete became popular in conjunction with clear-span construction, principally in bridges and stores.[45] Not until a publicly owned parking garage built in 1960 in Beverly Hills, California, was pre-stressed concrete used with clear-span construction to build a parking garage.[46] Lift-slab construction further facilitated wide adoption of pre-stressed components and further reduced costs.[47] A computer precisely lifted and positioned precast slabs in this system.

To control and account for traffic without the cost of staff on site, machines were invented and installed. In 1953, Josef Diamond had a device designed locally to complement his self-park operation in Seattle for the first park-by-number system. Entrepreneurs moved toward ever more slightly staffed garages through the 1950s. Self-park meant one man per floor to direct traffic, according to the *Architectural Forum*'s 1953 article, and by 1963, *Parking* featured an operation to be built the following year in

Dallas with an automatic ticket dispenser and personnel on each floor if needed.[48] Ticket dispensers and the relentless pressure for lower labor costs eventually enabled operations with only a cashier at the exit to become standard.

Security problems increased in severity throughout the last half of the century and with them precautionary responses. Security went unmentioned in the 1953 and 1958 architectural trade publications. Ricker's only advice in 1957 provided for what in 1993 was ranked low risk, items fraudulently reported stolen from parked cars.[49] But the 1970 article registered the "problem of assaults and attacks on women in garages." Television monitors, two-way intercoms, and random 24-hour patrols in a parking deck in Harrisburg, Pennsylvania, in 1971 were a newsworthy exception reported a year later. Charles Boldon attributed rising security problems to the ever larger self-park facilities that forced people to park in "remote, unattended areas within the structure, frequently in areas with very little pedestrian activity."[50] Whereas lighting gained little attention in the parking trade press before the 1990s, and then chiefly for a psychological reassurance to customers, as shown above, a rash of articles appeared in the early 1990s about lighting as essential for customer safety and a deterrent to criminals.[51] Women were no longer the principal victims. As security concerns rose in the last half-century, restrooms moved from a bothersome maintenance problem but an essential inclusion in garage design to become a liability because criminals often successfully hid there. Restrooms were less seldom built into garages by the end of the century.[52]

Garage design's broader outlook on efficiency gained further impetus from the Americans with Disabilities Act of 1990. The regulations of 1992 made it illegal to deny services to the disabled, necessitating auxiliary aids and services, removal of barriers, and requirements in new construction. A scale was adopted and enforced stipulating the minimum number of "accessible spaces" in all parking facilities. Those spaces were 8 feet wide and had an adjacent 5-foot-wide aisle marked for any special requirement. Location was also stipulated in relationship to entrances.[53]

Previous accommodations of differences irreducible to statistical measures regularly cited anecdotal information about women customers. By the 1950s, it was widely believed that women did not like to drive on ramps.[54] Paul Box was one of the first designers to doubt the sexist lore on which his colleagues relied: "Somehow the concept that 'women shoppers prefer angle-parking' has become a commandment." Indifference actually prevailed, Box thought, noting that designers in the early 1970s never catered to the need for parking stalls wide enough to accommodate doors opened fully for women exiting cars with infants or children.[55] Absent traffic engineering studies of women parkers, it is possible that garage designers at midcentury felt more comfortable with a science that reduced all parking behavior to statistical averages heedless of subgroups. From the 1950s through the 1970s, new garages were marvelous displays of technological virtuosity satisfying human needs to be sure, but in the aggregate.

Changing demands on the garage's contributions to the quality of urban life can be traced in the function of shops located inside garages. Ground-level stores were popular features through the 1950s because their rent could greatly augment the low profit margins that garage owners habitually decried. A garage on leased land had the potential to operate rent free in the event of profitable ground-floor stores.[56] With the rising traffic tide and the increasing cost of land, shops in garages were viewed less as profit sources than one of several services garages incorporated in a symbiotic urbanism.

"Mixed use," "vertical mix," "dual-purpose structure," "sandwich" building—there were several names for structures incorporating parking levels within offices or apartment buildings—gathered momentum as the last half-century progressed. The 1958 article in the *Architectural Record* discouraged their use because they imposed more expensive standards such as heavier columns and more elevators on the floors below and, without zoning variances, yielded low profits.[57] Their engineering, entrepreneurial, financial, and governmental synchronization was too complex for the new post–World War II entrepreneurs rushing to profit. The 1970 article in *American City*, however, catalogued garages as more attractive through time, and later that year the National Parking Association, in its first public revelation of parking data, noted that nearly one-third of the new parking garages were of mixed use.[58]

The conception of the city as a living entity with free-flowing traffic and ample parking akin to a circulatory system was well demonstrated in the 5-level, 2,200-car parking deck at the Cascade Plaza in Akron, Ohio, in the 1970s. Parking was no longer only a big city imperative. In 1948, when Bluefield, West Virginia, opened its 4-level garage for 800 cars, it was the first municipally funded and owned garage and was considered vital for the small town (20,641 residents in 1940) to remain the regional shopping center for an estimated 300,000 people.[59] Downtown garage design had advanced from a largely private opportunity with public effects in the 1920s to an integral component of an urban vision.

"Garages" began to be called by other names by the end of the twentieth century, a testimony to the changing demands, entrepreneurial initiatives, and technological capabilities that remade them periodically in response to the voracious appetite for urban parking. Early in the century, "garage" had certainly been appropriate for the place to store vehicles, repair them, and resupply their fuel and oil. Even as those services were provided by separate businesses in separate locations, the term "garage" remained current, however illogical. The first three of the four sources framing this chapter's discussion, those through 1970, unanimously used the term "garage." The last of the four sources, *The Dimensions of Parking*, issued in 1993, used various terms in addition to "garage" and offered one of the first extensive glossaries defining the alternatives. A "ramp garage" was "composed entirely of ramped floors connected at various levels." "Facility" could include lot, deck, or garage. "Parking structure" encompassed any "building for parking underground, aboveground, or both." "Garage" retained reference to its original protective function, a building "generally enclosed on all sides" although for storage or repair.[60]

"Garage" remained current in the vernacular although specialists in parking design preferred their own names. Correctly underscoring the building type's unique characteristics, the large 1996 guide of Walker Parking Consultants/Engineers preferred "parking structures" for its title but alternated with "facility" throughout the text. "Parking deck" or "parking ramp" were substitutes acknowledged in the glossary. "Parking garage" appeared in the glossary too, although it was unlisted in the index, having virtually disappeared from the Walker consultant's vocabulary. The accomplished International Parking Design firm, staking claim to be the largest parking design specialist in the western United States, used "parking structure" in its promotional literature. "Deck" was preferred among architects.[61] Complication and sophistication thus reoriented the very naming of the building to house parked vehicles.

The Uncommon

A vigorous industry such as parking was bound to generate variations from the norm. The endless quest for satisfaction characterized an enterprise trying to bring order out of change in numerous variables — in land values, entrepreneurial opportunity, structural improvements, governmental regulations, and consumer demands. Creative members of the parking industry pursued persistently receding horizons in parking garage design.

Mechanical parking garages or mechanical parkers, dallied with during the depression, returned briefly with force as viable, although minor, alternatives to the open-deck garage of concrete or steel. Mechanical parkers continued their inner-city, small-lot niche, suitable on frontages from 24 to 100 feet and were vast improvements in control, speed, and reliability over their forerunners of the first half-century. It was argued, too, that these mechanical parkers greatly reduced labor costs. In the mid-1950s Pigeon Hole Parking of Spokane, Washington, and the Bowser Parking System of Des Moines, Iowa, led the way. Their 5- or 6-story machines were common, and capacities varied according to lot size. A 5-level Pigeon Hole in Madison, Wisconsin, had a 146-car capacity, and a 10-level Bowser in Des Moines, the company's first model, had a 430-car capacity. Both companies built their first models in 1951, but the Korean War stalled sales for several years. Pigeon Hole was a manufacturer and installed its parkers with franchised operators. Bowser sold its parkers to parking companies. Whereas Pigeon Hole's apparatus was more completely mechanized than Bowser's, calling for an operator to command a dolly that pushed the car onto an elevator, Bowser's required a driver to move the car onto the elevator operated from a panel outside the window of the driver's seat. The two companies were enthusiastically received through the 1950s, but quickly thereafter entrepreneurs lost interest in them for a host of reasons. They were unsuitable for most lots. Clear-span construction was better suited to changing car sizes, and self-park satisfied customers' general impatience better than mechanical garages, which still required waiting. Periodic failures and unrepaired examples revived the prewar reputation of the mechanical parkers as impractical gadgets. The president of the National Parking Association discredited mechanical parking machines in his 1964 report to the association, and the *American City* article of 1970 did not mention them. The devices thereafter took the form of racks stacking one car above another, looking rather like trailers used to transport cars by truck. The ambitious high-rise mechanicals disappeared, but promoters insisted the short versions were established in the market. About 7,000 such units were reported in use in 1992.[62]

Underground parking was more widely used after San Francisco first proved its practicality in certain circumstances. The need to relieve traffic congestion, however, did not always hasten adoption. The Los Angeles Downtown Business Men's Association, for example, planned for parking beneath Pershing Square in 1931 and 1932, but it was not until the late 1940s before city officials and financiers agreed on plans. Construction began in

1951, and a year later, a 2,000-car garage, the largest underground facility built at that time, opened. Chicago surpassed Los Angeles with the opening of the largest underground parking facility (with a 2,359-car capacity) in 1953 under Grant Park. In the early 1950s, a trend seemed under way toward the wider adoption of underground parking.[63] Underground garages helped alleviate their respective cities' traffic congestion, served to coalesce public and private cooperation in many cases, and displayed handsomely landscaped parks above. They, however, were multimillion dollar undertakings, unsuited for every city that might have benefited from them.

Above ground, roof-top parking was more widely used during the late 1940s in the rush to rescue inner cities drowning in traffic. Some roof-top parking was exclusively a service to shoppers downtown. Other cases combined private initiatives for public parking. Overall, this type of parking was judged well-suited for one- and two-story department stores but ill-suited for higher-volume and faster parking.[64]

Engineering virtuosity in the 1960s produced "portable parking" or demountable modules that could be erected on site and respond to changing traffic patterns by relocation to a better site as the need arose. Charles Bentley invented the demountable garage.[65] By the 1960s, urban life seemed unthinkable to many without the parking garage. In that decade, downtown traffic's persistent crush produced use of the legal innovation of "air rights" resulting in garages above and between other structures. Air rights represented use of the legal concept that enterprises could purchase from other enterprises the height that remained unbuilt below the local building code. They did not invariably demand exceptionally engineered parking facilities, but they certainly indicated the imaginative resourcefulness that urban dwellers exercised in pursuit of their automobility.[66] Parking garages also began passing into history toward the last quarter of the century. In 1961, the parking industry's own trade magazine *Parking* acknowledged the Downtown Garage. Built in 1926 in Winston-Salem, it was the first urban garage in North Carolina.[67]

AN INDIANAPOLIS RETROSPECTIVE

Parking in Mile Square continued to swallow more space once the process began. In 2000, no one in Mile Square was farther than a block from a parking garage or lot. In the layperson's eye, parking must have seemed the ubiquitous urban form (fig. 6.5). No longer clinging as a novel business to low-

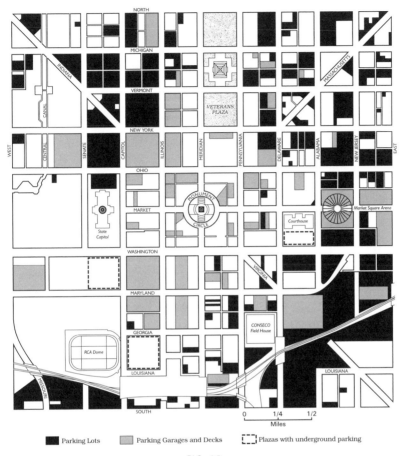

FIG. 6.5

Parking areas in downtown Indianapolis, 2000. *Source:* Authors' field survey, January 11 and February 5, 2000.

value back lots as in 1914, parking lots and garages occupied entire blocks in 2000. On the east side, surface lots and garages immediately adjacent to two sports buildings, Conseco Arena and Market Square Arena, responded to recreation, apart from shopping, as a traffic generator. On the west side, garages occupied whole blocks diagonally across from the state capitol. Those far exceeded the proportion of garage space assigned immediately east, in front of the capitol, where garage and surface lots remained substantially the same as they had been in 1942. Garages underground, connected to adjacent buildings, or integrated into buildings attest to how

| 153 |

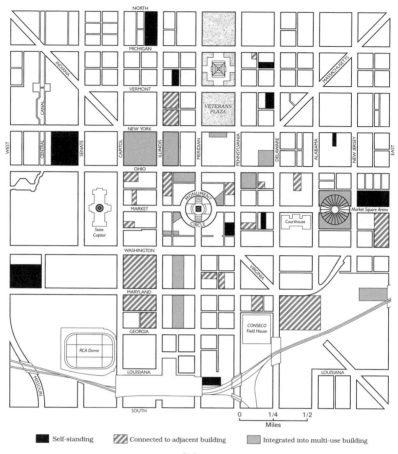

FIG. 6.6

Parking structures in downtown Indianapolis, 2000. *Source:* Authors' field survey, January 11 and February 5, 2000.

tightly entwined parking had become in the urban fabric (fig. 6.6). None of those types existed in 1942. Free-standing garages, progressive in 1942, were far less numerous in 2000 than the other types of parking structure.

Many interests converged to form the urban parking garage from its inception early in the twentieth century to the end of that century. Initially a collateral opportunity for mechanics and auto body repairmen offering winter storage, garages became a primary business in the general prosperity of the 1920s. A new building type sprang up across American cities as entrepreneurs razed urban cores for their enterprise or renovated buildings of previous purpose. Most of these businesses failed in the depression, but the scramble through mechanical parkers, mixed-use buildings, and the dawn of underground parking demonstrated the need to answer how the rising tide of traffic could be harbored in the inner city. Prosperity's return and persistence in the last half of the twentieth century ushered in a new round of entrepreneurs to provide the most sensible answer for how to end the growing downtown traffic glut through off-street storage in multitiered facilities. Efficiency measured in terms of profitable operation for entrepreneurs and affordability and rapid service for an arithmetically constructed average consumer brought traffic engineering to the fore as the dominant arbiter on garage design teams. Mega-structures with minimal attention to beauty generally resulted in an aesthetic backlash, the traffic engineers' acknowledged tour de force in ending "the traffic problem" notwithstanding. Diversity in cultural considerations such as facilities more sensitively fashioned for the eye and the disabled came just before the century's close. Specialized facilities for shopping centers follow.

7

PARKING AND
DOWNTOWN REDEVELOPMENT

The automobile wrought substantive change in American cities, and nowhere was its effect more pronounced than in downtown business districts. Although motor vehicles had come unobtrusively at first, their numbers quickly exaggerated street congestion, precipitating the widening of streets and the constructing of new thoroughfares. Municipal regulation of curbside parking rationalized streets as arteries for traffic movement. Encouraged was off-street parking, which led to the demolition of economically marginal buildings in and around central business districts in favor of utilitarian parking lots. Although downtown cores might be reinforced by tall buildings, and increased in density accordingly, the peripheries of central business districts were systematically invaded by parking and, thereby, substantially reduced to open space. There the solid infrastructure of the traditional city was replaced by the vacuousness of asphalted lots. Not only could cars be profitably parked in the short term, but land, once cleared, stood ready for redevelopment in the long term, or so it was argued. Thus was the commercial parking industry born.

Traffic congestion dampened retailing downtown, with many retailers moving to suburban locations even before World War II. Other kinds of business activity followed, especially during the 1960s and 1970s. To retain office, convention, entertainment, and traditional political and cultural functions, if not a residue of downtown retailing also, downtown business interests sought to stem the tide of downtown decline through aggressive redevelopment. Parking garages (or parking decks) came to play a critical role in downtown rebuilding. Indeed, zoning codes required in most cities that new buildings be provided with parking garages according to set formulas.

By stacking parking floors at locations immediate to commuter and shopper destinations, degrees of automobile convenience could be achieved reasonably competitively with that of suburbia. When employers and retailers fully subsidized the parking costs of individual motorists, then the parking advantage that had previously accrued to suburban business locations was substantially evened out. If the parking lot was a means of "sanitizing" downtown real estate for eventual redevelopment, then the parking garage was the actual energizer of that development.

CHANGE DOWNTOWN

By the mid-twentieth century, city commentators well understood that cities were decentralizing, and that decentralization was the result of downtown traffic congestion intensified by a general lack of parking. Although business district cores sported many new office towers during the 1920s, areas peripheral to downtown witnessed only decline, wastage induced by parking lot expansion. Around every business district, parking lots invaded previously residential areas, converting them into what urbanists frequently called "transitional" land use zones. But by 1940 even downtown cores were thinning out, with tall towers and open parking lots often directly juxtaposed. Newer outlying business districts, on the other hand, were thriving, encouraged by ease of auto convenience. The parking manual of the American Automobile Association provided a simple diagram descriptive of the change at hand (fig. 7.1).

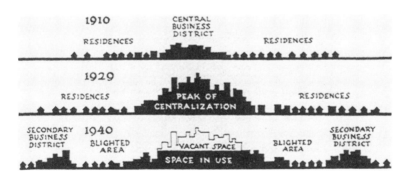

FIG. 7.1

Urban change in America illustrated. The diagram's original caption reads: "Inaccessibility due to lack of parking space is one of the causes of business decentralization. Provision of adequate parking facilities will, however, help greatly to stabilize downtown values." *Source: Parking Manual* (Washington, DC: American Automobile Association, 1946), 27.

It is surprising, however, how many scholars today either ignore the automobile's role in engendering downtown change or subsume it by emphasizing other factors, thereby focusing causal explanation elsewhere. Geographer Larry Ford assigned the leading cause of downtown metamorphosis to skyscrapers. Ford outlined change in America's big city downtowns through both the nineteenth and twentieth centuries in terms of six historical stages of growth: inception, exclusion, segregation, expansion, replication, and redevelopment. Downtowns emerged as special city places when commercial functions began to concentrate spatially in the nineteenth century, especially to the exclusion of residential activities. Segregation of specialized commercial land use occurred when different business activities were sorted out on the basis of required interaction: retailing, wholesaling, and office activities tending to cluster, for example. Expansion, especially in the case of office activity, involved vertical growth through high-rise building construction especially after 1900. Intending his sketch to be a kind of predictive model, Ford wrote of the late twentieth century: "The replication stage may be reached when expansion becomes difficult and a replica of the CBD must be located elsewhere in the city or even in a suburban area. Finally, successful CBDs are rebuilt continuously so as to compete for the highest-level activities and most prestigious buildings. This is known as the redevelopment stage." What were missing, of course, from Ford's sketch were the automobile and the logistics of both auto movement and auto storage. Ford wrote of the transition zones around downtowns, but without mentioning the increased commuter and shopper reliance on automobiles. Tall buildings encouraged economically marginal zones of semi-abandoned smaller buildings, he asserted: properties that "suffered from disinvestment as owners waited expectantly for a skyscraper builder to express interest in their property." [1]

A careful examination, however, of commentary of the period (that published in trade journals and popular magazines as well as in scholarly treatises) places emphasis elsewhere. It makes explicit the role of parking, or the impulse to overcome lack of parking, as the principal motivating force in downtown change. As regards skyscrapers, what truly mattered was how office workers chose to come downtown. Increasingly, people came by car to high-rise offices, as they also came to low-rise offices, stores, theaters, museums, and every other category of downtown place. Large skyscrapers did generate more traffic, and thus more automobile congestion. But it was the congestion, and the associated parking problem, that engendered the bulk of the land use change downtown, and not merely the anticipation of tall buildings per se.

Urban planner Kent Robertson also undertook to outline downtown change. Downtown office districts, he wrote, evolved for a variety of reasons. Expanding industry needed more space for management, with corporate owners preferring to separate office locations from factory locations in part to amplify interaction not only among themselves but, most especially, with banks and other sources of financing. Corporate administration engendered the nearby clustering of support services (e.g., legal advice, advertising expertise, printing, and other activities). Impressive skyscraper buildings rose, both as real estate speculations and as corporate symbols signifying power and influence. Drawn by the volume of increasingly affluent workers concentrated in central business districts, and by the fact that city transportation focused there, theaters, movie houses, sports arenas, restaurants, museums, and other attractions concentrated in downtowns also. By 1950, however, rise of auto ownership and use, and the outward spread of residential development fostered by it, enabled much of this downtown activity to decentralize. "Rising automobile use," Robertson wrote, "has allowed activities that had been the exclusive domain of downtown (e.g. department stores, movie theaters, business offices, hotels, medical services) to follow middle class residents to suburbia."[2]

In 1954, downtown retail sales still accounted for nearly 20 percent of the nationwide metropolitan total, but by 1977 it was only 4 percent.[3] Such statistics had been accumulating for years. In Detroit between 1939 and 1948, for example, the central business district's share of city retail trade dropped from 26 percent to 20 percent.[4] Between 1948 and 1954, general merchandise sales in the city's downtown declined an additional 19 percent. In Pittsburgh, it was 39 percent. In both Newark and Philadelphia it was 15 percent.[5] In downtown Cincinnati between 1937 and 1955, the number of downtown retail establishments fell from 1,375 to 1,087, a drop of 21 percent. Retail floor space declined 16 percent. Conversely, the number of parking lots in downtown Cincinnati increased some 70 percent, from 84 to 143, and the square footage in the lots increased by some 52 percent.[6] The pervasive parking lot increased its hold on downtowns everywhere. "The crux of the parking problem is that the ground space required to park an auto is as great or greater than the ground space required for the activities of the person its transports," one transportation consultant commented.[7]

DOWNTOWN REDEVELOPMENT

It is a truism that for every action there is reaction. For every force there is counterforce or, at least, invitation to same. Downtown decline brought to the fore in nearly every American city responses variously calculated to revive it. Redevelopment schemes emerged that were, in fact, widely shared from city to city. Planner Kent Robertson, extending his discussion to include this change, identified the most popular redevelopment options implemented in American city downtowns over the past half-century: the quest for enhanced pedestrian-orientation, the development of indoor shopping centers, historic preservation linked to themed district development and "festival shopping," the creation of event facilities such as convention centers and sports arenas, office development (the making of downtowns into "corporate centers"), and the addition of downtown housing stock.[8] Combinations of private investment, public-private partnering, and strictly public initiative were variously involved in American cities, with the federal government often assuming an important role through one or another program: urban renewal, urban development action grant, block grant, and other initiatives, most of them administered by the Department of Housing and Urban Development.

As retail and other activities departed, as traditional building stocks eroded, and as the "auto space" of streets and parking facilities became increasingly dominant, not only did downtowns change functionally, but their very character changed as well. Substantially reduced, if not gone altogether, was vibrant street life. The term "street life," popularized by Jane Jacobs and other critics of what automobiles had done to American cities, was, perhaps, a misnomer.[9] It was actually "pedestrian congestion" that was missing, the kind of lively sidewalk activity that supported a real sense of urbanity.[10] The strongest voice for reconstituting downtown around pedestrianism, as opposed to automobility, came from architect and planner Victor Gruen. In his book *The Heart of Our Cities; The Urban Crisis: Diagnosis and Cure* and in articles published under his byline in numerous magazines both professional and popular, Gruen derided urban America's full embrace of the automobile. What he dubbed as the "traffickist" gleefully sped along the new freeways, eyes fixed on the automobile in front while watching, as well, the rearview mirror for the car behind. Driven by a one-track mind and by a devout belief in the infallibility of the motorcar, Gruen mused, the traffickist proceeded in his work of destruction. First of all, he (most traffic planners, indeed, were male) brought to the city center as many automobiles as could be found "lurking" in the metropolitan region.

For this he constructed freeways, bridges, and tunnels, which bankrupted mass transit. "He thus proceeds to bring garages and parking lots on sites where people used to live and work and watch theatrical performances, or otherwise engage in urban activities, and thus loosens the fabric of the city," Gruen argued. Thus it was that American cities, especially when seen from the air, resembled the bombed out cities of Europe immediately after World War II — "with only isolated buildings remaining forlornly in a vast sea of tin automobile roofs."[11]

Gruen called for a strict separation of pedestrians and motor vehicles. His plan to redevelop downtown Fort Worth was outlined for readers of the *American City*. He called for the following:

1. Creation of a pedestrian central business district where automobiles, buses, and trucks would be prohibited, and comfortable, noiseless, battery-powered shuttle cars made available for the convenience of pedestrians.

2. Construction of underground freight and cargo delivery facilities there.

3. Construction of a loop or belt line highway ringing the central business district to receive traffic from the city's freeways and other tributary roads and funnel traffic into strategically placed parking garages and terminals where buses, taxis, and airport limousines could discharge passengers.

4. Location of major parking garages inside the belt line highway so as to minimize walking distances within the pedestrian zone.[12]

The same basic concepts were used in a proposal for revitalizing downtown Kalamazoo, Michigan.

Neither Fort Worth nor Kalamazoo embraced Gruen's vision fully, although both cities did adopt selected aspects of his scheme in watered-down versions. In 1959, Kalamazoo converted two blocks of its principal retail street into the nation's first outdoor downtown pedestrian mall, a third block being added a year later. City manager C. H. Elliott reported that gross sales downtown increased some 15 percent during the first year of the mall's operation, and patronage in parking lots and garages increased some 14 percent, with cars staying slightly longer than previously. Indeed, because parking was key to the mall's operation, the city opened a 450-space parking deck immediately behind stores fronting one side of the mall.[13] By 1978, some 90 cities across the United States had established downtown malls by closing off a street entirely, or by closing one partially: for example, closing it to all vehicular traffic except buses.[14] One of those cities was Allentown, Pennsylvania, where Hamilton Street in the downtown was converted to a "transit mall." A cantilevered canopy system stretched the length of the mall to protect pedestrians in inclement weather and integrate the street visually. New paving, streetlights, planters, benches, and other street furnishings, patterned after the city's new outlying suburban shopping centers were installed.

Downtown malls simulated the outdoor spaces of shopping centers, complete with trees and flowerbeds and children's play equipment. But what worked in suburbia, with new, carefully integrated storefronts placed in close proximity to parking, did not work in most downtowns. As parking usually was located at a distance, if only a short distance, downtown stores remained, in the typical shopper's perception, less than fully convenient. What did not look old looked flimsy, especially storefronts with appliqués of cheap contrivance. Where sign ordinances eliminated sign diversity across storefronts, relative dullness often reigned. Outdoor malls did not suddenly crowd with multitudes of shoppers. Instead, they came to be seen as overly quiet and dull. Gone almost completely was active street life. Even the cars were gone. Amplified, instead, was the all-too-apparent failure of downtown retailing. In most cities, outdoor malls were quietly removed after only a few years of operation.

To the fore came two other downtown shopping ideas: the indoor shopping center, on cleared land rather than on closed streets, and the festival market, utilizing buildings rehabilitated to retain their historical character. The enclosed shopping center or mall represented rebirth of an old idea, the downtown shopping arcade, which was, in a way, the precursor to the downtown department store. Developed in European cities in the early nineteenth century and epitomized, perhaps, by the Galleria in Milan, arcades were developed in many American cities, among them the now fully renovated Euclid Arcade in Cleveland. Designed to service downtown workers, as well as attract suburbanites, new downtown shopping malls closely resembled in layout and range of services the new enclosed suburban malls popularized after 1960.[15] A principal difference was that they were linked with large parking garages or decks rather than surrounded by acres of parking lot. Many were organized vertically rather than horizontally, with shopping levels stacked one upon another.

The Indianapolis Circle Center is one of the more recent downtown malls (fig. 7.2). The center stretches for three blocks south from Monument Circle between Meridian and Illinois Streets and contains some 1.4 million square feet of retail space. It includes two anchoring department stores and

FIG. 7.2

Circle Center in downtown Indianapolis, 1997. The view east along Maryland Street includes a large parking deck on the right, with the shopping center spanning the street in the distance.

a 600-room hotel as well as a wide array of shops.[16] Although buildings on several city blocks were completely cleared, a former department store was retained, as were the facades of many smaller buildings in order that they be re-erected in simulation of pre-existing downtown street margins. Parking was made available in the lower level of the complex and in parking decks in adjacent blocks connected to the center by over-the-street walkways. Other downtown malls include Chicago's Water Tower Place, St. Louis's St. Louis Centre, San Diego's Horton Plaza, and New Orleans's Canal Place.

Created in many cities were "themed districts," or so called "festival markets."[17] At work was a commercial packaging of place employing rehabilitated historic buildings. Renovation of the Ghirardelli Chocolate Factory in San Francisco's North Beach neighborhood provided an early prototype, a demonstration of what could be accomplished in old warehouse districts in or near central business districts through embrace of historic preservation values. Boston's revitalized Quincy Market, undertaken by James Rouse's Enterprise Development Company for the Boston Redevelopment Authority, proved to be the real trendsetter (fig. 7.3). The city's wholesale fruit and vegetable market was redesigned as an upscale shop-

FIG. 7.3

Boston's Quincy Market, 1981. The market encourages an active pedestrian-oriented street life that is sustained by nearby car parking.

ping plaza, and its essential pedestrian-orientation was sustained by nearby parking decks. The Rouse Company, previously a suburban shopping center developer (and developer of Columbia, a "new town" outside Washington, D.C.), created similar downtown complexes in a host of cities including Baltimore (Harborplace), New York City (South Street Seaport), Norfolk (Waterside), and Philadelphia (The Gallery). In festival market areas, retail functions were oriented both to tourists arrived from beyond the metropolis and to day-trippers from within. Thus these areas often contained stores, museums, and other entertainment venues, especially restaurants. Dallas's West End, Denver's Larimer Square, and Omaha's Old Market are configured in former warehouse areas of late nineteenth-century origin. Chicago's River North, on the other hand, was formerly an industrial zone of early twentieth-century loft buildings.

Convention centers and sports stadia are "event-oriented" facilities also capable of concentrating large numbers of people in downtowns. No major city is without its convention hall and cluster of hotels nearby. Many cities used convention centers to drive major downtown redevelopment, including the anchoring of new civic centers, as in Detroit. Rarely were convention facilities developed in isolation; rather, they were carefully linked with other visitor attractions. In Indianapolis, the city's convention facility on the southwest side of downtown is linked directly both to the nearby RCA Dome, home of the city's professional football team, and to the Circle Center only a short distance beyond. Surrounding all these facilities is the specially zoned Warehouse Historic District with its large number of former wholesale houses variously converted to restaurant, shop, office, and residential functions. Anchoring redevelopment on the southeast of the Indianapolis downtown is the new Conseco Field House, new home of the city's professional basketball team. Downtown redevelopment in St. Louis is anchored on the east by a large convention facility, linked directly to the city's large football stadium, the TWA Dome, and on the west by its large baseball stadium, Busch Stadium, with the St. Louis Centre, a multilevel shopping mall, serving as a "bridge." At the riverfront nearby is Laclede's Landing, a themed entertainment zone, as well as the famed St. Louis Arch, another popular visitor attraction. All these attractions are serviced by parking decks.

Big cities have vigorously embraced professional sports as a means of promoting downtown redevelopment.[18] As in Indianapolis and St. Louis, new baseball, football, or basketball facilities have been opened in recent years in downtown Baltimore, Buffalo, Cleveland, Denver, Detroit, Memphis, and New Orleans, among other cities. Indianapolis has adopted sports as a theme not just to "repackage" its downtown area but to re-energize the entire city with a new sports-oriented image. The city considers itself the amateur "sports capital" of the nation. Numerous facilities were built to house the Pan American Games in 1987. So also did the city attract the headquarters of various national sport federations with administrative oversight for amateur competition in such sports as canoeing and kayaking, diving, gymnastics, rowing, swimming, tennis, and water polo.[19] In 1999, the headquarters of the National Collegiate Athletic Association (NCAA) relocated to Indianapolis. So also has Atlanta been successful in using amateur sports for urban development, with the city hosting the 1996 Olympics.[20]

The skyscraper, however, has come to be the most important symbol of downtown resurgence. The skyscraper captures the imagination both as an architectural form and as a contributor to the city skyline. The power and energy of American cities is seen to be symbolized in clustered tall buildings. "Make no little plans" is the adage attributed to Chicago architect and planner Daniel Burnham, with the "bigger is better" syndrome brought forcefully to city planning and to city building early in the twentieth century. Skyscrapers originated mainly as real estate speculations, as developers attracted to their respective buildings businessmen involved in specific industries: coal agents here, jewelers there, lumber agents somewhere else. Then newspapers, insurance companies, public utility companies, and industrial corporations built skyscrapers for symbolic value as well as to cover their space needs. Hotels, department stores, and other specialty buildings also reached skyward in the years before the Great Depression. Building booms in the 1960s and 1980s repeated earlier patterns, although banks did come to participate more fully, and federally chartered banks (and many state-chartered banks as well) were forbidden by law from speculating in real estate, but they were allowed to speculate in rented floor space in new headquarters buildings. Especially important in the 1990s was mixed-use development intended to house a variety of functions either in a single large building or in a complex of adjacent buildings.

Debate over the impact of tall buildings, begun early in the twentieth century, continues today. Most cities have zoning codes designed to ameliorate what was, and what is, seen to be the skyscraper's most negative spillover effect: parking. Planner Frederic Delano outlined prevailing thought of the 1920s in an article for the *American City* that he simply entitled "Skyscrapers." He pointed out, in assigning "the growing menace of high buildings," that city planning was no longer a problem of two dimensions, but was, rather, a problem of three dimensions. There was much to recommend skyscrapers, he said. They represented a more intensive use of land that was often necessary if fair and adequate return was to be made on high-priced real estate. They displayed magnificent views of cities, thus amplifying rental value in high-up offices. There was great savings of time and energy incident to business activities being concentrated in tall buildings closely clustered. "Horizontal distance," he wrote, "is converted into vertical, making, by reason of the rapidly moving elevator, for greater convenience." On the other hand, tall buildings could be a burden on a community. "It is a real question," Delano wrote, "as to whether high values of land compel high buildings, or the reverse. Apparently we have a vicious circle in which one can hardly say which is cause and which is effect." True, offices high up offered fine views, but tall structures could cut off views from other buildings. As for concentration of people and activity, skyscrapers could spell congestion, especially congestion on downtown streets. "A forty-story building occupying an acre and accommodating conservatively 10,000 persons, is served usually by only one important artery of traffic, he observed." [21]

Zoning first came to the fore in the United States in New York City. The

Building Zone Resolution adopted in 1916 governed the height of buildings as a function of adjacent street width and block size, concern being to prevent dark shadow from completely enveloping Manhattan streets. As well, city officials were concerned to ensure free flow of air at street level. Formulas dictated building setbacks, guaranteeing angles by which sunlight could reach streets below. By 1930, concern had shifted in New York City and other places to the skyscrapers' traffic-generating implications: skyscrapers placed undue traffic loads on city streets. But Ralph Robinson and I. S. Shattuck, both traffic specialists in San Francisco, argued that tall buildings were but one cause of congested downtown streets. More important was the fact that most commuters chose to come and go to big city downtowns at the same time rather than at staggered hours. "Desynchronizing" the opening and closing hours of offices and stores would substantially reduce street congestion, they argued. So also would the regulation of curbside parking, for the "constriction of roadway space" was the real culprit of congestion. Eliminating curbside parking would encourage the financing and building of parking garages, they asserted, which might make tall buildings benign as traffic generators. Skyscraper development did bid up downtown property values, which in turn did encourage additional skyscraper building. "As soon as one high building is constructed," they wrote, "it tends to detract from the desirability of low adjacent buildings and to create a desire on the part of owners of low buildings to also build high buildings."[22]

Of course, what tall buildings inclined other property owners to do, especially those at the peripheries of downtown, was demolish low buildings for parking lots. Nonetheless, Robinson and Shattuck argued for new zoning emphasis whereby parking would be required either in or immediately adjacent to new skyscrapers. That is exactly what innovative developers were doing in the late 1920s. In Detroit, for example, the National Bank of Detroit Building and the Fisher Tower both had parking garages integrated. Most imaginative of all such buildings was Chicago's Jeweler's Building with its elevator-operated "automated" garage located at the core of its first 14 floors. Thus, by 1960, nearly every large American city included parking requirements in its zoning program not just for tall buildings but for all buildings. This included Houston, a city without zoning, but with a tradition of land use control sustained through deed restriction. Whether for the right reasons, or for the wrong reasons, as advocated by one or another planner or traffic engineer, new skyscrapers began to sport parking garages either directly integrated or closely connected. Today there is not a large city

FIG. 7.4

Woodmen of America Tower in downtown Omaha, 1997. Adjacent is a multiple-level parking deck with pedestrian access directly into the building.

in the United States without a landmark skyscraper soaring up over or beside a giant parking garage (fig. 7.4).

After 1980, more and more new skyscraper buildings were designed as part of mixed-use developments combining office, retail, and residential functions. In St. Louis, the Mercantile Tower, with its 1,400-car parking garage, was connected by skywalk to the St. Louis Centre, which incorporated shops in a central atrium that connected two pre-existing department stores.[23] Original plans allocated the top 6 floors of one store building to a hotel and called for a 20-story office tower to be constructed over the atrium. The 900 North Michigan Avenue Tower in Chicago was built with a 200,000-square-foot shopping center organized around an 8-story atrium and a 250,000-square-foot department store also on 8 floors. Some 500,000 square feet of office space occupied floors 9 through 28. Residential apartments occupied floors 30 and 31, hotel guest rooms floors 32 through 46, and condominiums floors 48 through 66. A parking garage for 1,700 cars was built immediately adjacent.[24]

The 30 largest American metropolitan areas added more downtown office space between 1960 and 1984 than had been built in all the years before, a total of some 1,300 new buildings.[25] Fostered substantially by tax and other incentives offered by municipal governments, the construction spree substantially overbuilt downtown office space nationwide. Older office buildings became harder to lease, expanding the amount of vacant (and thus devalued) real estate. Declining property values, in turn, led to declining property tax revenues at the very time that cities were improving downtown streets and other infrastructures in accommodating new development.[26] Precipitated were another round of building demolition and a further eroding of central business districts for surface parking.

Although new development, especially skyscrapers, vastly increased building densities at the cores of most downtowns, quality of street life was rarely enhanced. Indeed, large "superblocks" with integrated parking garages functioned largely as self-contained places, there being little reason for shoppers or workers to venture out on to downtown streets. Many new buildings presented blank walls of glass and metal to adjacent streets. Especially sterile were the walls that parking garages presented to view. The "superblock," argued Barton Myers, is "the scourge of a vital urban environment. Activity tends to be internalized, inevitably at the expense of surrounding streets. . . . The modern prototype for commercial development provides office towers, food courts and stores within a single structure: an isolated, self-contained world contributing little to the rest of the city."[27]

At the end of the twentieth century, advocates of downtown redevelopment began to emphasize housing as a land use. Downtown residents in substantive numbers would, it was argued, support a more diverse retail infrastructure, perhaps even sustaining small shops once common to downtown streets. Downtown residents also would enhance the customer base for downtown restaurants, nightclubs, and other entertainments. Another argument favoring downtown living was elimination of the long commute to city-center jobs. Increased concentration of white-collar workers in new downtown office towers substantially increased traffic loads on freeways and surface streets serving central business districts. As suburban development continued apace ever outward from city centers, commutes became ever longer. Sustained, therefore, in many cities was rapid gentrification of close-in residential neighborhoods, such as Federal Hill in Baltimore, German Village in Columbus, the Lincoln Park Area in Chicago, and Society Hill in Philadelphia.

Sustained also was apartment and condominium development in the heart of big city downtowns, especially in conjunction with new mixed-use development. Some cities promoted loft living in residual low-rise buildings, usually in conjunction with festival market initiatives. In most downtowns, however, old buildings did not survive in adequate numbers, or in numbers sufficiently concentrated geographically, to sustain such conversion, so asphalted parking lots dominated instead. In the 1990s, many small towns across the country launched initiatives to fill second- and third-floor apartments long empty above main street stores. And many small cities followed suit, using tax increment financing, zoning incentives, building code modifications, tax abatements, and other devices to stimulate investment. Nonetheless, bringing people downtown to live went counter to decades of transportation and land use planning concentrating on movement away from downtown. Nationwide, the results from such promotion are as yet negligible.

FRAGMENTATION DOWNTOWN

Traditionally, the prime objective of urban transportation planners was to reduce the cost of travel to and from downtown in terms of both travel time and money expended. With emphasis on automobile ownership and use, streets were widened and new streets, including freeways, built. With automobiles increasingly affordable, and with gasoline prices holding very low, Americans tended from the 1920s until the present day to substitute longer commutes from lower-priced land in the suburbs for shorter trips from more expensive central city locations. Each decade, Americans have spent less than 9 percent of their household budgets on travel, most of it by automobile.[28] Even the gasoline shortages of the early 1970s, prompted by the Arab oil embargo, failed to change commuting patterns and alter auto-oriented transport planning resolves. Gasoline prices more than tripled, and the American economy's dependence on petroleum was highlighted by the rapid rise in cost of living that followed. And yet by the end the decade Americans were spending no larger a share of their income on transport, most of it still involving automobiles, than at the beginning.

In the "transition zones" around the downtown on land increasingly stripped of buildings, very cheap parking could be found. Sustained by appraisal and taxing policies that saw parking as the "highest and best use" for marginal real estate, parking came to be valued merely as a "tax payer": where income was barely sufficient to cover property taxes.[29] And yet, it must be remembered, net earnings could and did accrue sufficiently to energize a commercial parking industry nationwide.[30] One might think of federally subsidized urban renewal as most influential in clearing city centers of old buildings, especially in the 1950s and 1960s. But it was not Title I of the Housing Act of 1949 that precipitated most of the land clearance around and in downtowns in American cities. It was, in fact, the parking lot syndrome. Two large American cities, Indianapolis and San Diego, did not participate in federally subsidized urban renewal, and yet land use change in and around their downtowns was exactly the same as elsewhere.

Economically redundant buildings were demolished and replaced with open-lot parking. Erosion by parking lot proceeded in a kind of nibbling fashion. It was not spectacular at first. Small nibbles were taken initially, wrote Jane Jacobs in *The Death and Life of Great American Cities*, but nibbles added up eventually to hefty bites.[31] No one step in the process was, in itself, critical, but each step tended to accelerate the process overall, the cumulative effect being enormous.

Apologists for the parking lot's wasting of traditional downtown land spoke of "parking urban renewal." Under the federal program, wrote Jerome Gottesman of New York City's Edison Parking, Inc., land was purchased, cleared, and assembled into sites, a process that proceeded "at vast cost to the taxpayer." Parking lot urban renewal produced, on the other hand, the same results and strengthened rather than weakened the tax base during the process.[32] What is more, much of the land actually cleared in Title I projects was turned into parking lots, much of it remaining in parking for years, with federal urban renewal projects, on average, requiring 12 years to complete.[33] In theory, municipalities were obligated to shoulder one-third of the cost in urban renewal projects, but part of a city's share could be contributed in nonmonetary form: donating the land in public streets, for example. So also was it possible for a municipality to provide public parking for a finished project and receive, as a local grant-in-aid, credit toward a portion of its obligation.[34]

Nowhere was the parking lot's fragmentation of downtown more noticeable than in Detroit. Home to the nation's largest automobile manufacturers, Detroit had become almost completely automobile-reliant by the 1960s. What had been one of the nation's finest streetcar systems was dismantled. Major thoroughfares—Fort, Michigan, Grand River, Woodward,

FIG. 7.5

Aerial view of downtown Detroit, circa 1965. Shown is Detroit's riverfront substantially shorn of buildings. Parking lots fill the voids. The city's new Civic Center is shown at an early stage of development.

Gratiot, and East Jefferson streets — radiated outward from Kennedy Square (the renamed Cadillac Square) with streetcar lines once located down their centers. But with street widening and increased flow of motor vehicles, accessing streetcars at the center of the street became increasingly dangerous. Increased hazard, along with increased auto ownership, caused streetcar ridership to decline precipitously after World War II. A subway system proposed in the 1920s never resurfaced as a political issue. Instead, plans were laid, beginning in the 1930s, for an expressway system, construction of which proceeded apace through the 1970s. Two north-south freeways, named for two auto industry pioneers, John C. Lodge and Walter P. Chrysler, came to define the western and eastern edges of downtown respectively, and a short east-west connector, the Fisher Expressway, replaced Vernor Highway across the north of downtown.

Also in the 1950s, demolition began south of Jefferson Avenue in the aging wholesale district along the Detroit River (fig. 7.5). There a new civic center would be built, in part using urban renewal monies. Cleansed of what most observers considered merely old and dysfunctional buildings, the open space of a new civic center, anchored by a mammoth convention center, Cobo Hall, would, it was argued, attract private capital for downtown redevelopment. One widely circulated illustration projected the utopian vision of a technologically sophisticated future 1975. Skyscraper towers would loom over an expansive plaza five to six blocks long. From under the convention center the Lodge Expressway would enter downtown along Jefferson Avenue, ultimately to connect with the Chrysler Expressway. Helicopters would hover overhead. And although the plaza was to be dominated by cars (the stick-figures signifying people being hardly noticeable), mass transit would be included in the form of an futuristic monorail. The illustration, as used in one advertisement, was captioned as follows: "Detroit in 1975 is efficient — and beautiful. Smart stores, handsome apartment and office buildings abound. . . . Gardenlike downtown squares increase the pleasure of shopping. Motor traffic flows smoothly in the pattern of a master plan. Ample parking space is available under, on or above ground."[35]

By 1965, the civic center dream was well under way but proceeding at a very slow pace, and private development downtown was negligible. Private capital was being withheld because investors were reluctant to gamble on an increasingly unstable city center when more secure opportunities awaited in the suburbs. Beyond the city, shopping centers and office and industrial parks were rising amid a multitude of new residential subdivisions. Expanding rapidly, therefore, was a new decentralized metropolis made possible by the expressway system. Once Cobo Hall was completed with a huge parking deck atop, and the new City-County Building was finished as well, construction of the remainder of the planned center was put on hold, and much of the cleared land was given over to surface parking. Only three new skyscrapers had been added to the skyline, and only one of those faced directly onto the proposed civic center itself.

In 1965, based on the amount of space consumed, parking dominated the renewed and renewing riverfront (fig. 7.6). So also did parking ring the downtown, amplifying the process of parking lot intrusion that began in the early 1920s (see fig. 2.6) and greatly accelerated in the early 1930s (see fig. 2.8). Parking lots were now spread nearly uninterrupted block after block along Cass, First, and Second Streets on the west side of downtown (fig. 7.7). The very heart of the business district was also fragmented by surface lots (fig. 7.8). Finally, downtown Detroit did have underground parking, long after plans for a subterranean garage under the length of Washington Boulevard were defeated in the courts before World War II.

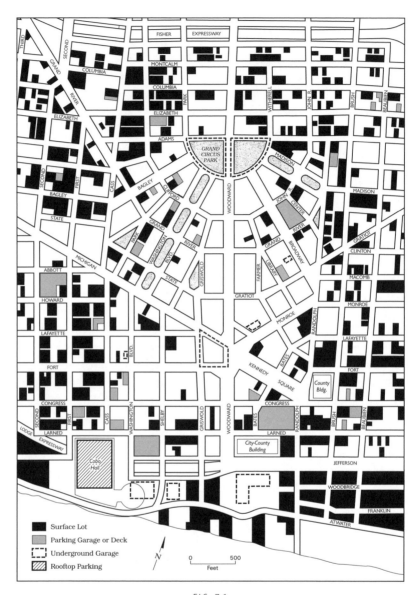

FIG. 7.6

Area devoted to parking in downtown Detroit, 1965. *Source:* Adapted from A. George Basmadjian, *Parking Facilities Manual: A Report of TALUS, the Detroit Regional Transportation and Land Use Study* ([Detroit]: TALUS, 1967), 10.

A municipal parking authority, itself delayed in formation through court challenge, was well established, and its prize operations were the underground facilities at Kennedy Square and Grand Circus Park and the rooftop deck at Cobo Hall. Blocks south of Jefferson Avenue and east of Randolph Street, cleared of buildings and turned to surface parking, awaited civic center completion but would instead provide a footprint for the Renaissance Center, Detroit's answer to the 1967 riots. Only recently occupied by General Motors as its world headquarters, the Renaissance Center was originally the work of the New Detroit Committee, an investor syndicate headed by Henry Ford II. Its construction was meant to re-energize the downtown, but like most new mixed-use developments in cities else-

FIG. 7.7
View of Detroit north from Cobo Hall's rooftop parking deck, 1963.

FIG. 7.8
View of Detroit's Penobscot Building from the southwest, 1960.

where, it actually diverted activity from the downtown's older buildings, exciting further parking lot expansion.

In 1975, with the Renaissance Center nearing completion, relatively little of the riverfront remained in parking lots (fig. 7.9). Parking atop Cobo Hall and in several nearby underground parking garages continued to service the still yet-to-be-completed Detroit Civic Center. Elsewhere downtown, the removal of buildings for parking lots continued rapidly apace. Pictured in 1977 are blocks just north of the Renaissance Center surrounding the old Wayne County Court House (fig. 7.10). Immediately north and south of Michigan Avenue, much of the old skid row area had been demolished, in part for a new federal building. Most of this area remains as parking lots over a quarter of a century later.

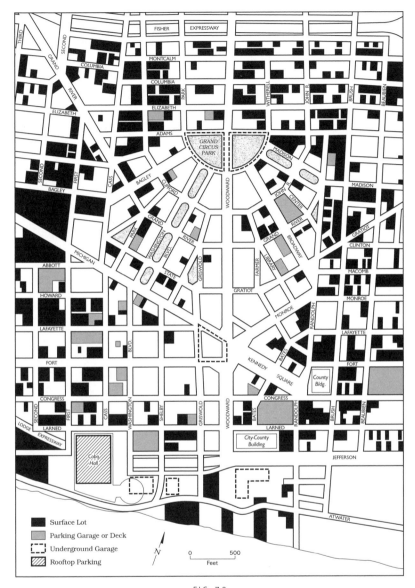

FIG. 7.9

Area devoted to parking in downtown Detroit, 1975. *Source:* Adapted from Kenneth W. Karket Jr., *Regional Parking Inventory and Analysis: Part I—Supply and Costs* (Detroit: Southeast Michigan Council of Governments, 1975), 38, 41.

FIG. 7.10
View of Detroit north from the Renaissance Center, 1977.

In 1999, with the Civic Center nearly complete and the Renaissance Center undergoing new expansion, only token space along the river was in surface parking (fig. 7.11). But parking lots remained the dominant use of land on both the east and west sides of downtown. Only on the far northeast had lots been eliminated. There, with two new sports stadia under development, surface parking had proven, indeed, to be a transitory land use, as at the Civic Center and the Renaissance Center. But it was not development of the expected sort. Development was delayed not years but decades, with many lots, indeed, standing for over a half-century. When development came, it was not through private investment but public investment well beyond the ordinary. It was public investment of the heroic kind. It was development mandated by the failure of anticipated regrowth.

Throughout Detroit's downtown many remaining office and retail buildings stood empty in 1999. One 40-story building served little purpose beyond that of supporting a radio and other communication antenna. The site of the J. L. Hudson Department Store was but a gaping excavation, although plans were underway for a giant mixed-use development both there and on adjacent blocks, the planned complex to house offices, condominiums, hotel space, and retail stores in skyscraper towers linked to a 1,100-car parking garage. The city's financial district, centered at Congress and Griswold Streets, had been reinforced by several new skyscrapers and was the only part of the traditional downtown to display active street life.

Rising in place of the traditional pedestrian downtown was a new auto-centered business district. New office buildings were "self-sufficient," as they were provisioned with parking garages. Just as along suburban roadsides, structures stood variously isolated as objects in open spaces given to parking. Implicit was not only speed and convenience of auto use, but also the sense of security that came from staying close to one's car. And so it was that the Renaissance Center, the leading symbol of downtown Detroit's intended rebirth, rose fortress-like above its own parking deck in a surround of parking garages and parking lots (fig. 7.12). In contrast, a new phenomenon was evident at the northwest edge of downtown Detroit (fig. 7.11). There abandoned parking lots could be found. So empty of commercial activity was this part of Detroit's downtown, that even parking, the presumed commercial nadir of downtown real estate, was no longer sustainable. Grass grew in crumbling asphalt where operators had walked away from lots, leaving signs and other paraphernalia to weather and rust. Only in 2002 were plans for a massive casino complex (the MGM Grand Casino) announced for this section of downtown.

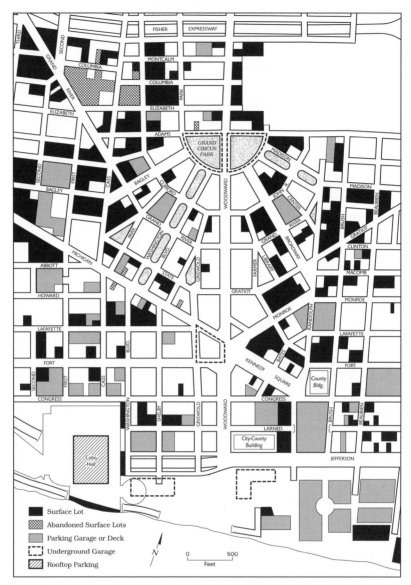

FIG. 7.11
Area devoted to parking in downtown Detroit, 1999. *Source:* Windshield survey by authors, 1999.

Downtown Detroit was not alone in being subsumed by the ubiquitous parking lot. Perhaps the city's central business district may have suffered an exaggerated case of parking lot conversion, given the decades of economic hard times suffered by the city. Detroit also suffered from rampant racism that precipitated massive white flight to the suburbs.[36] Yet even in Allentown, Pennsylvania, reputed to have one of the more stable downtown retail districts and to have relatively stable central city residential neighborhoods as well, the central business district was substantially changed by parking lots by the twentieth century's end (fig. 7.13). Parking lots even dominated at the very core of downtown. The city where Park and Shop originated had succeeded no better than most other cities in keeping downtown retailing and, indeed, downtown intact.

FIG. 7.12
Detroit's Renaissance Center viewed from the east, 1999.

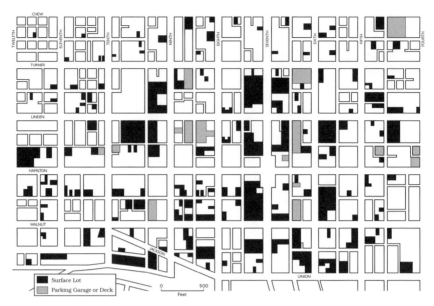

FIG. 7.13

Area devoted to parking in downtown Allentown, Pennsylvania, 1999. *Source:* Windshield survey by John A. Jakle, 1999.

Parking became the arbiter of downtown urban form after World War II. Mandated in most cities by zoning ordinances, parking impacted the design of new buildings, influencing not only their size and shape but also their relation to sidewalks and streets and to one another. "Form follows parking requirements," wrote planner Donald Shoup.[37] In most cities, parking demand produced a vast wastage of traditional built environment. In most downtown districts today old and new buildings stand isolated in surrounds of asphalted parking lot, the play of solid form and open space creating a new visual aesthetic.[38] Today, the typical American central business district appears fragmented and disjointed, giving cities, at their centers, a "half-developed look."[39] As well, many central business districts are substantially dysfunctional, despite (and probably because of) massive investments made over the years in automobile convenience. The pedestrian has become a largely vanished breed in many downtowns, and street life, the traditional definer of urbanity, is largely gone. And traffic congestion, for its part, remains, certainly at rush hour, as much a problem as ever.

With parking mandated for new buildings through zoning codes, commuter and shopper parking costs have been substantially subsumed by employers and merchants to be passed along in wages paid and prices charged. Consequently, what appears inexpensive, or even free, to the individual motorist only reinforces the motorcar as the transport mode of choice. Free parking, which is arguably still the ideal sought, continues to act rather like, in Donald Shoup's words, "a fertility drug for cars." The cost of parking is obscured by bundling it into higher housing prices, higher consumer prices, lower urban densities, and, overall, lower land values. Seemingly, everyone but the motorist pays for parking.[40] Nowhere has the quest for free parking been more successfully realized than in the outlying business districts and suburban shopping centers long competitive with America's downtowns. It is to suburban shopping, as an auto-induced ideal, that we next turn.

PART

3

PARKING AS
MODERN NECESSITY

Near universal quest for automobile convenience in America mandated that parking play an essential role in development and redevelopment. Should we be surprised, therefore, that automobile parking has become so universal, underpinning, as it does, the functionality of most places? Should we be surprised that the parking of cars has become an imperative in landscape making? The nation would come to a halt without it.

The journey to shop, for example, is now almost always anchored in a parking lot or parking garage. Stores without off-street parking stand substantially disadvantaged. As traffic congestion built up in city centers, greatly aggravated by lack of parking, retailers abandoned big city downtowns for outlying shopping districts. The shopping center was born as a cluster of stores fronting onto a parking lot. From the shopping center sprang the shopping mall set in a parking lot surround, later to be reinforced by parking garages or decks. So also is the journey to work usually anchored in parking, with most employers providing employees with "free" parking, or parking at very little cost. Indeed, few institutional activities, be they commercial or governmental, thrive in modern America without parking convenience. Even other transport modes remain tied to the car's demands. Air travel is fundamentally knit to the convenience of airport parking. Do most Americans think it could be any other way?

8

PARKING
FOR SHOPPING
Development in the Suburbs

Parking has seldom been a consideration in its own right. It has most often been a facilitator of other activities. Planners and traffic engineers might address parking as a central concern, but the general parking patron usually does not. As one parking professional recently said to us, "parking is something everybody expects but nobody wants to think about." [1]

In this chapter we address parking's subservient yet critical role in retail commerce for customers looking for places to park and merchants determining how to provide it, frequently on pain of economic death if they did not. How did parking influence the passage of retailing from downtown stores to neighborhood centers and finally to suburban shopping centers throughout the twentieth century? What physical configurations for parking were proposed for its silent yet seminal force? What alternatives were considered? What forms prevailed and why?

We view parking as an essential factor integral to broadly patterned commercial developments. We want to know why conditions prevail, perhaps in the manner most people would want to know if parking were something that most people did contemplate.

Decisions to locate parking for commerce did not commence rationally, if "rationally" involves awareness and evaluation of alternatives and steps taken in satisfaction of a long-term agenda. Rationalist critics of commercially located parking—many planners and anti-automobile critics—hold the nation guilty of drifting toward automobility's consequences without full consciousness of its meaning or intent to reach anything but short-term goals. [2] Practice through time demonstrates that the overwhelming majority of Americans concerned at all about the parking by-product of automobility were satisfied with how and where parking was provided before the lack of parking deterred mobility, and some arose to doubt, criticize, and suggest solutions to the parking problems resulting from their fore-bears' best intentions.

Americans have generally taken the opportunities for maximum physical mobility, individualism, and decentralized settlement in which the automobile stirred some of the latest expressions. Geographers have underscored the American passion for movement through the landscape variously in quest of economic renewal, especially before the twentieth century, in the process of resettlement or recreation through tourism. Literary scholars have more recently pointed out the emergence of a road genre in American letters with various dimensions all treating the automobile highways on which people traveled as "sacred space." Writers, using the highway as metaphor or means, speculated about where American culture has been and whither they believe it is headed. Historians have traced the emergence of the automobile industry and those industries dependent on it to claim they, too, have determined much of the nation's and overseas nations' life during the twentieth century. Southerners, often considered the nation's most conservative people, commonly altered their lifestyles to include automobility. Americans have tended to fill the vastness of their nation's midcontinent with outsize buildings and structures in quest of a finite location although ceaselessly celebrating the politically unchecked passage from place to place. Long-distance travel by automobile has not deterred Americans. Shorter distances such as through and across towns and cities has never daunted Americans who could afford the means, preferably in personal conveyances. The "king's highway" concept, traceable to the Middle Ages, gave legal credence to the belief that people had a right to unencumbered travel through a right-of-way. In the twentieth century it combined with the automobile's physical superiority vis-à-vis other forms of transportation and pedestrianism to produce a hubris about the automobilist's rank in using the road and parking as an extension of the road.[3]

Americans have generally resisted government programs that increase taxes, for they are perceived as impositions impinging on individualism. The absence of a strong socialist movement in the nation's history confirms the preference for individualism. Perhaps the most remarkable exception was the rapid adoption of the gasoline tax in each state (beginning in Oregon in 1919) to build a system of highways within each state and enactment of a series of federal aid–highway acts (beginning in 1916) to build a national trunk highway system. Even in states with strong anti-statist values, the highway system's proponents quietly acquiesced to driver licensing and speed limits. Communal and urban life have been minor American modes.[4]

Joseph Interrante has attributed the unusual way the automobile influenced settlement patterns to "metropolitanism," a term adopted from the Hoover Commission's *Recent Social Trends* of 1933: "By reducing the scale of local distance, the motor vehicle extended the horizon of the community and introduced a territorial division of labor among local institutions and neighboring cities which is unique in the history of settlement. . . . Moreover, formerly independent towns and villages and also rural territory have become part of the enlarged city complex." Interrante, although providing inadequate explanation of how the car became a prerequisite for survival in a metropolitan settlement pattern, correctly notes it did not have to turn out as it did. Automobility might have been reserved for recreation and movement beyond areas that railroads and trolleys served.[5]

The urban middle classes introduced the idea of using the automobile not only for recreation but also to solve a host of urban problems accumulated at the end of the nineteenth century. Many cities at that time had become undesirable places to live, and their once vaunted advantages were in serious doubt. Disease and psychological problems were attributed to city life by many social reformers. In the Progressive Era suburbs were offered as panaceas, and cheap transportation to them became a major political objective against the streetcar companies that were the major providers of public transportation. It has been proven in the important example of Chicago that corruption, mismanagement, and poor service weakened public transportation, while the automobile simultaneously improved service for the city's political elite and ended, through a series of complicated developments, as the dominant mode of transportation. Specifics differ between cities and their suburban hinterlands, but automobility and the outcome of low-density population centers were strong components of the solutions many people idealized. One historian argues convincingly that municipal reformers foresaw at least that the automobile threatened to kill street life, but they were incapable of checking the automobile's high esteem with middle-class urban dwellers who were their power base.[6] Automobility introduced unintended liabilities, such as parking eventually brought, but its complete hegemony was welcomed initially.

Alternatives were conceived to avoid urban traffic congested further by the automobile, but they all presupposed the automobile was a means of social satisfaction for whose owners the instincts for harmonious community life would be elicited. Those conceiving alternatives failed to foresee how almost all Americans who could afford a motor vehicle, at least through most of the twentieth century, would act on their individualistic proclivities to drive their vehicles, not with mostly centripetal force in community building, but equally as centrifugal agents pulling settlement further away from high-density cores. Alternatives ranging from theoreticians to suburban developers illustrate the faith in automobility harnessed. In 1914, philanthropist Mary Emery planned Mariemont, Ohio, within 19 miles of Cincinnati for the urban working poor. An American adaptation of the English garden city, a pastoral alternative to the overpopulated, polluted, and poorly serviced inner cities, Mariemont embraced the automobile, and a highway was provided to Cincinnati. "Concrete roads assure cleanliness, smoothness, and permanence" within the village, according to one description.[7] In 1932, Frank Lloyd Wright's "Broadacre City" envisioned a model for 1,400 families where automotive transportation was integral, and the settlement was extended over 4 square miles. Travel was not emphasized between such settlements, however; satisfaction was spiritual within the life of the self-nurturing community.[8] Radburn, New Jersey, 13 miles outside New York City, was planned to overcome the growing objections to noisy motorcars along the highways where many new towns were founded and yet be "the town for the motor age." Radburn's planners avoided the typical gridiron that permitted the ceaseless whir of automobiles passing for a series of cul-de-sacs on which houses were situated. Greenswards entwined the settlement intended for a population of 25,000.[9]

Such places were predicated on the belief that automobility was an adjunct to the good life within a community, and they were anti-urban. Advocates assumed no growth in the number of people within each settlement and no growth between settlements. They abandoned existing cities and posed refuge in pioneering new settlements in the open countryside, namely, suburbs. They did not anticipate the degree to which the automobile, initially a means of transportation, eventually became a formative agent with reforming rather than integrating capacities. Many people enjoyed motor travel, and commuting did not deter them from residence in suburbs and work in distant cities. Advocates of the eventual pattern of most settlement along highways in the open countryside and concentrated in intermittent centers with stores outside the urban core begged the question of that pattern by extolling consumers' demand for "convenience." Over 53,000 housewives were asked in a survey by the Scripps-Howard newspaper chain and another by the Kroger Grocery and Bakery Company in 5 cities why they shopped most frequently with a particular grocer. The answer was convenience for 27.2 percent in the Scripps-Howard survey and 70.5 percent in the Kroger survey.[10] Who but those with a vested financial interest in opening outlying settlements conducive to more automobiles polled people about their preferences initially? Bias toward suburbanism likely skewed reports.

Convenience is a catchall term masking a confluence of many more specific reasons. Convenience is relative. What is convenient for one person might not be convenient in the estimation of another person. Empirical data influencing businesspeople's decisions about location is scant. We do not know, most of all, how far early shoppers were willing to drive to their destination. The first drive-in markets in Los Angeles, those in the 1920s, may well have been located according to the would-be owners' impression of the volume of sales suitable for profit at a prospective business site. There appear to have been no traffic studies akin to those made for parking garage entrepreneurs. The small size of drive-in shops and markets may account for the absence of data because its collection was deemed an unnecessary expense. A study for a chain store grocery published in 1941 revealed that 76 percent of the automobile-borne customers traveled more than one-fourth of a mile, and 34 percent drove more than three-fourths of a mile. Some people, thus, were likely willing to drive beyond quick walking distance to their destination. Convenience may have been the pitchman's jargon, but most people did have a very specific set of expectations upon arrival. Those expectations have been voluminously elaborated and repeated in the trade literature since the 1920s.[11]

Americans were unwilling to shop in downtown stores where congestion beset their destination. Values played a primary role, helping to configure the look and accessibility of shoppers' destinations. How could one reconcile the taste for individual expression, distaste for involuntary commitments to authority, spaciousness, and faith in freedom through automobility when confronted with traffic jams? The very synchronization of one's life with other motorists while probing downtown for a good place to park or payment to a meter, lot, or garage for something many people believed overpriced, whatever the charge, represented incursions on many Americans' libertarian streaks. Other factors helped push them from downtown shopping: poor selection of goods and services, unpleasant and unsafe environment, and distance from their suburban homes. But many Americans also quickly felt crowded in space and preferred generous distances between themselves and other shoppers. The absence of plentiful and free parking pushed consumers away; parking itself was a potent factor. Automobility, fully dismissing subdued alternatives such as Broadacre City, Mariemont, and Radburn, triumphed in dispersed settlements and commercial strips because many did not mind or even enjoyed travel, for shopping as well as recreation, when arrival promised quick parking and egress so long as the settlements stretched ever farther beyond the sequence of congested inner-city and earlier outlying shopping centers left behind. Looking back on the origins of the strip and the suburb, some scholars concur that those place-types demonstrate that Americans want to simplify where they live, where they shop, and how they arrive there, and embrace informal settings.[12] But this is hindsight.

The results were neither foreordained nor obvious to those evolving the present paradigm. In 1927, John Ihlder, an official of the United States Chamber of Commerce, appreciated the importance of parking but did not understand that parking correctly arranged could draw customers. Ihlder warned that parking restricted downtown would not spur commerce, but he failed to encourage public storage garages—likely because they seemed untested novelties to him—and instead proposed street space be increased through regulated building occupancy. Insufficient downtown parking in the following decade damaged retailing. A chamber of commerce survey in 1944 of downtown Montclair, New Jersey, for example, disclosed that the city had the highest per-family purchasing power in the East and the third highest in the nation, yet almost half the money spent in shopping was in nearby cities.[13]

Frank R. Hawkins, general manager of Unterecker's, a candy store chain in Buffalo, was one of the imaginative entrepreneurs and acknowledged his trial-and-error method for accommodating the automobile-borne trade beginning in the 1920s. Hawkins realized that "nearly everyone today who is in the mood to buy candy and feels like spending the money for that purpose, also has an automobile." At one store in a congested downtown location adjacent to a movie theater, where a brisk trade could be expected, most customers, in fact, came in the daylight hours, not on nights with heavy attendance at the movie theater. At another store, not in a congested location in a shopping district, "our customers can almost always find a place to park in front of this store or very close to it. They do not have to come on foot or to drive around the block once or twice looking for a place to park, as is often the case in the congested portion of this district." The difference in patronage was due to the availability of parking, and Hawkins astutely planned for Unterecker's future, not only with a quality product, but based on geography.

> In the future, the locations which we pick will be those which assure us of ample parking space for customers and which are in the center of good residential communities. The number of people who pass the store on foot really does not matter so much, as does the number of people who pass in automobiles, have the inclination to stop and the parking space which makes it easy for them to pause and buy.[14]

Parking, clearly visible from the car and easily accessible, was an incentive. Hawkins was disarmingly candid contrasted with the many merchants who later postured that they knew the primacy of parking all along, and Hawkins gives rare insight into early entrepreneurship sensitive to the new trade source.

Most of the evidence for stores rendered convenient to automobile parking, however, must be studied through mute material culture. Founders of roadside businesses left virtually no written records. Dallas was one of the first scenes of off-street parking for commerce, and it began in that city about 1921 as an option not originally intended by those eventually welcoming it. Absent a zoning prohibition against neighborhood stores, several stores moved onto corner sites where they were set back at least 22 feet from the curb to invite head-in parking. Chain store demand for that spatial lure to motorists in subsequent real estate transactions made it popular with property owners. Los Angeles simultaneously accommodated a more extensive array of parking-dependent shops. Longstreth has correctly seen in suburban stores a radical departure from traditional merchandising. Parking drew the motorists' eyes to a series of architectural arrangements in the store.[15]

Planned parking came quickly to shopping centers once entrepreneurs set the shoppers' bait with parking. Country Club Plaza in Kansas City, begun in 1923, was the early model many businesspeople adapted. Founder J. C. Nichols wanted parking to be more than easily visible and accessible. Parking was one aspect of vehicular flow, calculating parking angles, delivery unloading and loading, and block length, to name a few keys. Risk-taking businesspeople began to appreciate parking's potential by the late 1920s.[16]

Convenience came to be understood intuitively as several things in such shopping centers. Ample, accessible, and visible parking was certainly among them. Nowhere in the trade literature was parking's rank made explicit, but its frequent inclusion in statements about good retailing clarifies parking's potency. Such comments as "Patrons have the convenience of parking in front of shops" and "this marked growing need for convenient parking" typify references from the 1930s.[17] "Convenience goods" meant commodities bought impulsively, presumably because opportunity permitted. Parking helped induce impulse. Location of shopping centers, their design, and the design of the individual stores within them contributed as well, but parking was that curiously unlovely partner. A void waiting for patrons, attractive by implication, it was singularly different from the overt geographical and architectural attractions of shopping centers.

We turn briefly to those other attractive features completing the view of shoppers arriving by automobile. We take up geography first. The early retail suburban nodes can be named "outlying shopping centers," a name J. C. Nichols helped popularize, to connote their break with traditional retail places downtown.[18] The macro view of those outlying shopping centers has been described often and well. We can reliably generalize from a traffic engineer's description in 1942 of Los Angeles, the preeminent automobile-convenient landscape. Outlying business centers began at every major road intersection and followed or anticipated traffic's direction. "As growth continues, the arms of the numerous crosses on the gridiron of the major streets meet and thus every major street and highway in Los Angeles has become or will soon become closely built up with every class of business establishment."[19] On the ground, a planner characterized their right-of-way as narrow; the intersections, speed-limit zones, and stop signs as numerous; highway frontage as teaming with competitive small stores, dwindling residential use, and billboards; and nightclubs, stands, and salvage yards overwhelming any surviving open countryside. Outlying shopping centers colonized strips.[20]

Once parking beckoned customers, they were shown goods in ways most likely to clinch a sale. Clear visibility seemed to reinforce the customer's discretionary power. Clear visibility also suggested product reliability; what you saw was what you got. Weights and measures and purity of products had long created problems in the marketplace. Retailing in the automobile age attempted assurances. Longstreth pointed out the open forecourt in the Los Angeles drive-in market, one of the first forms in automobile retailing. The display windows of the outlying shopping centers, more common nation-

FIG. 8.1

A 1930 advertisement in a building trades magazine illustrates how shoppers arriving by car looked through their windshields directly onto the goods that merchants most wanted to sell. *Source:* "Good Design Lures Customers to a Store," *Building Age* 52 (April 1930): 71.

ally than the open bays of Los Angeles because of weather and security, occasionally encouraged owners in "taxpayer" strips for trolley car and pedestrian shoppers. ("Taxpayer" properties were created to earn income to pay the taxes on them in anticipation of greater earnings from them at a later time.) Peering through large store windows from trolleys or on foot had been key to the aggregate of "taxpayers" in blocks, and recessed and arcaded fronts and window cases centrally located in "islands" had been developed to multiply precious store frontage three to four times. Automobiles heading directly toward display windows to park afforded a dramatic new twist in merchandising to the arrivals, different than viewing the windows from parallel parking. The merchant made the point immediately upon the customers' arrival that goods in front of the windshield were most covetable (fig. 8.1).[21]

In keeping with most merchants' slow grasp of parking potential through the late 1930s, however, most outlying shopping centers provided modest parking volumes. Many combined taxpayer blocks with its curbside parking and some off-street parking in front of the store anchoring the ensemble. The Woodlawn neighborhood on Chicago's near South Side in 1940 typified the parking problem for older taxpayer blocks; instead of the desired 2:1 or 3:1 ratio of square feet of parking space to square feet of store space, Woodlawn suffered a 0.8 ratio.[22] Some of those taxpayer blocks with cramped parking provisions survive, and some are built new, proof of a neighborhood vicinity or a traditional anchor store. Those represent modest business horizons.

Parking helped formulate the location and appearance of the outlying shopping centers, but certain individual business types most often led the way. Grocery stores and movie theaters pioneered, perhaps because the large investments behind them could feasibly plan for more profits by improvising extensive new trials.

Grocery stores suffice here to illustrate the seminal pattern. People most often bought their foodstuffs before the 1930s in three shops, one each for groceries, meats, and produce. Goods had to be weighed and packaged upon selection, and clerks waited to provide those services in addition to stocking and selling each customer's accumulations.[23] Grocers seeking increased profits restructured their business in several ways. Relocation to sites outside habitually congested city cores was critical to take advantage of the increasingly automobile-borne consumer who was likely to have a greater income than many living in traditional confines. Atlanta proved what was likely true nationally: because customers shopped frequently and regularly at grocery stores, the stores could not survive traffic congestion that deterred patronage.[24] In 1925, the Safeway Stores' farsighted realty director in Los Angeles described the most desirable site as one close to a busy intersection, where traffic was voluminous yet rent was cheaper than at the corner, and on the same side of the street as homebound travelers. "The automobile is becoming more and more a selling problem," and "convenience and parking space are necessary for this trade."[25] Aggressive merchants, usually budding chain store moguls, puzzled how to fully and most effectively integrate automobility into their prospects.

Visions of increased mechanization, periodically characterizing various lines of motorized services, turned up in the Automarket in Louisville in 1927. In the prototype, customers drove their car on a track alongside rotating shelves from which goods were selected. At various newly styled grocery stores, convenience incorporated two factors: the purchase of all foodstuffs at one store — "one-stop" locations, as they were called in various automobile-dependent businesses — and parking that was plentiful, with spacious berths, and close to the store. MacMarr Stores, headquartered in

Portland, Oregon, understood that 70 percent of its customers arrived by car, so the company built "drive-ins" with parking immediately beside each facility.[26]

Progressive grocery retailing since the late 1920s combined various strategies, both inside and outside each grocery as well as printed advertising, but cuing customers from the roadside became imperative. Parking evolved first, perhaps because it seemed to require the least cost and imagination. A random selection of model grocery store plans from the 1930s through the 1950s uniformly included parking.[27] Early roadside grocery stores customarily restricted signs to boards on the roof ridge or on the fascia above display windows. Large signs, either on a corner tower beside or above the entrance or at curbside came later. By the 1950s, designers more exactingly calculated intended effects. A grocer in Hot Springs, Arkansas, believed signs attracted customers initially because they were novel, implying that their messages had to be continuously novel to work best. Patrons feared they would miss something if they did not stop, and many turned around to carefully read the sign's message.[28]

Parking advanced from a courtesy to a means of increasing sales and a variable for predicting sales. Regional variations on the relationship of parking to stores in general had persisted since the automobile's appearance. Los Angeles preferred parking in front of the stores, and Houston preferred parking in the rear. One supermarket architect spoke for utilizing both front and rear parking and various stall layouts arranged diagonally, depending on how many cars a grocer wished to accommodate. Diagonal parking was accepted as the most capacitious arrangement. Close parking proximity was a cardinal dictum: the maximum distance between parked car and store entrance was 500 feet, and preferably 300 feet. Details of access, egress, maintenance, and drainage occupied the remainder of the substantial elaboration on parking. In 1964, colossal supermarkets, over 20,000 square feet and not in shopping centers, averaged room for 400 cars; that was more than the number of spaces that multilevel parking garages provided inner-city customers a quarter of a century before. Typical supermarkets parked 194 automobiles.[29] Parking had become its own sign, and few grocers were deemed worthy of patronage without parking (fig. 8.2), in deference to many consumers' automobile dependence.

While movie houses and supermarkets gathered smaller merchants into nodes at outlying shopping centers beside automobile arteries in the late 1930s, another place-type emerged to utilize parking in an even more spectacular manner—the strip. The strip differed from its automobile-

FIG. 8.2

The Red and White cooperative grocery chain chiefly promoted new architecture for its post–World War II stores but also accented parking in striking silhouettes at the stores' perimeter. *Source:* "Include a New Store Front in Your Post-War Plans," *Red and White Hy-Lites*, Jan. 1945, 6.

convenient forerunners by substantial degrees. Strips were more extensive and more given to unmasked commerce. Small entrepreneurs utilizing no architectural pretense situated their buildings beside one another in a series paralleling the road like a motorist's bazaar. Elite arbiters of public taste recoiled contemptuously, conducting campaigns of beautification to regulate existing practices and improve future operators alike.[30] Parking space that rendered all roadside business feasible was not the beautifiers' primary target; rather, it was the scrap that accumulated on the junk dealers' grounds.[31] Postmodern architectural theorists championing the look of brash roadside commerce briefly alluded to the parking lot's contribution.[32] Typically, opportunistic small roadside entrepreneurs meanwhile wedged their niche with ample and obvious parking lots. The nascent roadside petroleum industry beginning after 1910 and the restaurant industry and the lodging industry beginning in the 1920s led the way. A chain of Rodomes to be launched in Sacramento, California, in 1922, for example, announced the novel plan for each site to provide storage garages for each lodger and a "central paved court." About 90 cars and 420 lodgers could be accommodated at each Rodome.[33] Many motorists enjoyed parking their own cars and carrying their baggage to their rooms without porters, thus making self-parking adjacent to one's lodging a trait distinguishing the increasingly popular motel.[34] In 1958, the Downtowner motel chain deviated from the motel's self-park characteristic when its founder, a partner in two regional parking chains, depended on valet parking, not as an amenity, but to maximize parking space on Downtowner's characteristically small city lots.[35]

Drive-in businesses, some restricted to a service window where motorists parked momentarily while transacting business and others involving that plus parking in a lot for a longer duration, founded an entirely new sales strategy. Banks were among the first to provide an automobile service window.[36] Shoe stores and airline ticket offices were among the plethora of drive-in businesses that followed with their momentary and long-term parking components and thereby substantially defined the strip.[37]

Automotive vehicle and parts dealers, especially for passenger cars and trucks, have perhaps influenced the landscape through parking more to elitist displeasure than any other roadside commerce. New car sales were first offered in adapted buildings, and then around 1910 some dealers began lavishing great sums on automobile showrooms where new annual models were surrounded in palatial trappings (fig. 8.3). Displayed cars were parked cars, but the inventory of many unsold models was kept on upper floors of the showroom in shipping crates as unassembled parts from the manufacturer. The demand for storage space lessened accordingly. Numerous photographs of dealerships presenting a group of the most saleable vehicles in tight formation at curbside pointed toward the camera suggest the possibility of storage outside in adjacent grounds. Those were fanciful settings. By the 1960s, parked cars waiting for sales in lots adjacent to the showroom and garage rivaled for visual attention. Used car dealers, however, availed them-

FIG. 8.3

A 1940 Chevrolet dealer's showroom demonstrating two important parking themes. 1) New annual automobile models are given resplendent staging. 2) Parking's ubiquity is confirmed in the receding set of parking venues: the dealer's floor, curb parking, and parking lot. *Source:* Detroit Public Library, National Automotive History Collection.

selves of more extensive parking displays requiring the least possible expense. Refinements evolved sporadically in this vernacular landscape.[38]

Junk automobile dealers operated "graveyards" that occupied the lowest aesthetic rung along the roadside, there being little reason, except for compliance with zoning regulations, to arrange the scrap otherwise. In 1929, Connecticut enacted one of the most effective regulations of automotive graveyards. By that time, the dealers' counterparts in other states were considered contributors to an "automobile 'graveyard' menace" depressing values of adjacent property, according to a New York real estate developer.[39] Idle cars and dismantled parts were variously stacked atop each other or akimbo in piles strewn in sizeable roadside acreages and small city lots. Size varied, but the impact on viewers seldom did. Although new vehicles carefully aligned in dealer lots differed markedly from disheveled graveyards, in either case roadside viewers saw automotive products pushed forward from the comparatively small offices or salesrooms of those preeminently parking-based businesses.

Cities continued responding slowly to automobility's potential. Arlington, Virginia, was regarded as farsighted for adopting an ordinance in June 1938 to provide off-street parking for any residence, but the ordinance required amendment five months later to avoid vehicles backing onto streets and stopping traffic flow in the meantime. Further amendment in 1941 stipulated that no residential building could occupy more than 35 percent of a parking lot in order that vehicles could maneuver in the lot and move quickly into the stream of traffic rather than interfering with other parked vehicles. Finally, in 1942, parking provisions became part of the zoning requirements in commercial or manufacturing areas. Those incremental adjustments signified the general inability to grasp automobility's full potential. Inner-city merchants also had the weight of tradition on their side in remaining staunchly dedicated to their practices. For example, merchants in Passaic, New Jersey, a "buying center" for a huge metropolitan area, were not easily persuaded that a city parking authority should be empowered to purchase property for three parking garages to be built on the fringe of the shopping district. Exemplifying the failure to embrace change and face customers positively, one store owner forced shoppers to go to the rear of his store and up one floor to have their parking ticket validated for a discounted parking rate. Atlanta, subject of a detailed study of how the automobile re-created a city's physical layout, showed that a traffic-congested downtown pushed customers to outlying areas. Parking demands far exceeded the capacities of many older outlying shopping centers. Proponents of shopping on main streets advised "radical surgery" of prevailing practices.[40] Others seized the initiative elsewhere.

Developers, investors, and consumers ranked automobility so far ahead of other factors in the frenzy to profit from the American landscape after the mid-twentieth century that parking set the exterior pattern of the next commercial place-type developed—the suburban shopping center. A rich literature documents and argues for the great growth and vast relocation of population to the suburbs after 1945. Hardly a city or town with accompanying shopping center or centers seemed lacking ambition to rise beyond the once prosperous city cores. Success came to the suburban shopping centers so quickly and so dramatically, judged by profits, numbers, and aerial extent, that the numerous novel decisions risking great sums of money are too often overlooked without historical introspection. To repeat what was true of earlier automobile-based business liberally applying the parking ingredient, the steps to the suburban shopping center were neither obvious to those taking them nor foreordained as cultural outcome.[41] Jerome

McDermott, a founder of the International Council of Shopping Centers in 1957, recalled 20 years later, when the shopping center was regarded as something of a financial miracle, that only 60 people attended the meeting, that a vote was taken to disband the organization because of the low attendance, but that he voted against the measure because they needed to share what little information existed.[42] Suburban shopping centers were a new concept immediately after World War II, but by 1960 there were 1,281 suburban centers. The year 1956 witnessed the peak number of large centers started, totaling 13,757,00 square feet, and 1959 witnessed the peak number of centers started, 206.[43]

Victor D. Gruen, shopping center planner and guru, insisted that community building was his aim. In an oft-quoted speech in the boom years of the shopping center, Gruen stated that individual needs ideally took a secondary role to "the integrated, controlled one-ownership shopping center." An oasis "without the pressures and sounds of typical downtown areas," "the shopping center can and should become a community focal point" with club rooms, meeting halls, auditoriums, and nurseries. He envisioned an "architecturally organized space" in contrast with the "anarchic wilderness of our urban landscape" and the "excitement of the battle of parking ratios." In an article published in 1948 in *Chain Store Age*, Gruen described the shopping center's commercial functions, and the editors, consistent with his philosophy, stated succinctly in a legend for one illustration, "shopping centers would be spacious, park-like, free from automobile traffic." In Gruen's own words, "in order to create psychological comfort, we propose to separate traffic, automobile parking, delivery truck lanes, and foot traffic completely from one another." Individualism, automobility, and parking as their manifestation were regulated for a higher and spiritual, not a commercial, good.[44]

Pietro Belluschi, another shopping center visionary and architect, wrote ardently of the center's redemptive power.[45] Gruen and Belluschi shared a pastoral fantasy in which cars came to rest, and then passengers afoot shared life in the original sense of park as a serene, protected enclave.

Gruen's utopia was taken instead for a commercial scheme by, in his words, "fast buck promoters and speculators." In 1979, near the end of his life, he especially isolated the parking lot for attack: "Even when other community facilities were built beside shopping centers, they were separated by roads and acres of asphalt parking lots, creating a non-walkable, inhumane environment" (fig. 8.4).[46] Gruen might have pointed out that popular demand contributed heavily to his dream misbegotten in lesser hands.

FIG. 8.4

The J. L. Hudson Company, headquartered in downtown Detroit, sought rejuvenated income from its suburban shopping center, Northland Center. The illustration depicts Victor Gruen's original idea of smoothly flowing traffic amid cars parked in artful surroundings.

In the late 1940s and through the 1950s, numerous shopping center plans and descriptions of built examples detailed what satisfied consumer appetites in parking. A summary of the Community Builders' Council of the Urban Land Institute in 1944 correctly acknowledged that "no authoritative books have been written on the development and management of shopping centers and the enterpriser must proceed largely by trial and error."[47] Despite the disclaimer about received knowledge, parking was prescribed in specific terms. Two square feet of parking space to one square foot of store space was the minimum allowable; a 3:1 ratio, which newer stores used in California, Texas, and Florida, was preferable. Another designer reported a larger ratio in California.[48] Ample and convenient parking meant a host of things. "Parking area should be generous enough so that there will always be an empty space," was the first rule. Parking was both functional and symbolic. Open space implied a welcome. Twelve years later, the Urban Land Institute published a successor guide acknowledging that the parking ratio depended on variables—trade type and number of customers each store attracted daily—but "in general, a 3 to 1 ratio is an acceptable measurement for parking demand."[49] Empty parking spaces remained no less important than occupied ones.

Automobiles seemingly required parking and displays of commodities in long linear arrangements, be it pedestrian Main Street or outlying shopping centers. Inchoate needs for clear and instant comprehensibility resolved the spatial arrangements of many shopping centers. Entrepreneurs and planners played to those factors, however much idealists wished for better ways. "In the early centres the mall was similar to the traditional street but without the vehicular traffic," shrewdly observed a British designer, with the characteristic insight cultural outsiders often bring.[50] The Nob Hill Business Center in Albuquerque, New Mexico, built between 1948 and 1949, illustrated the detractions of an enclosed courtyard. Although it merited inclusion in the Urban Land Institute's series of shopping center case studies in 1949 for several reasons, including "all cars within a minimum distance of surrounding stores," it lacked a capacity for future lateral expansion. Parking too was inefficient because a centrally located line of stalls was "omitted in the interests of movement and visibility of the rear stores," leaving too much empty parking space.[51]

Evidence, scientific and anecdotal, showed that customers wanted close proximity and clear visibility. Thirty minutes was the most time shoppers were willing to spend driving to a shopping center, according to a study by the American Society of Planning Officials. Three minutes seemed the most time that designers expected customers to walk between their auto and their intended store to shop. A random survey of 14 supermarkets included the respondent who declared that customers did not park in a lot across from the main lot unless directed there.[52]

It seemed incomprehensible to Gruen's thinking that by 1953 he observed parking frequently arrayed in huge areas perpendicular to long lines of stores, "strips" as he borrowed from the vernacular. He characterized the opposite end of those strips as "marginal business enterprises which cannot afford higher rent" and consequently are "inhabited by car lots or honkytonks" that "slowly debase the character of the shopping area and residential section itself." He marveled that "those shopping centers continue to spring up and repeat the same mistakes," but he felt certain "the better centers will lure customers away from these strips."[53] Gruen himself was too busy at first with other aspects of shopping center design to throttle the quantity of parking and eschewed control until, he stated, "the parking problem, which is relatively new, has been solved so many times in so many places for so many store types doing varying volumes of business, that the parking requirements can be estimated from a chart."[54] In 1960, when Gruen did enunciate the principle that alacrity in filling and emptying a parking lot should determine its capacity, and that it should not be built to the maximum number possible, others were building according to sheer volume.[55]

Women, counted the majority of the automobile-borne customers at shopping centers, were thought by one observer especially appreciative of "being able to see their cars while moving from store to store." The *Chain Store Age's* editor reporting this generalization from discussions with shopping center staffs added that "early centers which provided ample parking at the rear and little at the front now find themselves handicapped, particularly if new centers with plenty of front space are competing with them."[56]

Shopping center designers responded to popular interests. On the controversial question with designers on whether the angles of the parking stalls should be 45 degrees or 90 degrees, one chain store construction head asserted, "unless you set up a parking angle that agrees with local custom when you build a new store, the women who shop there will always complain about the parking lot." An architect cited in the same source advised 90-degree stalls because "empty parking stalls are more easily seen at a greater distance, and driving distance inside the shopping center's parking lot is reduced." By the mid-1960s, no axiom about the angle of parking stalls dominated.[57]

A people schooled to the highly visual character of the consumer culture consequently exercised a complicated set of expectations in their selection of a shopping center among the many in competition. A rare behavioral study of shopping centers, done in 54 centers in Arlington, Texas, reported in 1981 that what prospective customers saw from their cars correlated strongly with those centers' success: "Centers without visibility problems had a vacancy rate of 13.75%, while those with major visibility problems had a rate of 60.8%."[58] Parking's obvious availability and ample supply were not included in the resulting visual calculus, perhaps because the study hoped to explore hitherto unresearched factors, for parking visibility was a constant in various earlier design guides and vignettes of individual shopping centers. The vast number of customers, in effect, had voted with cars for plentiful parking immediately in front of their primary store objective at the shopping center. Traffic circulation including ease of access and egress, the location of stores with particular goods, and the easy visibility of those goods enhanced by displays played key roles. But parking contributed powerfully.

In the halcyon days of shopping center speculation, in the late 1940s through the early 1950s, trade literature typically carried references to parking's essential virtues. "Note the ease of circulation, and freedom from all the through traffic," a description of the Bellevue Shopping Square in suburban Seattle ballyhooed in 1946.[59] The Crenshaw project in Los Angeles, also announced in 1946, was described as both a shopping center and dedicated residential suburb that "will house 2,000 cars. A new feature that will free this lot from track congestion is a 2,000-foot-long service tunnel having basement entrances to all stores."[60] The Ridgeway Shopping Center in Stamford, Connecticut, was announced in 1948 as "one of the first efforts in the East to meet the challenge of automobile shopping . . . which will eliminate parking snarls and traffic jams." About 1,000 cars could be parked simultaneously, and the article in the *American City* boasted "Thirty-three Cars to a Store."[61] What was one of the most impressive aspects in 1948 about the second shopping center that the Conant Real Estate Trust and Middlesex Trust built in suburban Boston was that it would have more parking spaces, increased to 4,000.[62]

Magnitude impressed — not only money spent on design and construction, population of the consumer hinterland, and number of stores, but also parking capacity expressed in raw numbers. Gargantuan parking lots connoted progress. Welton Becket, a prominent shopping center architect who early on warned that too much parking space was as bad as too little parking space, reminded developers that many customers arrived by public transportation. He believed that those arriving by car, although numerous when the shopping center was new, declined in numbers if given the option of public transportation.[63]

Straight linearity weighed heavily in popular impressions, too. Most shopping centers defaulted to parking plans locating vehicles before storefronts, be they on a strip or in a multisided shopping center. Some designers and developers introduced above-ground parking, both in freestanding ramps and roof parking, and raised the shopping center above the parking at grade level. Those remained exceptions through the 1960s.[64]

Kenneth Welch and Bruno Funaro lectured that "the simple pattern of stores with their fronts facing the parking area (front parking) is, undoubtedly, the best for directness of access to the stores, but is obviously only suited for the neighborhood center made up of convenience good stores." Untested alternatives included one form of straight linearity, namely, arcaded entrances that usher customers from the parking lot without undesirable exposure to service entrances. A "more costly" alternative was underground parking or underground service passages.[65] Those could satisfy the consumers' desire for clear sight lines to their target store.[66]

Parking without charge or "free parking" added further incentive to patronizing suburban shopping centers. Although not a design but a management feature, "free parking" was and is important. When downtown merchants and municipal authorities wrestled with various options, park and shop or reduced rates, for example, no shopping centers in the major trade literature recorded any example of parking for any fee. Leaders in the parking industry said the contrast between downtown and suburban shopping centers was invidious. Josef Diamond, president of the National Parking Association in 1963, drew special attention to this issue in his address to the association: "Downtown will lose more and more shoppers to these attractive suburban shopping centers with ample free parking until such time as not only convenient parking but 'free' parking is made available for downtown shoppers."[67] Parkers seldom thought of the cost for parking lot design, construction, and maintenance that shopping center merchants passed on to shoppers as added costs. They also perceived parking as something they should pay a minimum for if at all. Amid all the material written on parking design and examples given, "free" parking was not gainsaid. Again, parking was a silent but potent force in many recalculations of the American landscape.

Spatial definers, straight linearity and great magnitude, however, yielded the design of surface lots providing ample parking in front of each store. By the 1970s, changed expectations combined to put the conventional parking format of shopping centers in serious doubt.

Conditions inspiring many smaller parking areas for shopping centers began in the 1960s. Several factors combined. Economic opportunities no longer lay in the construction of the large, regional shopping centers that required commensurate parking spaces. Existing centers often earned less than their potential, and few sizable undeveloped sites remained; those factors persuaded the Urban Land Institute, which had reported periodically on the shopping center phenomenon since 1944, to issue a conclusion in 1960: "there is no longer a wide open field for new shopping center developments as there was in 1950."[68] Shopping center analysts foresaw several trends with special relevance to parking lots: the advent of smaller centers because they did not require the special cost of delivery and interstore tunnels or elevators and the "discounter" or stores dealing in discounted goods.[69] Keeping costs low, regardless of analysts' encouragement of better landscaping, reinforced the tendency for parking lots to be comparatively vast expanses with the stores they served.

Detractors arose. Elitists criticized shopping centers for their bland sameness, an especially American phenomenon that the parking lots magnified. Complaints ranged from "mall ennui" to pointing out the irony that accommodations to automobile convenience produced buildings spread apart by parking lots and fewer people willing to walk between them. Gruen had ideological descendants. Joel Garreau, first a journalist and by 1994 head of the Edge City Group, lectured and wrote about the lack of identity and community in the consequent landscapes. Geographer Edward Relph observed that the dysfunctional landscape was part of the general phenomenon of "placelessness." Grumbling about traffic congestion was more common, however, a facet of the enduring demand for those factors summed up in the word "convenience."[70]

Shopping center design diversified in the entrepreneurs' search for novelty, economy, and the new aesthetics. Enclosed malls were one result. They created pedestrian interiors with walkways through and on several sides of the stores housed under a common roof and separate from outdoor parking. Mega-malls played to the same cravings albeit in larger settings overtly combining entertainment with shopping. The Mall of America in Bloomington, Minnesota, which opened in 1992 with floor space for 88 football fields, is the largest U.S. mall. Occupancy costs in older, larger shopping centers drove some chains to start strip centers that they occupied exclusively. Some automobile service chains and independents combined to operate "car-care malls" combining a car wash, tire and accessories store, and muffler shop on comparatively small and low-priced lots to which customers were attracted because they needed the services.[71]

Parking's persuasiveness varied from place to place. Statistical studies in the last quarter of the twentieth century characteristically dealt with remedies for specific circumstances; parking's significance had been conceded long before. Numerous downtown redevelopment organizations or stores built parking garages to push economic recovery. A 5-tier parking ramp serving Macy's department store and a 2-level shopping mall were claimed essential to the revitalization of downtown New Rochelle, New York, beginning when the ramp opened in 1968. Some downtown garages charged for parking; others gave it free. Regardless of the rate or its absence, parking worked best when it was connected closely to nearby stores. In Tysons Corner Center in McLean, Virginia, rapidly revitalizing area shopping, 4 parking facilities opened in 1988 with space for a total of 8,000 vehicles and provided several levels of horizontal paths between the parking area and the mall. Studies in 1981 and 1985 illustrated a rising fear of crime and increased shopping at small centers while support for adequate parking space hardly varied. It remained the second most important factor at neighborhood strip centers and enclosed large malls alike. Technological improvements provided increased lighting at lower cost, first as a spotlight on shopping centers and the provision of clear visibility and later as a security measure.[72]

Parking space as shopping incentive became more fully engaged by the end of the century when convenience businesses were carefully situated on shopping center lots. Those stores could also increase income for the shopping center owners, but from the shopping centers' inception it was understood that they could disrupt rapid traffic flows and sight lines to the main stores. Hugh Potter, developer of River Oaks in Houston, a pioneer shopping center begun in 1937, stated during the shopping center boom of the early 1950s that to be profitable filling stations must be handsome and kept clean, but just as important, their traffic must be separated from other consumers.[73] Car washes and photograph kiosks were some of the options strategically situated in parking lots through the century's end.[74] Those businesses added to the generally ephemeral nature of the shopping center as a landscape feature because most were leased on short terms until chances arose for greater profit through shopping center expansion or the construction of higher-income businesses.[75] On land at the fringe of shopping centers that remained unoccupied, developers began in the 1980s to arrange for businesses — motels, fast-food restaurants, and offices, for example — that induced shoppers to linger at the center after parking at those business located peripherally.[76] The principal of the highest income use for commercial frontage enhanced with parking space remained a cardinal principle amid the other periodically refashioned elements (fig. 8.5).

Commerce did not provide the first parking space. The automobile, bus, truck, and motorcycle were too widely used for merchants alone to have insight into their motorized patrons' special needs. But commerce made the first spectacular use of parking by absorbing the largest swaths of landscape and displays consistent in its breadth of scope with mass retailing since the late nineteenth century. Commerce on the highways set the templates that many others first explored for their own parking uses.

Downtown merchants, however, slowly countered their narrowing fortunes with parking but permitted new opportunities in outlying districts and roadside lodgings, food stands, gasoline stations, and a host of followers. Parking became the sine qua non of automobile-convenient businesses with big intentions by the mid-twentieth century. Space had to be manipulated, enclosed, and defined to point potential customers to sales. Entre-

FIG. 8.5

The Post Oak Shopping Center, about six and one-half miles from downtown Houston, 1996. The suburban shopping center, with a canopied walk perpendicular to 90-degree parking stalls and minimal landscaping, typified parking lots at the end of the twentieth century.

preneurs, planners, and architects opposing indiscriminate consignment of space to parking as an afterthought in the commercial scramble helped found the shopping center in the mid-twentieth century, but common capitalist aspirations and consumers satisfied with easy access and short distances from their car to their destination store left the landscape to pragmatic but unlovely parking lots and garages often spatially two to three times greater than the stores. Parking truly was something consumers wanted without having to think about. Is there something deeply satisfying after all in such a landscape to a people deeply imbued with a taste for open expanse and frontiering?

Generally unquestioned commitment to automobility necessitated parking support for institutions as well. We turn now to the schools, hospitals, airports and other noncommercial origins and configurations of parking.

9

PARKING FOR INSTITUTIONS, AIRPORTS, RECREATIONS, AND INDUSTRIES

Parking for institutions, airports, recreations, and industries, when reviewed in the confines of a single chapter, makes certain the complexities and connectivity of the different groups and places in a technological and suburban society. Parking is a common need. Anyone who drives also parks, obviously. Parking also reaches far beyond to affect financial and environmental resources and invites problem-solving imagination as well. The "parking problem" conversely takes various forms depending on the group for whom parking is permitted. Although a certain degree of frivolity may seem to undergird a discussion of parking for shopping, since shopping often departs from a search for essentials, parking for institutions, airports, recreations, and industries forces serious consideration of how Americans have handled and are handling the storage of automotive vehicles; for it is in the widely different activities here grouped that we pass our lives as social beings.

We examine a wide range of special parking needs in this chapter to make our point about parking's numerous effects and relationships. Although it might be claimed that those unities are forced due to the large number of parking categories framed in this chapter, the parking industry itself has conceived this omnibus category. The progressive expansion of the category is central to the facts of parking during the past half-century.

Parking was a matter of either commerce or parking-supported "institutions" in the mid-twentieth century. Residential parking was a specialized subcategory unto itself. Institutions included social, educational, and religious organizations, all of them distinguishable as not for profit according to Wilbur S. Smith, a parking consultant who in 1960 published the first comprehensive study on many of the categories of parking in this chapter.[1]

An article he coauthored 13 years before, in 1947, indicated how little concerned cities were with parking for theaters, hospitals, and industries; for parking at such places, between 10 and 25 cities out of 70 cities surveyed had ordinances stipulating off-street parking. Whatever parking space existed for those places was accepted.[2] A rather hurried response due to the galloping demand for institutional parking, Smith's 1960 publication concluded with hope "that this analysis points up some of the problems, needs and approaches of institutions in their attempts to grow and function in urban settings."[3] Smith subsumed stadia, auditoriums, and coliseums in his book as functions of a city or institution. He did not mention that some of those recreational facilities were profit-making businesses. Urgent planning needs did not permit scholarly taxonomy. Subsequent parking studies distinguished between institutional and special events parking but discussed them as a group apart from parking for shopping and residences. Airports have recently been added to the group including institutions and special events. The list of parking categories presented in this chapter, thus, has expanded rapidly.[4]

America's voracious appetite for new forms of healthcare, schooling, and recreation in turn fostered specialized parking. Spokesmen of the newly formed traffic engineering profession understood their charge within the context of historical change for those specialized demands. They believed, with many others, that America was very different after World War II than earlier in the twentieth century regardless of any continuities. In 1960, Smith wrote of significant alterations and consequently alarming conditions because parking planners were unprepared: "The picture has undergone drastic change; crowded classrooms, more people, greater mechanization and more extensive use of the automobile have combined to bring about the present chaos." An engineering and landscape firm's authors of *Parking for Recreation* in 1965 referred to the population as undergoing an "explosion," leisure as "ever-growing," and "the versatile automobile with its appetite for space" as stymieing planners. Enthusiasm for a consumer- and leisure-oriented break with the past ironically seemed to border on an unpleasant future. "Complicating the picture is the growing concentration of population in urban centers." What historians later referred to dispassionately as the "baby boom," Smith saw through a very different filter: "The phenomenal increase in the country's population within the past 15 years is one of the major contributing factors to present problems."[5]

Urgency waned, to be replaced with faith in the rational solutions by the time the next parking study on institutions and special events was published in 1982.[6] Heightened sensitivity to geographic needs occurred to planners at the same time they accepted constant and rapid change as facts and abandoned their earlier stance of heroically addressing historic changes. The only constant they acknowledged was the rising demand for parking. The future was at once to be organized according to each parking site's idiosyncrasies and with generalizations induced from numerous cases. Parking professionals had gathered much data and had time to reflect on it since Smith's study of 22 years before.

A 1990 study restated the precept that each parking circumstance should inform effective planning and management. The 1990 study also repeated many of the 1982 study's conclusions about parking for the several categories on parking considered in this chapter.[7] We turn next to those specialized venues.

HOSPITALS AND HEALTHCARE FACILITIES

Increased population and rising healthcare expectations, especially among more affluent groups, have pushed parking developments at hospitals and healthcare facilities in the last half-century. Admissions grew 67 percent in the 25 years after 1946. Exclusive of those arriving by taxi, a survey reported in 1973 indicated that employee trips by automobile varied between 56.3 and 61.5 percent while long-term patient, outpatient, and visitor trips by automobile varied between 42.9 percent and 75 percent. Hospital administrators appreciated the rapid growth in healthcare demand with its parking consequences, but the lack of a comprehensive study before 1973 reflects the disorganized response to parking before then.[8] Healthcare meant mostly medicine heretofore.

Hospital administrators thereafter quickly turned to experience from shopping centers to calculate financially efficient plans. Sorting through a hypothetical hospital administrator's considerations for an efficient surface lot, authors of a 1977 article reasoned as follows: "As a guide, the experience of the shopping center industry may be cited, the shopping center industry being a particularly useful source because careful, accurate records of operating costs are kept, which isolate the costs associated with a parking area."[9] More fully rationalized parking derived rapidly from the generally stronger business orientation of the healthcare industry in the last quarter of the twentieth century. Administrators determined their parking responsibilities were both unique and similar to other settings. Hospitals and medical centers received more people with different parking needs —

administrators, physicians, nurses, technicians, visitors, outpatients, volunteers, clergy, and students, to name most—than other institutions at the same time as administrators confronted the common demand for increased parking space. Finally, adhering to traffic engineers' admonitions for nearly a half-century, parking needs were to be determined according to detailed studies of traffic peaks and flows. Like other institutions insinuated in residential areas, hospitals and healthcare facilities advised their staff and visitors not to park in those areas. Despite their initial attraction to the shopping center model with no fee charged for parking, administrators were persuaded that rising costs made free parking unrealistic and learned their patrons were willing to pay for parking.[10]

With their reputation as fundamentally humane services linked in some cases to particular neighborhoods, hospitals and healthcare facilities often faced especially difficult conflicts in their expansion programs. Some seemed to have unfairly gobbled up adjacent residential areas. In the late 1950s, St. Elizabeth's Hospital in Youngstown, Ohio, sought to retain its location in an older residential neighborhood near downtown and add facilities for the nursing school, personnel housing, specialized health agencies, and their consequent parking. Federal involvement facilitated planning. An interstate was scheduled to open just north of the hospital, and urban renewal funds were available to acquire and raze neighborhood residences considered substandard. The Youngstown Health Center Development plan proposed a layout featuring three parking garages immediately accessible to drivers off the interstate. The plan envisioned not only a "pleasant place in which to live and work" but a more efficient healthcare operation and traffic pattern. St. Elizabeth's Hospital remained the heart of a complex dedicated to old Youngstown; this was a public relations coup.[11]

Increased costs, increased demand, specialized services, and limited available land have converged to generate a unit dedicated to hospital parking within many parking consultant firms. Site plans periodically redeveloped to address changed circumstances have especially upset the traditional provision of parking by hospital main entrances. Surface parking was frequently surrendered to building expansion, with the result that parking was in too short a supply or considered remote from the "front door." Patron maps are one solution, but like shoppers, physicians and visitors expected convenience, that is, primarily parking close to their destination. How to provide it? Safety for night-time workers, the employment of more part-time workers, and compliance with the federal Americans for Disabilities Act compound the problems.[12]

Commercialism also strongly informed parking considerations. Access and attraction are keenly conceived because healthcare managers "know that users of their medical facilities, now more than ever, have a choice regarding which healthcare provider they use," according to one head of a design firm. It became more acceptable to charge patients for parking by 2000.[13]

SCHOOLS

Colleges and universities obviously are by no means the only educational institutions requiring parking, but they have received the most attention in print. No surrogate for other school levels or churches, if the behavior-transforming mission of churches categorizes them as educational, university parking has raised essential geographic and historical issues similar to those raised by other institutions regarding parking. Institutions with smaller traffic volumes raise proportionately smaller-scale, but important, problems.

Parking on college or university campuses required incremental responses from administrators until the latter half of the twentieth century, when the automobile turned from a relative luxury into a required transportation mode. Unanticipated high enrollments, fixed quantities of land with little chance for more, and the new move toward suburban locations produced a constant flux of factors necessitating an entirely new member of the campus planning committee, the parking coordinator in charge of a campus parking plan. A survey of 114 colleges and universities between 1956 and 1957 disclosed no common patterns for managing parking, much less planning for it. The survey director typified the belief of many college administrators that traffic and parking problems were intensifying. "Drive-in" campuses for student bodies comprising a high percentage of commuters, or "rubber-tire schools," began in the 1960s to take a place along with the traditional colleges, the preponderance of whose enrollees were pedestrians in residence. College towns, those with a largely full-time resident student body, have adopted and effectively enforced student driving regulations, but the challenges of traffic volume and confluence with city streets and intercity highways have been devilish at universities near big cities.[14]

San Jose State University wrestled with key aspects of the "parking problem" in the early 1990s. The campus occupied 92 acres in downtown San Jose, California, and 62 acres with athletic fields 1.5 miles south of the city. Approximately 5,700 spaces or 88 percent of the university's parking was available in 3 large multitiered ramps on the main campus and a surface lot for 1,000 vehicles on the south campus. Notwithstanding the total available supply, the surface lot was remarkably unoccupied while approximately 3,500 spaces were occupied in the neighborhoods adjacent to the main campus. Neighbors complained about students parking near their homes. "Parking is an emotional issue often triggering over reaction on the part of those who perceive a negative impact upon their lives," responded two university campus planners. California law required a traffic study before the university could build an additional parking garage, and the city of San Jose undertook a downtown study, which the university funded, before responding to the university request to close a major street downtown to alleviate traffic congestion. The study resulted in improvements for getting in and out of the garages and the installation of signs on the interstate and major streets to notify drivers of available garage space, but no additional garage. San Joseans in the university neighborhood responded cautiously but amicably to the decreased traffic on residential streets.[15]

Additional problems were numerous. Regarding the politics of who gets parking, students have traditionally been considered tertiary. Faculty, staff, and visitors have ranked as those groups to whom parking space should be assured first. No less than parking for shoppers, many members of university communities expect parking space within short walking distance from their campus destination. Financial considerations influence decisions mightily. Students often prefer commuting because, at least in the early 1980s, it required one-third the cost of living on campus, and they valued parking second only to quality of instruction in a 1993 poll. Universities, however, faced the fact that parking one car required more space than housing one student or classroom space for 15 students. A summary of campus parking in 1995 declared it wasteful and impossible to plan the future on the previous ratio of one space per person on campus. Carpools, shuttles from outlying parking lots, alternative transportation (walking, bicycles, and motorcycles), but less garage construction were recommended to provide every member of the campus community with a reasonable way to work. Members of that community resisted paying their share of parking's rising costs. Although colleges and universities paid more attention to parking costs by the end of the twentieth century, they never viewed parking as a commercial prospect, as did hospitals and healthcare facilities. Underground garages, a calculated expedient only for some campuses, such as Ohio State University, ultimately seemed too expensive, and by the early 1960s they were recommended to campus planners as a last re-

FIG. 9.1

Parking ramp at Western Michigan University, Kalamazoo. Hobbs and Black Associates, with consultant Carl Walker, Inc., designed the parking ramp to absorb 1,200 automobiles in three levels over 350,000 square feet instead of a far more extensive lot. The ramp was built in 1993 at a cost of $6.3 million. *Source:* Courtesy of Hobbs and Black Associates, Inc.; Ken Perkins, photographer.

sort.[16] Aesthetics, proximity, security, cost effectiveness, and the confines of a particular location within the campus often helped prescribe garage design (figs. 9.1 and 9.2).

Tension erupted between parkers and parking managers on San Diego State University's campus, where four garages had been built in 20 years, while one official insisted student parking was actually plentiful. "It's that they cannot park where they want to park, when they want to park there."[17] The hallowed role of the university as a community apart from the workaday world perhaps militated against adaptation of the practices outside where parkers more commonly expected to pay for parking at rates higher than university campuses.

High school parking has received far less attention than college and university parking despite its reflection of similar trends. High school students driving cars became commonplace by 1960. Their curbside parking exacerbated morning traffic snarls but drew no attention beyond local solutions. Occasional notes in the parking industry's literature nonetheless reminded people of the lingering problem. At rural Katy High School in Katy, Texas,

FIG. 9.2

A glass-enclosed stair and elevator tower on the parking ramp at Miller Auditorium on the Western Michigan University campus affords access to the facility's three decks and clear surveillance for security purposes. Source: Courtesy of Hobbs and Black Associates, Inc.; Ken Perkins, photographer.

for example, the student body tripled since 1980 to 3,000 by 2000, and with the increase in enrollment came parking lots (a 110-car and 2,500-car lot), a policy of lost parking privileges for disciplinary reasons, and the possibility of a multitiered parking garage. Katy's assistant principal was as surprised about the flood of student automobiles as parking planners and managers had been 40 years before about the general increase in automobiles.[18]

AIRPORTS

People wishing to park at airports leaped in number during the last half of the twentieth century. Demand at Hartsfield Atlanta International Airport, for example, jumped 47 percent to 1.4 million passengers in 1952, that is, a 500 percent increase in 11 years. A classic pre–World War II planning study of airports throughout the United States and Europe did not include parking although its author was aware of how quickly other influences on airport design had changed.[19] The "Jet Age," colloquially named for the advent of commercial jet airline travel beginning in the 1950s, introduced more travelers, both for business and recreation. Like their counterparts parking elsewhere, airline travelers were not eager to walk far from their car to their immediate destination.

Airport parking more closely approached traffic engineering's ideal of participation in a transportation system than perhaps any other place of parking treated in this chapter. This is consistent with the tendency for Americans to see airports less for their potential as members of metropolitan life than as travel facilitators.[20] The large airports commanded idealized attention partly because they were fewer in number and at the same time had the potential for colossal traffic snarls and dissatisfied patrons who could bring down unfavorable publicity. People who traveled by air were among those groups accustomed to and capable of making their opinions known.

O'Hare International Airport in Chicago was the nation's largest airport in terms of "enplanements," to use the airline industry's argot for passenger boardings, and had a garage to park 9,300 vehicles. This made O'Hare's garage the largest in the world and the world's fourth largest building of any kind at the time. Parking at this airport was prohibited on the access roads to free them for maximum capacity in this beehive of activity. Patrons passed through tunnels under access roads for greater efficiency and safety, and moving sidewalks hurried them to or from flights. The $40 million garage on 79 acres posed problems for finding one's vehicle, alerting motorists to which areas were vacant to prevent the congestion resulting from a slow search for parking space, and ventilation of automotive exhausts. Faced with unfinished construction on the garage, the relationship between the garage and a hotel (the world's largest airport lodging), and planning for future expansion, planners of parking at O'Hare were faced in 1973 with even more congestion, confusion, and delay. It was foreseen that within a year or two after opening, the 11 tollgates would reach capacity, and cashiering was to be moved to the elevators that people used after parking their cars. Doyen of Chicago architects and planners, Harry Wiese, outlined a series of improvements.[21]

By 2000, information available on the Internet reinforced the effort to ease access to O'Hare. In addition to the central garage, the facilities comprised an arrangement of long-term and short-term parking by 3 of the airport's 5 terminals and outlying parking and space for brief stops by automobile passengers with shuttle service ("Kiss 'n Ride") at two locations. A free shuttle covered 2.7 miles and operated around the clock. Kiss 'n Ride was especially intended for the suburbanites to the immediate north and northwest from whence 80 percent of the vehicles originated by 1983.[22]

Parking at airports was of so vast a scale and dedicated to such a clearly commercial enterprise that perhaps not surprisingly it was one of the first parking venues commodified. The reason for calculating cost efficiency from the exorbitantly expensive airport facilities meshed with regularly scheduled flights to permit industrial precision in the calculations. Traffic volumes moreover were constant, high, and inelastic. Whereas shopping center experience helped early parking administrators in the healthcare industry, it shed little light on airport parking because shopping centers did not operate around the clock as did airports. Cleveland airport's tradition as one of the few American airports profiting before World War II perhaps fostered expectations giving birth to modern airport parking following the war. Edwin M. Roth, who started in the parking industry in 1946, originated the first parking services especially for air travelers three years later at the Cleveland airport. Airport managers gladly passed on the work of running parking facilities rather than adding it to their already considerable responsibilities. Entrepreneurs such as Roth tapped the potential earnings. In 1951, his APCOA earned $200,000; it earned $2 million by 1956 and $200 million by 1985, although the company was no longer exclusively in airport parking.[23]

Entrepreneurs persistently refined the business of airport parking. In the parking industry's customary citations of low profit margins, airport parking owners were among the industry's most ardent accountants of costs and earnings. Howard Metzenbaum, a founder of Airport Parking in Cleveland, which was the predecessor to Roth's APCOA, told the National Parking Association at its annual meeting in 1963 that airport parking space was often expensive to acquire, improve, and operate. He explained insurance rates were exceptionally high because the land was usually publicly owned, and public complaints could explode disproportionately to the grievances because they were usually addressed to elected public officials. Roth understandably reckoned as very important his creation in the 1960s of equipment combining a cash register, gate arm, and detectors to accurately charge all exiting parkers. Electronic computers improved those devices.

Such seemingly humble measures were the boast of the Jet Park garage opened in 1996 adjacent to Lambert International Airport in St. Louis. Porta-King Building Systems of St. Louis devised machinery for entrance and parking fee collection that relied on magnetic strip technology to also speed customer service.[24]

Airport parking has also earned incomes special to it from long-term storage and high percentages of travelers on business expense accounts or leisure. Valet parking also has come increasingly into vogue despite its added cost. The Los Angeles International Airport (LAX), one of the few airports with valet parking in the early 1960s, had numerous valet parking businesses at the time of this writing. Light automotive services are often combined, reminiscent of earlier downtown parking with ancillary services such as that at the first site of Denison Service Parking (fig. 6.1). For example, Car Barn Airport Parking, begun in 1980 at LAX and owned by PRG Parking Century in Chicago, in 2000 advertised as the only parking lot at LAX to offer car wash, wax, detail, and lubrication while customers flew.[25]

Airport parking has been exceptional in the parking industry for its frequent overbuilding. Richard C. Rich, who in the 1960s designed the parking garage for O'Hare International Airport, observed that early airport parking garages commonly provided more parking space than was needed at peak traffic flows. Downtown garages with mixed short-term and all-day parking and low overnight occupancy provided the only antecedents from which to design airport parking, but airport garages built to those models actually served a more even stream of patrons. Parking provisions were adjusted accordingly. In 1997, parking owners and planners observed the apparent anomaly that the demand for airport parking spaces exceeded boardings. Boarding traditionally had been the basis of planning for expansion. Increased leisure travelers due to increased expendable income and low-fair airlines induced longer trips by air and lower turnover in parking spaces, one member of the industry hypothesized.[26]

RECREATIONS

Hereunder we group several venues that parking professionals treat under separate headings. We, however, see greater similarities than dissimilarities in the parking needs of auditoriums, stadia, special events, museums, and parks.

In the last half of the twentieth century parking for auditoriums and stadia grew more important in planning those facilities. The rising travel and other consumer industries following World War II motivated retailers and hotel associations to expect "a bigger, a newer, a more elaborate municipal auditorium" in many cities, according to a report on 175 municipal auditoriums published in 1949. Little had to be shared in print before then because the design and role of auditoriums had been concerns of a comparatively few municipalities. The survey published in 1949 aimed principally at improving function, capacity, facilities, and location; parking was but one consideration.

Officials at 34 of the surveyed auditoriums nonetheless provided the basis of observation and considerable commentary about parking. Indicative of parking's previous insignificance, 11 of the auditoriums providing public parking excluded its maintenance from operating costs, and an unspecified number, simply characterized as the "bulk," charged no parking fee. Inadequate to adequate parking: that was the first comment about the existing auditoriums. Every auditorium lacked abundant parking or plans to expand parking. Over half of those providing public parking did not provide that parking when built; they reported "inadequate" parking on their questionnaire. Auditoriums providing parking when built reported no more than "adequate" parking. Parking must be provided at auditoriums built in the future, the survey advised. It encouraged use of mass transit but also recognized automobile dependence and consequently further metropolitanism. Future auditoriums would be better if not "located in the most central of locations — as the economic value of the land would make the cost of the land acquisition exorbitant. A location on the outer periphery of the central business district is likely to be the wisest location for most auditoriums."[27]

Geography and history took a somewhat different turn than was anticipated in the 1949 report. Within 20 years efforts at downtown revitalization fixed on auditoriums and stadia for epicenters that planners hoped would restore the entertainment and financial vitality drained off from downtowns by midcentury. Special events including the periodic performances of professional athletic teams named for cities or regions would restore the city as carnival, it was planned. Auditoriums and stadia opened in the suburbs, to be sure, but those downtown especially strove through low fees, easy entrance, and voluminous parking to dispel the persistent downtown image of a place impossible to drive through and park within. Older facilities did not accommodate much parking and contrasted starkly with those newer facilities designed for visitors coming by car. According to a 1975 survey, 10 percent of the visitors to Yankee Stadium (built 1923) in New York

City arrived by car whereas 85 percent arrived by car for games at Dodger Stadium (built 1962) in Los Angeles.[28]

Parking's contribution to escalating expectations was well documented in 2 cities. In Detroit, Cobo Hall and Convention Arena on the eve of completion in 1960 was planned to simultaneously hold 4 major trade shows, 33 meetings, and a 3-ring circus with a total of 9,600 spectators. Approximately 1,150 cars could park on the roof. In New Orleans, the Superdome, constructed between 1972 and 1975 adjacent to downtown, could park 5,000 cars. With space wasted when no event was held or the event did not demand full occupancy, Superdome parking induced substantial private redevelopment in its vicinity. Interstate access and new boulevards added impetus, but coincidentally, the same year the Superdome opened the city government enacted minimum parking-per-square-feet requirements for adjacent buildings. Low-cost parking at the Superdome for potential customers and complete avoidance of its construction costs magnetized developers who constructed 7 office buildings, a motel, and a shopping mall on the fringe of the Superdome. Developers saved between $39.2 and $43.6 million between the city ordinance and the serendipitously available Superdome parking. It was asked, why not combine public authority for minimum parking requirements on private development and construction of adjacent cheap public parking as a general economic development strategy? It had been reasoned for at least 25 years that reliance on nearby business or municipal parking for patrons attending live theater was an effective way to lower an auditorium's land acquisition costs and still draw audiences with parking convenience. This lesson from live theater auditoriums may have derived from the earlier practices of movie theaters in outlying shopping districts. In 1980s, however, it became a popular strategy for capital gain apart from the auditoriums or stadia themselves. For cities, parking finally emerged from a financial afterthought to become a powerful instrument in its own right.[29]

Parking for recreational attractions developed traits both unique and common to parking in general. The time drivers take to leave after an event—"dump time," in the specialized vocabulary of parking for recreational events—dictated parking designs to clear crowds within an hour. That standard was identical for other facilities with high-peak usage pulsations. Unlike shoppers at malls, however, special events patrons were willing to walk up to 2,000 feet between their vehicle and the event. Reversible lanes and portals were possible in parking at many recreational destinations because traffic was seldom coming and going simultaneously.[30]

FIG. 9.3

A parking salesman at the Illinois State Fair in Springfield, shown in a 1998 photograph. Such entrepreneurs typified the petit bourgeoisie historical foundation of roadside industries and parking in particular.

Events of infrequent occurrence manifested eccentric parking traits eluding easy generalization. Perhaps the case most widely known in the parking industry was the professional football championship game held in 1981 in the Silverdome stadium at Pontiac, a Detroit suburb. Special parking provisions for this unique special event failed traffic engineering's test for efficiency in many regards. The secret service guarding the United States vice president's attendance at the game denied Silverdome's traffic coordinator his usual vantage point atop the stadium to monitor traffic. The normal 10 seconds required to charge spectators at the stadium entrance swelled to one minute because everyone, including those who paid in advance for the exclusive privilege of parking immediately adjacent to the stadium, was directed into the lot. Whereas the Eno Foundation advised against property owners adjacent to special events with insufficient parking from becoming "one-day parking entrepreneurs" in locations where the practice was illegal, such lots thrived in places where it was legal (fig. 9.3).[31]

A few big aquariums and museums specialized their parking in keeping with the general trend to maximize this expensive resource's utility. Parking garages became entrees, not adjuncts. International Parking Design won an award for its creation of the Queensway Parking Structure in Long Beach, California. In 1998, the Museum of Science and Industry in Chicago restored the historic greensward foreground that existed after the Columbian Exposition of 1893 by removing the parking lot and built an underground parking garage. Not only was the capacity increased from 1,300 to 1,500 vehicles in the shift, but a railroad exhibit was installed for visitors in the passage between the garage and the galleries inside the main building. The Getty Center in Los Angeles enforced an unusual management policy. To avoid long traffic lines, delays, and possible denied entrance due to the site's filled capacity, only automobile-borne visitors with parking reservations were admitted. Those innovations were farsighted exceptions.[32]

The demand for recreational retreat from urban settings where most people lived in the last half-century brought high expectations for open space. While on the one hand highways and park roads within were to facilitate arrival and departure with no less efficiency than city garages, they had to be landscaped to retain the wilderness illusion. Parking lots came under special scrutiny. "A shiny new car may be a thing of beauty, but a thousand of them lined up in a bare parking field suggests a used-car lot or a factory shipping center," snorted the writer of a primer on parking for recreation published in 1965. Safety islands separating parked vehicles from traffic passing through, picnic tables assigning specific locations, and plantings, albeit in parks and woodlands, were some of the ameliorating features adjacent to the parking lots.[33] Yet some widely acclaimed natural landscapes were reduced for spectator convenience (fig. 9.4).

INDUSTRIES

Finally, we draw attention briefly to industries' growing need for parking. Although the working class owned fewer automobiles and drove them less than the middle class through the 1930s, as best as can be concluded from the few studies of this subject, occasional circumstances spurred industrialists' plans for their workers arriving in automobiles. Production increases on the eve of World War II, however, often resulted in sprawling parking lots or cramped traffic in the haste to spur manufacturing inside factories. A survey of steel mills in Pennsylvania and West Virginia reported that in 1940 60 to 80 percent of the workers arrived by car and that new plants were forced to provide parking space. More workers were able to purchase automobiles because of wartime prosperity, and displays of automobiles in industrial parking lots symbolized to many Americans their side's invincibil-

FIG. 9.4

Curb parking and a road flanked this postcard view, about 1920, of Niagara Falls from the Canadian side.

ity in the war (fig. 9.5). Following the war, industrial parking became another specialized field.[34]

TRANSIT VERSUS AUTOMOBILE SOLUTIONS

The foregoing chapters on urban garages and this chapter on various parking venues to this point bear out conclusively the huge commitment of landscape, entrepreneurial imagination, finance, and popular satisfaction with private solutions to the need for parking. A dialogue of doubt instilling public modifications of the private solutions has engaged many Americans since the 1920s, if only sporadically and only in certain locales. Although it is premature to assess the outcome of this private-public tension, landscape studies would be remiss not to account for its emergence.

The public alternative to inviting all automobilists to their destination at profit-making garages and lots along publicly financed roadways strangely did not take root in the altruistic institutions where hesitancy about purely private motives might have been expected. Not universities, not hospitals, and not churches but struggling transit companies founded the alternative perhaps best known by the name used to promote it with prospective customers — "park and ride." One parking professional defined it succinctly: "P & R facilities are vehicular parking lots which are located at some intermediate point along the route of a trip being made partially by a private passenger car and partially by a second vehicle for the balance of the trip."[35] Private cars used for part of a trip and public transportation used for another part of a trip thus constitute a private-public amalgam. Once transit companies introduced park and ride to attract additional riders and income, doubts about the capacity of city centers to park all the cars of motorists preferring to drive the entire trip then caused government officials and planners, especially in large eastern metropolitan areas, to spur the present stage of park and ride. Parking entrepreneurs and managers have traditionally focused institutional parking inward, more on the institutions served than on the context of their service. Linking institutional, airport, and special events parking here with park and ride underlines the premise of this chapter. Parking has profound consequences for the immediate landscape it occupies as well as the areas beyond where many of its parkers originate, and those areas are impacted by pulsating traffic flows into the street and highway network.

FIG. 9.5

Parking in the unpaved lot at Ford Motor Company's River Rouge plant, circa 1953. *Source:* Collections of Henry Ford and Greenfield Village.

A few cities in the 1920s assigned their vacant land to parking lots outside the downtown to assist motorists willing to use them. Pittsburgh, Akron, and Michigan City, Indiana, were among those charging a parking fee. Many cities charged nothing, and those often took a short-term view. Michigan City, for example, charged only on days of anticipated high traffic, and most cities assigned lots where space was available rather than where lots were needed.[36]

Mixed results discouraged further exploration before World War II. Philadelphia's Rapid Transit Company, the example most remarked upon in the parking news, began in the fall of 1925 with 3 lots ranging from a 100-car lot to a 500-car lot outside the city's center. The transit company owned and operated the lots. The parking fee raised between 25 and 35 cents for a day's parking according to the value of the property that the lot occupied plus the transit tickets to and from the city. Parking duration was not limited, but an additional fee was charged for occupancy in excess of 24 hours. "Park With Us and Ride With Us," the transit company's slogan, failed to attract many motorists; the 870 total spaces available by 1929 were seldom fully occupied. Summer days witnessed 600 cars parked on average and many fewer on winter days. The transit company nonetheless declared success in a report of 1927, citing the approximately 500,000 additional riders who boosted income and the 209,000 parked cars that were kept out of the downtown.[37]

Parking companies operated the lots adjacent to streetcar and elevated transit systems in Baltimore and Boston for far fewer cars than in Philadelphia. Pittsburgh and Poughkeepsie abandoned their experiment after a short trial because their lots were not patronized.[38]

Private transportation companies seemed relatively more satisfied with parking operations, probably because they were accounted as loss leaders hopefully paid for by increased commuter numbers. Intercity railroads led the way. The Northern Ohio Power and Light Company, a traction line between Cleveland and Akron, operated a garage at Akron with valet parking in the 1920s to induce travel by rail. The Northern Texas Company, a traction line to Fort Worth, provided a lot 8 miles out of town for 50 automobiles, charged no fee, and left the lot unattended, with the result that 10 to 20 automobiles generally were parked there according to a 1929 report.[39]

Most suburban travelers to the inner city, however, faced serious difficulties at the commuter railroad stations. Travelers believed the stations were too far from home, were inhospitable inside, and lacked sufficient space. Because many stations were the products of the pre-automobile era, parking operators took advantage of the dear supply to charge high parking prices. Their reputation as a setting for social exchange with infrequently seen neighbors greeted after the train left the station did not offset what one writer named the "drop-run" traffic.[40]

Park and ride operations increased in number after the mid-twentieth century in municipalities determined to alleviate traffic congestion. The mayor of Summit, New Jersey, arranged for a parking study in 1952 that resulted in funding renovation of an existing lot and construction of another. The former, a gravel-surfaced lot that was wet and muddy in spring and winter, was paved, drained, and well lit, and the latter was built across from the Delaware, Lackawanna, and Western Railroad station in 1953. Parking was charged for and limited in duration. In 1954, the village of Valley Stream, New York, the westernmost station outside New York City on the Long Island Railroad, operated 3 "public fields" mostly for the 1,979 daily commuters who made up 8 percent of the village's population.[41]

Varieties of park and ride proliferated too. Suburban gasoline stations cooperating in Pittsburgh with public transportation permitted shoppers to park in available adjacent space and ride buses or streetcars into the city in a plan publicized in 1955. Philadelphia's traffic consultant encouraged cities to consider several different methods of shuttle bus service in an article published in 1955. Shoppers at Atlanta and Dallas downtown stores could charter a bus. People in Cleveland could travel by bus through the downtown or to parking lots on the fringe. St. Louis exemplified a shuttle system with regularly scheduled runs to fringe parking lots and downtown stores. The first proposed federal grant for the Tri-State Transportation Committee, including Connecticut, New Jersey, and New York, was awarded in 1963 to provide matching funds for construction of a 300-car parking lot near the Pennsylvania Railroad station at New Brunswick, New Jersey. After a traffic study of downtown Columbia, South Carolina, reported a 385-car parking deficit, the city and chamber of commerce in 1967 started a "parking mall" for 550 cars at the edge of the downtown. An automated collection system was installed at the lot's gate, and an articulated bus stopped downtown and at intermediate points between the lot and the downtown.[42]

Beginning in the late 1960s, new reasons were added to the list for park and ride. West New York, New Jersey, operated a free bus service for the city's senior citizens (approximately 8,000 by 1973) if they wanted to shop downtown. Environmentalism in the late 1960s and the energy crisis of the mid-1970s brought new urgency of fuel economy to transit alternatives. Here parking's global implications were obvious. In Illinois, for example, state highway officials and communities in metropolitan Chicago cooperated in design, planning, financing, and building of commuter facilities including parking. The shuttle service to O'Hare International Airport mentioned above evolved as part of the new farsightedness. In 1971, East Brunswick, New Jersey, started operating a park and ride service making an 80-mile round trip daily into New York City. For a $12.25 weekly charge, commuters could park 5 days a week in a 402-car lot and save on gasoline and tire consumption. Advocates added that other tolls were avoided en route, and commuters could relax and arrive in air-conditioned buses. Popular demand was high; the lot was almost filled to capacity daily.[43]

In the late 1980s, support for transit solutions moved from the largely pragmatic to include ideological rationale and new visions of settlement with considerably subdued automobile dependence. Robert McGarry, director of the Montgomery County, Maryland, Department of Transportation, in metropolitan Washington, D.C., said on behalf of his area's park and ride program: "People are going to have to consider alternative commuting options because, quite simply, there's not going to be anywhere for them to park."[44] Suburbs then became glutted. Michael Bernick and Robert Cervero wrote in 1997 of "transit-supported design" to replace planned urban developments with "patterns reminiscent of earlier streetcar suburbs and pre-World War II traditional communities."[45]

"Intermodal" supplanted park and ride by the 1990s in traffic engineering jargon. The stronger emphasis on comprehensive transportation and often regional planning that underlay the new public thinking about parking justified the new term.[46] An extensive survey in 1985 disclosed that 72.6 percent of the people arriving at an intermodal facility to exchange transportation came alone, 97.2 percent were on the way to work, and 86.8 percent traveled 5 or more times each week.[47] Road quality to and from the parking location and the quality of the transit service greatly influenced the use of the facilities, but most parking lots, unlike those in the first half of the century, were over 90 percent filled, and some were always full. Rail transit served the travelers to many large city airports, although most workers arrived by automobile. As noted above in the case of O'Hare International Airport, the parking garages had huge capacities. Americans were increasingly thinking about interconnected travel means.[48]

Suburban living stretched Americans' resources considerably in the last half of the twentieth century. Americans, nonetheless, willingly spent the money to live in one place, work in another, and create yet two other places, the highway to travel between work and home and the parking place framing both ends of this traveling experience. Technology, most obviously the automobile, made possible that consequent landscape of low-density residence and high-density highways and parking places. Universities, hospitals, airports, stadia, and special events evolved a similar pattern. People flooded roads to arrive at ever larger and more sophisticated facilities to handle parking demands. Not the least of the consumers were the staffs at those institutions.

Parking planners and managers insisted on the peculiarities of traffic engineering at every site. Although this was correct in the technical sense that numerous variables could result in many different parking systems, noteworthy traits were shared from place to place in this field of growing design sophistication. Parking came increasingly to be commodified by hospitals and healthcare facilities figuring how to recover costs and parking administrators in higher education ruminating about whether it was time to charge higher rates. Close and easily accessed parking was a feature secondary to the reasons why patients, students, physicians, and faculty selected their locations to study, work, or receive medical care, but parking was a factor. Those shoppers for parking were not far behind customers at shopping malls in seeking the sacred convenience. "Dump time," jargon applied only to stadia and auditoriums, should not exceed one hour according to traffic engineers, thus driving those facilities' intolerance for time into the same one-hour test of efficiency for city garages. That universal emerged from the thicket of data, making every parking place different in other regards. Popular demand and professional dictates agreed essentially on maximizing automobility. Crosscurrents did come.

Reducing traffic volume and fuel and oil consumption and protecting air quality from automotive emissions led to the park and ride compromise with automobility. Cars and motorcycles for single drivers with no passengers sustained appetites for privacy and convenience at least in travel to a parking location, after which joining others in park and ride saved individual tolls and fatigue in getting to otherwise congested destinations.

Might those shared experiences be harbingers of a metropolitanism in which common concerns bring people together? Will automobility help maximize mobility on the one hand without continually fragmenting community on the other? Is park and ride a future sign or another replay of individualism in popular vocabulary? Does its successor, "intermodal" travel, presage more cooperation or reemphasize the mode of travel and not the members traveling?

CONCLUSION

Allow us to organize our concluding thoughts around several questions: What does parking mean to Americans? That is, what is its importance historically? What are its social implications? Have we as a nation done well in our reconfiguring of built environment around parking need? Might we do better? How might we proceed in the future? If this book proves to have lasting value as a survey of parking's landscape import, it will not be through the certain comprehension of topics explored, but through the uncertain speculation of questions asked, both explicitly and implicitly. Awareness needs to be raised regarding parking's significance as an American landscape imperative. Parking has proven to be an easily taken-for-granted topic, with the act of parking perhaps too everyday and the places for parking too commonplace to excite much respect. By its insidious nature as a kind of necessary evil, parking commands not only little respect but also little affection. Nonetheless, fuller attention to parking, its history, and its potential as future organizer of American geography seems to us very important. Convincing others, however, is not necessarily all that easy. Few people question the role of parking in America. Most only dismiss it. Many of those who do question it see only negative implication.

PARKING'S HISTORICAL IMPORT

What does parking mean to Americans today? Perhaps we can only speculate regarding Americans as a whole, but we can be most specific when writing of our own interactions with specific people. While researching this book, one of us experienced on two successive days skepticism that, in retrospect, directly frames the questions we ask here. One curious associate laughed when the subject of our project—parking—was divulged. How could parking, a history museum educator wondered, be a subject for elaborated contemplation? The next day, a historic preservationist expressed fear that we might use information she provided about parking at an early suburban shopping center to somehow justify even more automobile dependence in such places in the future. A neighborhood conservationist, she complained of suffering healthwise from the deleterious effects of automobile-engendered smog. Thus utter foolishness or the breath of life itself were meanings two people ascribed to parking. Might not people in other walks of life, forced to think of parking's importance, likewise react? What of today's developers as they anticipate the nation's future? What, for example, of the "New Urbanists"? Whereas historic preservationists advocate saving the old, the New Urbanists advocate the adoption of traditional values in designing the new.

The varied locations where Americans park have come to make parking places one of the most multifaceted of place-types. In America, parking is so intertwined with so many aspects of life as to loom fully commonplace. Certainly, it is a dimension of modern living to be taken for granted. Many people, perhaps most, tend to be contemptuous of things overly familiar. One can hardly exaggerate this point. Parking tends to lack distinction as one of life's more profound considerations. Why else does parking, whether on vast asphalt reaches of open lots or in cavernous parking ramps, beggar people's memory as to where they might have parked their cars? How frequently does the average American walk around in circles looking for a parked car, the location of which stands temporarily forgotten? Except where parking is in truly short supply, the act of parking is something we do as if on "automatic pilot." It is a behavior of reflex rather than reflection.

In part to blame is parking's low-place imagery. Place-product-packaging, as a means of heightening place identity, is only minimally used in commercial parking, and in public parking as well, despite its effectiveness in other automobile-oriented businesses. Competitors in various other roadside activities strive for distinguishing architectural and other signatures ("curb appeal") around which to promote distinctive place-attachments. Parking customers do not repeatedly seek out the brands of distinctive parking companies. Instead, they park at generic locations that serve primarily to minimize distances walked to intended destinations. What else induced utilitarian surface lots to be so ubiquitous and curbside parking everywhere to be so popular? What else drove, at least in downtown cores, the widespread replicating of utilitarian parking decks seemingly ad nauseam?

Whereas people occupy the most personalized place-type, home, with its innumerable relationships and decorations, parking remains a contrasting place, an almost alien world. The house or apartment, as home, excites affection and the attention of continued contrivance through refurnishing and redecoration. Yards and gardens declare one's personal tastes through constant manipulation, but parking spaces, even at home, usually stand as someone else's creation to be neither celebrated nor elaborated. Parking is not described through a diversity of words (despite early confusions at naming), in contrast to home and garden, whose many nuances stimulate rich vocabulary. Parking space is parking space. A parking place is a parking place.

Nonetheless, parking in America has an ingrained history fully evident in attitudes and behaviors prevalent today. Parking implies arrival. It represents for motorists a destination almost reached. Coming to a halt in the parking lot at work, or at the valet parking stand of a restaurant, or in one's garage at home brings realization that a trip has all but ended, the act of parking substantially positioning the motorist in a process of completion. Parking is a transitional state from motoring to mooring. It thus punctuates life in cycles. It is part of the American ordering of time. The act of parking is a kind of work, if we understand work to include planned exertion. Continued outcries against lack of parking (or lack of parking where people impatiently want it) remain one of today's most common laments despite the nation's general oversupply of parking space. Arrival and departure calculations are made with allowances for parking necessarily included. Parking stands as an additive in Americans' estimation of time.

The history of parking in the United States is, in fact, quite rich: personalities moving off on entrepreneurial tangents, designers bringing innovations to the fore, politicians bending to the realities of a new "motor age." Parking has been quite changeful. Early on, owners of downtown parcels in cities regarded them as fit only for buildings, but the parking industry's founders provided viable alternative. They understood that an absence of structure need not leave land idle. Vacant lots could pay. When buildings ceased being profitable, they could be knocked down and made into parking lots! Profits could be had in the short run by renting space to parkers, and in the long run, cleared properties stood ready for eventual redevelopment. "Land banking" was not only clever but honorable in the search for real estate's "highest and best use." Municipal governments engaged in off-street parking when investment capital fled big city downtowns in preference for suburbia. Public parking followed from concern to stabilize downtown property values and thus safeguard municipal tax revenues. Legal precedent lay in city regulation of on-street parking and in regulation of land use through zoning. Efforts at downtown revitalization met the suburban challenge by "suburbanizing" downtowns through full embrace of parking convenience. Today, most large buildings in central business districts stand in parking lot surrounds or are tied directly to parking garages or decks. Nor is any large institution, whether hospital, university campus, or airport, without its close-at-hand parking facility. Change wrought ephemerality: old buildings torn down for lots, lots replaced by new structures, ways of organizing and operating parking facilities introduced and abandoned, and, of course, successive technologies adopted in the building of parking structures. Parking's history evolved a rich material culture.

This brings us back to our friend, the historic preservationist. What does parking's ephemeral material culture mean for preservationists as guardians against wanton change in America? Logically, most preservationists see as unfortunate the loss of buildings for parking. The stock of old buildings in some big city downtowns is shockingly low. To some preservationists, even parking garages might be worthy of landmark designation if proven outstanding examples of their ilk. Few parking lots, however, would so qualify unless, perhaps, they were incorporated into a worthy shopping center or some other building complex of historic merit. Parking lots are too much associated with loss — the loss too often, at least in retrospection, of historically significant architecture. The parking lot symbolizes a system gone wrong. "If those buildings come down, an ugly parking lot will replace them," is the common warning in the preservationist's continuing fight. Parking lots bespeak overwhelmingly of vandalism.

But what of the convenience afforded by parking to historically significant buildings still remaining? Too frequently historic preservationists have failed to appreciate the entire urban landscape. Significant buildings are valued as architectural monuments deserving of attention and esteem. But how might they relate to their surroundings today? How might they have related to past surroundings? Should they be valued presently, and historically, as mere islands in geographical space? What of the "tissue" that joins, and joined, landmark buildings in place? Early in the twentieth century, "pedestrianism" provided that tissue. Increasingly after World War I it was "automobility"—the nation's reliance on motoring. Shouldn't preservationists be concerned to preserve the evidence of such contextualization when it survives from times past? In protecting historic value in landscape today, shouldn't they seek to fully understand how the bindings of contemporary, auto-oriented landscape work? Parking, as part of urban history, should not be rejected out of hand by any history aficionado.

Others, some preservationists included, have stepped back from outright dismissal or condemnation of parking. They seek to comprehend parking as one of the automobile's truly significant landscape consequences. They may not like everything they see. Concessions were made to the nation's free-ranging automobilists. Their parking needs came to disrupt the city's traditional rhythms of mass and space. The automobile's needs became exclusive and accelerated increasingly.[1] Parking spaces expanded at an alarming rate, 5 times in towns between 100,000 and 500,000 people, and 12 times in smaller places between 1972 and 1980.[2] Governments at all levels—federal, state, and local—embraced the automobile, creating legal environments fully conducive to auto use.[3] Zoning ordinances required new buildings to have parking space. We have come to live in a world of "hyperplanning" totally encouraging to auto use. Should not preservationists and, indeed, all other students of history seek to understand this? Comprehensive direction, not only of the smallest detail but of the grandest goals, has swept aside the general citizen and the serendipity that formerly effected landscape evolution. Ensconced in power are planners and engineers with expert opinions and time-tested standards calculated to limit transportation and land use choices.[4] The parking experts have been prime among them.

PARKING'S SOCIAL IMPLICATIONS

Above all, parking facilitates car use. And many Americans find their cars central to their being, central to who they think they are. Automobiles can figure prominently in the defining of self or, in other words, personal identity. To the extent that parking is personalized, as, for example, through having an assigned parking space at work, it can be an important form of territoriality. It can represent an extension of the self through expansion of personal space car-defined. On a back alley in downtown Indianapolis we found a sign humorously worded, but not unusual for its intent and intensity. It read: "THIS SPACE RESERVED FOR TED. ALL OTHERS STAY THE HELL OUT OF IT. DO NOT BLOCK. WILL TOW, WON'T CARE."

People actually use parking space as creatively as any other place-type, humanizing it in many ways and affirming their agency. We borrow anthropologist Victor Turner's concept of liminality to elaborate. According to Turner, social order depends occasionally on people's passage between normative social structures where participants mutually consent to different codes of behavior. Individuals lose something of their previous identity in deliberately groping for self-redefinition. This playful or ludic dimension of life is especially important in societies shaped by the Industrial Revolution, where, for example, delineation between "work" and "play" is sharply defined in word and in deed. Work implies often involuntary exertion required for specified reward, whereas play connotes pleasurable release from the tensions of rigorously purposeful behavior through more voluntary action.[5]

Parking can be liminal. Parking, as a largely habitual and sometimes mindless endeavor (and contained, as it is, in substantially generic settings configured through formula), provides opportunity to act "out of place." Offered is invitation to informal social relationship. The parking lot, for example, provides setting for common neighboring: those fortuitous, spontaneous social interactions based largely on the coincidence of spatial propinquity. Chance encounter in a parking lot, as much as on a sidewalk or in a store or other traditional locale, dictates much of today's sense of belonging, especially in urban neighborhoods. Substantially it is in parking lots that the social glue of place identity in the city is stirred and thickened. Public parking lots and garages are humanized through chance encounters with friends and neighbors, and even with strangers.

In the post–World War II era, the co-opting of parking spaces at "drive-in" restaurants by teenagers offered opportunity for socializing. Cars, serving as status symbols as well as transportation, required not only streets but parking lots especially in sustaining "cruising" as a ritual. Accordingly, teens interacted between cars while they drove an informally designated circuit, stopping at intervals usually in the parking lots of fast-food restaurants. Citing the parking lot's critical role as a focal point for cruising, one observer elaborated: "Teen-agers may drive in, park and talk with friends, and leave after a short while to cruise some more; they may park and remain there watching the strip-activity; they may not park at all, but only drive through looking for 'action', or possible dates."[6] There, beyond the purview of parents and adult authority, generally, an adolescent subculture based on automobility thrived.

Teens periodically make subsidiary use of parking and occasionally with consequences rising to more than casual note. In the 1950s and 1960s, drive-in owners uniformly complained about teenagers drinking alcohol, revving engines, speaking in loud voices and obscene language, congregating on foot after arriving by car, littering with cups, paper plates, and food wrappers, drag racing, destroying food trays and condiment containers, and honking their horns excessively. All this was done almost entirely in parking lots and to a far lesser degree on adjacent streets. Much of this furor is attributable to the acute intensity with which the teenager was initially identified as a new social cohort. Thirteen- to nineteen-year-olds were always members of society, but not until the late 1940s were they identified as a group with distinctive behavior needs and (most importantly for arbiters of proper decorum) problems. Not until after World War II did a unique confluence of forces set off an articulate backlash. Youths' changing tastes in music, speech, clothing, and mores threatened many who feared chaos as a result of what seemed to be revolutionary. Roving teenage gangs were linked as sure consequences of the new rock and roll dances, for example. The movie *Blackboard Jungle* (1955) pitted teens against adult authority in the classic formulation of the era's newfound teen problem. America's children loomed as enemies.[7]

Most drive-in restaurant owners and managers were satisfied with private and local municipal curbs on teen behavior: use of private security guards, paternalistic chats with problem kids, elaborate prescriptions for rapid carhop service (to cut down opportunity for trouble), and municipal anti-loitering and other ordinances.[8] What most teens did in drive-in parking lots appears not to have been very disorderly or at all sociopathic. One drive-in chain in Pittsburgh had no problem with teenagers raising car hoods to show off engines except that the practice "discouraged" older customers. Assembling in parking lots fit teenagers' need to socialize. Sociologists even suggested that parking lots, as places to stop while cruising, offered special opportunities for teens to display themselves and their cars and thus attract and meet potential mates.[9]

As unencumbered open space, parking lots were (and are) frequently "colonized" for large assemblages that cut across age, gender, class, and other social lines. Organizers often assemble parades in parking lots before sending them off down city streets. Sometimes they even hold the parades there as well, especially when there are no major streets to carry strong community symbolism as ritual place. The fans' celebration for the New Jersey Devils' victory in the 1995 Stanley Cup took place in the parking lot surrounding the team's arena. Failure to parade on a traditional main street served editorialist Calvin Trillin's point about the nation's replacement of multipurpose public space (open to all) with commercial space (controlled by private property owners). The victorious team might more accurately have been renamed the "Suburban Sprawl Devils," Trillin quipped. The Devils' second championship was celebrated in another parking lot five years later, cause again for many to comment negatively on the sorrier implications of America's parking lot imperative.[10]

Important political events have been tied to parking. Bob Woodward, Carl Bernstein, and "Deep Throat," critical agents in the impeachment proceedings against President Richard Nixon, offer the best-known example of parking's great subsidiary power. Both the investigative reporters and the informant, after all, were collaborating to put a social construct right, in this case constitutional government, by revealing and publicizing truth. An underground parking lot made possible the liminality freeing each agent from normal constraints to move from the Watergate imbroglio of the presidency to a constitutional resolution. True, the conclusion did not come quickly or easily because Deep Throat felt safe in passing only fragmentary evidence requiring interpretation in a scenario of incremental steps. Clandestine meetings in an underground garage, however, sustained the interchange.[11] David Obst, Woodward and Bernstein's agent, charged that they fabricated Deep Throat, which, if true, eradicates the parking garage's liminal function in this dramatic case of subsidiary use.[12] We are not prepared to argue for or against an informant's existence, but we do observe at the very least that Woodward and Bernstein understood how parking space invited liminal behavior, permitting a translucent quest by holding back the troubled world's intrusion.

Finally, crime has long ranked high among parking's unintended social implications. Any environment fostering anonymity through fleeting occupancy or limited police surveillance potentially sustains criminal opportunity. Roadside locations have been long suspect for this reason. Of course, anyone using an automobile in a crime will park at some time in the conduct of that crime, making the parking facility ancillary in the criminal's "journey to work." Parking facilities are by nature characterized by transient, ephemeral activity: the rapid coming and going of proximate strangers in cars. Inconstant surveillance, whether by users or by attendants, offers invitation to unseemly behavior. Unsupervised lots and garages contribute substantially to parking's reputation, especially at night, as a time ripe for confrontational, often violent, opportunistic crime.

ASSESSING THE RECORD

Have we as a nation done well in reconfiguring built environment around parking needs? In answering, let us first assert that America's embrace of autos, and of auto parking, as changeful as it has been, has always been pragmatic if not rational. One can readily empathize with decision makers, the actions they took, and the trends that they established, realizing that historical events are always constrained by contextual circumstances: value system, political reality, legal environment, technological prowess, market functioning. Too easily can one wish that historical circumstances might have been different, and that history had played out otherwise. It is too easy to decry in retrospect the unintended negative impacts of past actions.

Some critics of the contemporary scene, and we must include many of the so-called New Urbanists in this category, pass judgment without reference to full historical context. Their profound dissatisfaction with the nation's present embrace of the automobile, and their dislike of its accoutrements, such as parking lots and parking garages, induce many commentators to develop incomplete historical explanations. Comprehension is rooted not so much in real history so much as in history imagined as viewed through prisms of present-day discontentment. Often it is a longing for an idealized past that never existed. These critics select from history what they want to know and what, in turn, they want to act upon. This enables them to be dismissive of many concerns and, sometimes, to be quite impractical in proposing problem solutions.

But for every outspoken reformer there are voiceless people by the tens of thousands, those who will leave no published record or enduring quote in open debate, and who, for various reasons, continue to think and to plan in established ways, thus to preserve a sense of status quo. They would leave things unchanged if they could. They are quite satisfied with how things are and with how things got to be the way they are. Freedom of choice and continued search for intense personal satisfaction, translated into liberally expended resources, constant economic expansion, and low-density settlement widely diffused, have long characterized for most Americans the desired American way of life. Those values have been the bulwarks upon which the nation's automobile dependence has been built. They are, in fact, the cultural foundations upon which we as a nation have committed an inordinately large amount of space to parking cars. Those values, and the conditions they produced, may have "caught up" with the nation at the dawning of a new century. But this did not happen through the malice or the stupidity of preceding generations, as some critics would have us believe. The landscape remains tacit evidence of the silent majority's past and present commitment to motoring as something to be preferred. At base, Americans like their cars. They do not mind committing space and time to driving, and to parking.

Many of the New Urbanists, rooting some of their thinking in the preservation ethic, seek to return cities to what they might have been. They seek to re-create in cities what some have called "the wonderful chaos of the past," in opposition, for example, to the homogenizing influences of the automobile's widespread embrace.[13] Many overlook, in their advocacy, much of past reality. In advocating vibrant street life, many see only a part of what the past was really all about. The view is selective in emphasizing the positive by ignoring the negative. Streetcars early in the twentieth century did sustain vibrant pedestrian activity, especially in downtown cores. But they also charged fares that consumers often believed unfair. Motormen and conductors frequently went on strike for better wages, with resulting inconvenience to riders. Transit companies failed to reinvest in track and rolling stock in taking profits. Streetcars, horse-drawn wagons, and pedestrians conflicted constantly, with injury and loss of life widespread. Streets were filthy from the droppings of horses, and street cleaners suffered from lung disease as occupational hazard. Sidewalks teemed with activity, to be sure, but in part as outlet for apartments and tenements too small to sustain much indoor life beyond eating and sleeping. In the past, chaos was not always wonderful. And the automobile offered respite from some of it. It enabled a fuller suburban escape. It cocooned its occupants in relative safely as they moved about cities. And, of course, it suggested speed and convenience in that movement.

Today, many urban reformers challenge Americans to push the automobile aside, to put it back into some more proper place. The call so far has fallen largely on deaf ears. The quality-of-life issues that have been raised simply have not been perceived by most Americans as important enough to demand attention, let alone redress. This is unfortunate since no society can ensure its successes without seeking betterment in appraisal of changeful need. Reformers are surprised by the indifference. "The problems of automobile subsidization have been well documented; this is old news," wrote one advocate of transportation reform. "And yet it is news which few people seem to understand, and which has barely begun to influence government policy in any significant way," he concluded.[14] In other words, how could the few know so much for so long, and the majority remain so uncaring? An alert, creative, and well-meaning minority—but a minority nonetheless—is alone aroused.

Many reformers suffer a current American myth: that America was once a community but has disintegrated into competing, selfish interest groups (prime among them the automobile and highway lobby). Reformers frequently take a singular view of life, misreading what was done in the past in setting future goals.[15] Parking malfunctions because we are in an "age of sprawl and social alienation," one leading critic has put it.[16] Community is implicitly understood as a cooperative network of mutually reinforcing individuals sharing a single perception of the past, present, and future. Many reformers work from such premise, finding it, in a reading of history, where it never really existed. The American small town, for example, is seen to have been a kind of communal utopia. Thus we should be building "small town" set pieces into urban designs. Perhaps so, but villages in the past were not idyllic havens. Villagers in real towns were divided—socially, economically, and politically—much like city and suburban dwellers are variously divided today. It might be argued that if community exists at all in America, it exists through values and things very widely shared and viewed as being fundamental to life. In this regard, nothing is as rooted in the American psyche as the penchant for automobile ownership and use. Is there anything in America more widely shared than the experience of motoring? Motoring has tied Americans together as, perhaps, nothing else in history! If this is true, then we may have done very well, indeed, in our reconfiguring of the built environment around parking needs. For every person a car! For every car a parking space!

SEARCH FOR BETTERMENT

Might we do better? The answer is obvious, but the question needs to be asked anyway. Of course, we must do better. The world changes, and we must change with it. Since maintaining the status quo is never possible, seeking change of positive implication is ever desirable. However, before anyone promotes change in defining and confronting problems, those affected, we believe, must first agree that the problems exist. Too much parking or too little parking? Parking that's too expensive or not expensive enough? The opinions are manifold. There are no simple answers.

The parking implications of the nation's automobile dependency are both positive and negative. The list of debits is long. Detractors of the status quo accurately observe that efforts in the past to end traffic congestion invariably led only to more congestion. Increased street capacity always excited increased traffic in cycles of stimulus and response. So also did increased parking create insatiable appetite for more parking, leading to the wholesale destruction of traditional city landscapes and to creation of new and highly wasteful suburban places as measured by the vast amounts of land consumed, among other measures.[17] Both land and money were wasted on "ugly and desolate car-dominated" landscapes to which parking contributed greatly.[18] Since 1970, acreage the size of the state of Delaware has been annually diverted from forest, farm, and countryside into new suburban development configured largely as an uncoordinated agglomeration of standardized single-use zones. This development displays little pedestrian life and less civic identification, being connected only by overtaxed roads, observed several critics.[19] Parking's contribution to sprawl is, indeed, substantial. The ravages are quantifiable and palpable and not a matter of judgment as aesthetics can be. Let us assert that automobiles today routinely require not two but three parking spaces: at home, at work, and at the shopping center. Add the space for entering, driving around, and exiting parking facilities, and the observation that "asphalt too frequently wins over architecture," as one architect put it, can be seen as all too true.[20]

The asset list is relatively short, with enabled mobility and perceived convenience standing out. Even the car advocates, and the apologists for current parking practice, falter in their enumeration of the positive aspects. It is hard to justify parking lots and parking garages, which presently dominate urban space, as clear aesthetic and environmental assets. Apologists can only emphasize functionality, and with present-day excesses, even that is questionable. Car parking, however, carries history's accumulated weight of affirmation. The present system grew in response to wide public dissatisfaction with conditions in the pre-automobile city and, especially, with the traditional forms of public transport then relied upon. Developers and affluent consumers cooperated to settle new suburbs dependent on privately owned automobiles and thus to recover and extend personal mobility, both geographical and social. Entrepreneurs and consumers cooperated in the relocation of shopping from downtown to outlying shopping districts and later to shopping centers, largely due to the perceived convenience added. New infrastructure, including that of parking, grew thoughtfully. Planners, architects, and engineers carefully calculated ideal street widths and traffic configurations through whole road networks and conceived and applied single-use zoning to spare new residential areas from earlier depredations of indiscriminately intermixed commercial and industrial activities. Parking requirements were included. Modernism undergirded those provisions with faith in the possibility of perfection through machine-like efficiencies, savvy economics, and dedicated public service. It was search for betterment.

THE NECESSITY OF PARKING

How might we proceed in the future? We have no choice but to meet an immediate future with automobiles and parking very much front and center. The automobile is probably here to stay. America's love affair with the automobile is simply too ingrained to imagine a future nation without substantial auto dependence. Producing automobiles and building highways, proven engines for economic growth, are far too important to phase out completely. As much as one should support the advocates of mass transit, and their attempts to provide urban Americans with alternative means of moving about cities, automobiles and motor trucks will dominate transportation and land use in most cities and towns over the foreseeable future. Parking, therefore, will remain a concern with substantive economic, environmental, and social implication for us all.

Those Americans outspoken on parking seem polarized today, perhaps a reflection of what appears to be increased political polarization in the country generally. Parking can be, and often is, a highly charged political issue. Conservatives, especially ultra-conservatives, resist any restriction by government over what they perceive to be inalienable rights: to move freely, to own and use property, to seek personal success. The automobile has become the nation's prime instrument of geographical mobility. It represents a prized possession for most Americans, usually standing second in value only to one's house as a form of property. As such, one's car (or possession of multiple cars) has very much come to symbolize success, with many lifestyles defined around car ownership and use. To conservative minds, restrictions that interfere with basic rights — those readily translatable into terms of auto use for example — are to be fully resisted.

The more liberal (or perhaps, in today's parlance, the more progressive) seem bent on curtailing the automobile's embrace nonetheless. They welcome restriction. They decry the wastefulness implicit in the nation's substantial reliance on motoring. The consumption of land for thoroughfares and parking space has, they realize, substantially reduced urban landscapes to machine or auto spaces. Cars and trucks consume an inordinate amount of petroleum, as does the asphalting of roads, streets, and parking lots. Auto use wastes energy resources. Near universal auto use, they see, severely damages the environment. When compared to pedestrian movement, as sustained by mass transit, and to the densely built (rather than sprawling) city spaces made possible, automobile dependence stands as wasteful of land if nothing else. Many progressives advocate total elimination of autos in certain kinds of urban area, and indeed, over recent decades, experiments with auto-free pedestrian zones have not been inconsequential.

As regards parking in the future, we would advocate a middle ground, one that recognizes the need for auto use everywhere but under degrees of containment tailored to context and need. Parking, we argue, should be available everywhere in cities and towns but configured imaginatively in limited amounts to meet specific demands. Avoided would be the simple formulas of hyperplanning. Introduced would be more design experimentation and even serendipity. Encouraged would be complementary forms of transport beyond motoring.

To allow automobile advocates free reign invites, as we have demonstrated, substantial oversupply of parking space resulting in urban landscapes much debilitated. The built environment suffers the exaggerations of machine space discouraging to, if not precluding altogether, alternative kinds of land use save through urban redevelopment involving truly heroic governmental intervention. The vast acreage of asphalted parking lot, which by the 1960s had come to fully dominate the peripheries of most American big city downtowns and intrude substantially into downtown cores, offers ready testament. The demolition of old buildings and parking lot operation in anticipation of redevelopment may have made (as it continues to make) economic sense. But the kind of urban environment produced was (and is) of the most degraded and demeaning kind. It is ugly. It is environmentally unsound. It is discouraging to most kinds of human interaction save the mundane act of car parking, and this despite the human penchant to convert and redirect parking facilities to other social uses at least on occasion.

Where, in fact, downtown real estate has been redeveloped in recent decades, the parking deck has played a central role. Usually mandated by zoning ordinance, parking garage capacity in most cities also has been overbuilt, with extensive surplus capacity available in most cities even at peak hours of demand. Employers and retailers universally subsidize parking for employees and customers, passing parking costs along in higher prices for goods and services. Parking, so treated as a cost of doing business, also makes economic sense. But discouraged in the process are other forms of transportation not so heavily subsidized, most especially transit. Discouraged also are other kinds of land use, such as downtown apartments and condominiums from which people can walk to work or to shop. Utilitarian parking structures with their blank walls, especially those attached to or integrated into other buildings, contribute little to active downtown street life, at least street life of a truly positive nature along sidewalks.

In post–World War II suburbia, where off-street parking has been part of commercial and residential development from the beginning, oversupply, again largely driven by zoning ordinances complemented by subdivision controls, is also evident. Such surplus carries clear landscape implication by spreading things out excessively, making things more disconnected both functionally and visually. In commercial areas, stores are pushed back from streets in parking lot surrounds and are thus difficult for pedestrians to approach. Driveways, tall signs, and sign-like buildings repeat endlessly in arrays of street-side monotony dissolving, in the view of many persistent critics, into chaos rather than into order. Street life is necessarily based on vehicle use only. Subdivisions sprawl, and substantive acreages are given to overly wide streets capable both of two-way traffic flow and curbside parking. Houses are often dominated visually by out-front garages and large driveway aprons. Produced in subdivision after subdivision are landscapes monotonous in such homogeneity. Although a minority, more and more Americans seem to agree that change is necessary. Needed is more diversity. Needed is more choice as to how people live.

To allow the opponents of auto use free reign is, however, inappropriate. The closing of downtown streets for pedestrian malls and the eliminating of cars and car parking from the centers of college and university campuses, among other planning strategies, has, for the most part, produced boring, lifeless places where people go only during rush hours, and across which windblown newspaper and other trash moves at other times. When vacant, as they usually are at night, these places can be outright dangerous for lack of human surveillance. They stand at best as neutral "no-man's-lands." What is missing is movement, not only pedestrian movement but also the movement of people in cars.

The idealized middle ground, we suggest, would involve parking everywhere, but parking in limited amounts. Some of it would be close to and some of it distanced from commuter, shopper, or other destinations. No destination would be totally denied, but then again, no destination would be fully supplied, dominated by parking and its infrastructure. The car would be accepted but placed under degrees of control. Parking integrated imaginatively into the making and remaking of urban place is the pragmatic choice. It may, indeed, be the only choice. Americans do find their automobiles important. The do like to drive them. They like the comforts that their cars provide. They readily overestimate the convenience that auto use pretends. They readily underestimate the costs of motoring. And many of those who know the costs do not care that the price is extravagant. Americans identify with urban landscapes seen through auto windshields. And they expect, to varying degrees, that those landscapes will contain other automobiles both moving and parked. Landscapes totally without cars appear to most Americans to be somehow impoverished, antiquated, or otherwise lacking. Much of the visual interest found in the American city, for better or for worse, is generated by the colors, shapes, and textures associated with automobiles moving and parked. To prohibit cars from city streets, including parked cars, is to reduce visual interest. Most Americans avoid uninteresting places.

The middle ground in big city downtowns would seem to involve small parking lots and modest parking garages close to work and shopping destinations, which would accommodate short-term parkers certainly. Additionally, it would involve increased on-street parking close at hand through added embrace of angle or other parking schemes calculated to maximize use of curbside space. Curbside parking would be part of a larger strategy for traffic calming whereby downtown streets once more would stand as destination spaces as opposed to being mere arteries for through traffic flow. It would be a return to degrees of traffic congestion calculated in part to the diverting of motorists to transit or to in-town living. At the distance would be long-term storage lots and garages, also of modest scale and substantially integrated with residential and other activities there. Overly massive lots would be discouraged. All lots would be broken up into module spaces carefully landscaped to stand more as "parking gardens."[21] Garages would be designed to blend with surrounding buildings and open spaces. Such is, perhaps, a utopian view, but one totally within the realm of possibility. Many cities, such as Portland, Oregon, are already well advanced in using such strategies in reconfiguring a much re-energized downtown. As for the parking garden idea, central business districts in American cities, in adapting to the automobile, have become substantially "suburbanized," as we have argued. Buildings stand isolated in parking lots just as along suburban commercial strips. Perhaps the pastoral ideal, around which American suburbs were first configured, might be given fuller play downtown as well. One suspects, however, that cities ought to be cities. Perhaps, they ought to be more architectural than pastoral in sustaining population densities fully urbane. It might be best if, over time, parking garages supplanted parking lots in downtown areas altogether.

The middle ground in suburbia also would involve relatively small parking lots and, in order to concentrate workers or customers near set destinations, increased reliance on parking garages or decks as well. Such is already very much in evidence in the nation's more affluent suburbs. Pedestrians there are receiving greater emphasis, with people walking into shopping centers, office parks, hospitals, or other places from a distance and motorists being turned into pedestrians upon alighting from parked cars in lots and garages. Imagination calculated to the opportunities of the moment, rather than dictated formula, is being brought more and more to the fore.

The parked car should be thought of not so much as a design problem as a design opportunity. Some containment will be necessary. As popular and as essential as automobile use is in American life, auto dependence cannot continue to grow indefinitely without totally subsuming people and the environment. Motorists, now substantially subsidized both in their driving and in their parking, need to assume more of the actual costs of car use. Motoring needs to be complemented by other means of moving about: riding in transit cars or walking most especially. Parking, in other words, needs to be thought of as part of a transportation and land use system much larger than a system merely automobile engendered. But proposals need to be based on real understandings of how things got to be the way they are. To base proposals on imagined past circumstances risks misdefining the problems to be solved. It risks the wrong solutions.

The history of parking in America has been one of constant shift. From the early use of small, long-term storage garages and attempts at accommodating short-time parking solely in the streets to the rise of large off-street parking lots and parking garages or decks, change has been unceasing. From commercial parking interests opposed to public involvement to full private-industry embrace of municipal parking subsidy, parking has proven a most changeful aspect of life in modern America. And the future will bring more change. Indeed, the nation may be poised for yet another historical turn. Rejecting homogenized landscapes that are substantially auto-oriented, both in post–World War II suburbs and in recently reconfigured downtowns, a vocal minority of Americans do express readiness for transport diversity. Choked traffic arteries, even in the suburbs, speak of long commutes and increasingly tiresome shopping trips that even the majority can now understand. Suburban sprawl, the precipitator of much inconvenience, is now widely noted as a serious urban problem. Such realization can only bring to the fore new governmental and private commercial approaches to parking based on new citizen and consumer expectations about parking's lot in life.

NOTES

INTRODUCTION

1. *U.S. Bureau of the Census, Statistical Abstract* (Washington, DC: 1998), 61, 636.

2. "The Future of the Auto in City Transportation," *Parking*, Oct. 1980, 46.

3. "New Report on Commuting Trends Shows Increase in Private Vehicles," *Parking*, Sept. 1996, 15–16.

4. William Leach, *Country of Exiles: The Destruction of Place in American Life* (New York: Pantheon Books, 1999), 55.

5. Roy D. Chapin, "The Motor's Part in Transportation," *Annals of the American Academy of Political and Social Sciences* 116 (Nov. 1924): 1.

6. Henry B. Churchman, "Hunting a Place to Park," *Hoosier Motorist* 22 (April 1924): 19.

7. Michael Bernick and Robert Cervero, *Transit Villages in the 21st Century* (New York: McGraw-Hill, 1997), 42.

8. Sandra Rosenbloom, "Why Working Families Need a Car," in *The Car and the City: The Automobile, the Built Environment, and Daily Urban Life* (Ann Arbor: University of Michigan Press, 1992), 39–49.

9. William P. Eno, "The Storage of Dead Vehicles on Roadways," *Annals of the American Academy of Political and Social Sciences* 116 (Nov. 1924): 169.

10. Mark C. Childs, *Parking Spaces: A Design, Implementation, and Use Manual for Architects, Planners, and Engineers* (New York: McGraw-Hill, 1999), 3.

11. Miller McClintock, *Street Traffic Control* (New York: McGraw-Hill, 1925), 139–42.

12. Hawley S. Simpson, "Downtown Storage Garages," *Annals of the American Academy of Political and Social Sciences* 133 (Sept. 1927), 84.

13. M. Christine Boyer, *The City of Collective Memory: Its Historical Images and Architectural Entertainments* (Cambridge: MIT Press, 1998), 2.

14. James Marston Fitch, *Historic Preservation: Curational Management of the Built Environment* (Charlottesville: University of Virginia Press, 1990), xi.

15. Victor Gruen, *The Heart of Our Cities: The Urban Crisis, Diagnosis and Cure* (New York: Simon and Schuster, 1964), 43.

16. Jane Holtz Kay, *Asphalt Nation: How the Automobile Took Over America and How We Can Take It Back* (New York: Crown, 1997), 83.

17. Peter Newman and Jeffrey Kenworthy, *Cities and Automobile Dependence: A Sourcebook* (Brookfield, VT: Gower, 1989).

18. Ronald J. Horvath, "Machine Space," *Geographical Review* 64 (April 1974): 168.

19. J. B. Jackson, "Auto Territoriality," *Landscape* 17 (1968): 1.

20. Newman and Kenworthy, *Cities and Automobile Dependence.*

21. "The Land Hungry Automobile," *Downtown Idea Exchange* 6 (April 15, 1959): 1.

22. Detroit City Plan Commission, *Urban Transportation and the Detroit Bus System* (Detroit, 1972), 16, 19.

23. Jane Jacobs, *The Death and Life of Great American Cities* (New York: Vintage Books, 1961), 257, 259, 338.

24. Bibliographic guides to the traffic engineering perspective on parking include U.S. Public Roads Administration, *Bibliography on Automobile Parking in the United States* (Washington, DC: 1946); Highway Research Board, *Automobile Parking in the United States* (Washington, DC: 1953); Anthony G. White, *Architectural Design of Parking Garages: A Revised Source List*, bibliography A1028 (Monticello, IL: Vance Bibliographies, 1983); Robert Weant and Henry Levinson, *Parking* (Westport, CT: Eno Foundation for Transportation, 1990).

25. H. F. Hammond, "Traffic Engineering: Its Origin and Purpose," *Traffic Engineering* 11 (Nov. 1940): 131–32.

26. Geoffrey Baker and Bruno Funaro, *Parking* (New York: Reinhold, 1958).

27. Childs, *Parking Spaces.*

28. Christopher Tunnard and Boris Pushkarev, *Man-Made America: Chaos or Control? An Inquiry into Selected Problems of Design in the Urbanized Landscape* (New Haven: Yale University Press, 1963).

29. Peter Blake, *God's Own Junkyard: The Planned Deterioration of America's Landscape* (New York: Holt, Rinehart and Winston, 1964); Ian Nairn, *The American Landscape: A Critical View* (New York: Random House, 1965).

30. See John Brinkerhoff Jackson, *Landscape in Sight: Looking at America,* ed. Helen Lefkowitz (New Haven: Yale University Press, 1997).

31. Robert Venturi, Denise Scott Brown, and Steven Izenour, *Learning from Las Vegas: The Forgotten Symbolism of Architectural Form* (Cambridge: MIT Press, 1977).

32. See E. Relph, *Place and Placelessness* (London: Pion, 1976); Edward Relph, *The Modern Urban Landscape* (Baltimore: Johns Hopkins University Press, 1987).

33. See John A. Jakle and Keith A. Sculle, *The Gas Station in America* (Baltimore: Johns Hopkins University Press, 1994); John A. Jakle, Keith A. Sculle, and Jefferson Rogers, *The Motel in America* (Baltimore: Johns Hopkins Uni-

versity Press, 1996); John A. Jakle and Keith A. Sculle, *Fast Food: Roadside Restaurants in the Automobile Age* (Baltimore: Johns Hopkins University Press, 1999).

34. For example, see Alan Hess, *Googie: Fifties Coffee Shop Architecture* (San Francisco: Chronicle Books, 1985); Philip Langdon, *Orange Roofs, Golden Arches: The Architecture of American Chain Restaurants* (New York: Alfred A. Knopf, 1986); John Margolies, *Home Away from Home: Motels in America* (Boston: Little, Brown, 1995); Daniel I. Vieyra, *Fill 'er Up: An Architectural History of America's Gas Stations* (New York: Collier Books, 1979); Michael Karl Witzel, *The American Gas Station* (Osceola, WI: Motorbooks International, 1992).

35. Richard Longstreth, *City Center to Regional Mall: Architecture, the Automobile, and Retailing in Los Angeles, 1920–1950* (Cambridge: MIT Press, 1997); Richard Longstreth, *The Drive-In, the Supermarket, and the Transformation of Commercial Space in Los Angeles, 1914–1941* (Cambridge: MIT Press, 1999).

36. Jan Jennings, "Housing the Automobile," in *Roadside America: The Automobile in Design and Culture, ed.* Jan Jennings (Ames: Iowa State University Press, 1990), 95–106.

37. Anne Vernez Moudon, "Urban Morphology as an Emerging Interdisciplinary Field," *Urban Morphology* 1 (April 1997): 7.

38. For introduction to the landscape concept, see John B. Jackson, *Discovering the Vernacular Landscape* (New Haven: Yale University Press, 1984), and D. W. Meinig, ed., *The Interpretation of Ordinary Landscapes* (New York: Oxford University Press, 1979).

39. For introduction to the place concept, see Relph, *Place and Placelessness;* Yi-Fu Tuan, *Space and Place: The Perspective of Experience* (Minneapolis: University of Minnesota Press, 1977); John A. Jakle, *The Visual Elements of Landscape* (Amherst: University of Massachusetts Press, 1987); Robert D. Sack, *Place, Modernity, and the Consumer's World* (Baltimore: Johns Hopkins University Press, 1992).

1. PARKING AT CURBSIDE

1. U.S. Department of Transportation, Federal Highway Administration, *Highway Statistic: Summary to 1985* (Washington, DC: n.d.), Table MV-201.

2. Morris A. Hall, "Motor-Driven Vehicles and Traffic Congestion," *Horseless Age* 30 (Dec. 11, 1912): 898.

3. "Too Many Cars for Town," *Tabor (Iowa) Beacon,* reprinted in *Jefferson Highway Declaration* 2 (Oct. 1917): 21.

4. T. Glenn Phillips, "The Traffic Problems in Detroit and How They Are Met," *Annals of the American Academy of Political and Social Sciences* 116 (Nov. 1924): 241.

5. E. S. Taylor, "The Plan of Chicago in 1924," *Annals of the American Academy of Political and Social Sciences* 116 (Nov. 1924): 226.

6. Miller McClintock, "The City Traffic Problem," *Buffalo Motorist* 20 (March 1927): 11.

7. Richard Longstreth, *City Center to Regional Mall: Architecture, the Automobile, and Retailing in Los Angeles, 1920–1950* (Cambridge: MIT Press, 1997), 13.

8. "Summing Up Street Perils: A Warning from the Record of Newark, NJ," *American City* 23 (Sept. 1920): 269.

9. Miller McClintock, *Report and Recommendations of the Metropolitan Street Traffic Survey* (Chicago: Chicago Association of Commerce, 1926), 16.

10. See "Three-Dimensional Planning," *Architectural Review* 90 (Sept. 1941): 84.

11. Burton W. Marsh, "Traffic Control," *Annals of the American Academy of Political and Social Sciences* 133 (Sept. 1927): 90.

12. E. A. Kingsley, "Street Widening in San Antonio," *Municipal Journal* 40 (Feb. 24, 1916): 263.

13. "Width of Streets," *Public Works* 55 (June 1924): 380.

14. Robert H. Whitten, "Width of Roadway and Corner Cut-off," *Municipal Journal* 45 (Aug. 31, 1918): 166.

15. A. F. Malo, "Putting Traffic Engineering to Work in Detroit," *Traffic Engineering* 22 (Jan. 1952): 133–34.

16. The Buffalo Plan of 1922 was an example of thoroughfare planning inspired by the City Beautiful Movement. "What the Buffalo Plan Means to All Motorists," *Buffalo Motorist* 15 (April 1922): 28–32.

17. For example, see Daniel L. Turner, "The Detroit Super-Highway Project," *American City* 32 (April 1925): 373–76.

18. Burton W. Marsh, "The Results of Eliminating Parking on City Streets," *American City* 39 (July 1928): 114.

19. Jerry P. Gilbert, "Off-Street Parking: Key to Urban Mobility," *Parking,* winter 1962, 26.

20. A. T. Erwin, "Streets from the Landscape Point of View," *American City* 4 (1911): 76.

21. "What Streets Are Used For," *Municipal Journal* 40 (Jan. 6, 1916): 1.

22. John F. Dillon, *Commentaries on the Law of Municipal Corporations,* vol. 3 (Boston: 1911), section 1168; quoted in Miller McClintock, *Street Traffic Control* (New York: McGraw-Hill, 1925), 138.

23. "To Park or Not to Park," *American City* 35 (Oct. 1926): 461.

24. Harold S. Buttenheim, "The Problem of the Standing Vehicle," *Annals of the American Academy of Political and Social Sciences* 133 (Sept. 1927): 145.

25. Harold S. Buttenheim, "City Highways and City Parking: An American Crisis," *American City* 55 (Nov. 1946): 116.

26. Richard Ingersoll, "The Death of the Street," in *Roadside America: The Automobile in Design and Culture,* ed. Jan Jennings (Ames: Iowa State University Press, 1998), 153.

27. "Parking Regulations: A Statement of General Principles and Specific Recommendations," *American City* 55 (Nov. 1946): 139.

28. Longstreth, *City Center*, 5.

29. Clarence R. Shethen, "Los Angeles Making Scientific Study to Relieve Traffic Congestion," *American City* 24 (Sept. 1924): 197.

30. Walter R. Lindersmith, "Less Parking—More Parking in Los Angeles," *American City* 43 (Dec. 1930): 120.

31. "Taxing Parking Privileges," *Public Works* 57 (April 1926): 105.

32. Robert H. Nau, "No Parking: A Year and More of It," *American City* 40 (March 1929): 85.

33. McClintock, *Street Traffic Control*, 153.

34. "Snow Removal in Detroit," *Public Works* 57 (Dec. 1926): 411.

35. "Automatic Auto Parking: The Advantages of a Systematic Method," *Modern Highway* 5 (Nov. 1920): 20.

36. "Painted Curbs Indicate Parking Rules," *American City* 25 (Oct. 1925): 420.

37. Ross C. Harger, "Simplified Curb Parking Control," *Traffic Engineering* 17 (June 1947): 377.

38. For other traffic rules see M. B. Barkley, "Some Phases of the Traffic Situation in Indianapolis," *Hoosier Motorist* 5 (June 1917): 15.

39. Wilbur S. Smith and Charles S. LeCraw Jr., "Progressive Treatment of Parking Problems," *Traffic Quarterly*, Jan. 1947, 77.

40. George J. Fisher, "Angle Parking vs Parallel Parking," *Traffic Engineering* 21 (Oct. 1950): 15.

41. "On the Shelf," *Traffic Engineering* 18 (June 1948): 423.

42. Robert A. Weant and Herbert S. Levinson, *Parking* (Westport, CT: Eno Foundation, 1990), 243.

43. Percival White, "Where'll We Park the Car? How 54 Cities Control Traffic," *Hoosier Motorist* 14 (March 1926): 6.

44. For example, see "How to Park," *Reader's Digest* 61 (Dec. 1952): 135 (condensed from *Woman's Home Companion*); Charlotte Montgomery, *Handbook for the Woman Driver* (New York: Vanguard Press, 1955).

45. See Leroy H. Fisher and Robert E. Smith, "Oklahoma and the Parking Meter," *Chronicles of Oklahoma* 67 (summer 1969): 168–209.

46. Hugh G. Corbett, "75 Cities Report on Parking Meters," *American City* 56 (March 1941): 71.

47. See H. G. Thusen and Leroy H. Fisher, "Reminiscences of the Development of the Parking Meter," *Chronicles of Oklahoma* 65 (summer 1967): 112–42.

48. O. M. Mosier, "Our Experience with Parking Meters," *American City* 51 (Jan. 1936): 97.

49. Ibid.

50. "Supreme Court Bans Parking Meters," *Buffalo Motorist*, 30 (Feb. 1937): 7.

51. "85 Cities Operate Parking Meters," *American City* 53 (Nov. 1938): 7.

52. Robert H. Burrage and Edward G. Mogren, *Parking* (Saugatuck, CT: Eno Foundation, 1957), 109.

53. "Parking Meters' Silver Anniversary," *American City* 75 (Aug. 1960): 103.

54. Nora Fitzgerald, "Expired Patience: Warsaw Residents Hate New Parking Meters," *Chicago Tribune*, Nov. 4, 1999, sec. 1, p. 10.

55. "Supreme Court Bans Parking Meters," 7.

56. Harold S. Butteheim, "City Highways and City Parking—An American Crisis," *American City* 67 (Nov. 1946): 116.

57. Walter R. Lindersmith, "Less Parking—More Purchasing in Los Angeles," *American City* 43 (Dec. 1930): 120.

58. Mosier, "Our Experience with Parking Maters," 97.

59. B. H. Cruce, "Pampa Merchants Learn True Value of Parking Meters," *American City* 41 (March 1953): 135.

60. Traffic Congestion, Parking Facilities and Retail Trade," *American City* 34 (June 1926): 664.

61. Arthur Pound, "No Parking," *Atlantic Monthly* 161 (March 1938): 387.

62. Fisher and Smith, "Oklahoma and the Parking Meter," 181.

63. "Curb Parking Is Big Business," *American City* 60 (July 1945): 13; "All about Parking Meters," *American City* 68 (July 1953): 149.

64. John F. Leahy, "A City's Parking Meters Are Big Business," *American City* 66 (Aug. 1951): 139.

65. Donald Townsend, "How San Francisco Chaperones Its Parking Meters," *American City* 66 (May 1951): 129.

66. Geoffrey Baker and Bruno Funaro, *Parking* (New York: Reinhold, 1958), 2.

67. Percy E. Wagner, "Appraising and Mortgage Lending," *Appraisal Journal* 28 (Jan. 1960): 66.

68. "Street-car Tracks Are Coming Up," *American City* 52 (March 1937): 85.

69. Alfred Brahdy, "The City Transit and Traffic Problem," *Civil Engineering* 8 (May 1938): 307–10.

2. COMMERCIAL PARKING LOTS

1. "Automobile Parking in Pittsburgh," *Horseless Age* 33 (June 3, 1914): 852.

2. See, for example, Lonnie Hackman and Norene D. Martin, *The Parking Industry: Private Enterprise for the Public Good* (Washington, DC: National Parking Association, 1969), 1-3, 9-1.

3. *Polk's Detroit (Wayne County, Michigan) City Directory, 1918* (Detroit: R. L. Polk, 1918).

4. *Polk's Directory, 1936.*

5. Hackman and Martin, *Parking Industry*, 9-1.

6. Butler Anderson, "Getting On in the World," *Saturday Evening Post* 202 (Nov. 2, 1929): 56.

7. "Develops Million Dollar Parking Business," *Motor Age* 16 (July 10, 1924): 16.

8. "Briggs Parks More Autos Than Anyone," New York *Herald-Tribune*, July 9, 1961; reprinted in *National Parking Association Newsletter* 9 (July 18, 1961): 3.

9. *Polk's Directory*, 1923; *Polk's Directory*, 1926; *Polk's Directory*, 1936.

10. John F. Hendon, "Private Enterprise in the Parking Field," *Urban Land* 9 (Nov. 1950): 3.

11. *Parking in the City Center* (New Haven, CT: Wilbur Smith and Associates for the Automobile Manufacturers Association, 1965), 1–2.

12. Howard Rudnitsky, "Take-away Game," *Forbes* 158 (July 29, 1996): 50.

13. Wilbur S. Smith and Charles S. LeCraw Jr., "Parking Lot Operations," *Journal of Property Management* 13 (June 1948): 263–64.

14. Ibid., 266–67.

15. Ibid., 267–68.

16. Robert A. Weant and Herbert S. Levinson, *Parking* (Westport, CT: Eno Foundation, 1990), 235–36.

17. William J. Porter Jr., "Managing Parking Lots," *Journal of Property Management* 14 (March 1949): 187–94.

18. Mark Heisenberg, "A View from the Booth," *Utne Reader* 55 (Jan.–Feb. 1993): 133–34.

19. John Julia, "Franchising, Can It Work with Parking?" *Parking*, July 1997, 52.

20. For discussion of place-product-packaging, see John A. Jakle and Keith A. Sculle, *The Gas Station in America* (Baltimore: Johns Hopkins University Press, 1994); John A. Jakle, Keith A. Sculle, and Jefferson Rogers, *The Motel in America* (Baltimore: Johns Hopkins University Press, 1996); John A. Jakle and Keith A. Sculle, *Fast Food: Roadside Restaurants in the Automobile Age* (Baltimore: Johns Hopkins University Press, 1999).

21. Diamond Parking, Inc., press release, March 1999.

22. George V. Dragotta, "Louis E. Meyers: Parking Mentor," *Parking*, spring 1983, 29; Rudnitsky, "Take-away Game," 51.

23. "Parking Pays: The Allright Way," *Business Week*, March 2, 1957; reprinted in the *National Parking Association Newsletter* 5 (April 9, 1957), insert; Rudnitsky, "Take-away Game," 50; "Central Parking to Buy Allright for $585 million," *New York Times*, Sept. 22, 1998, C-3.

24. Standard Parking Corporation, press release, October 1998.

25. Hackman and Martin, *Parking Industry*, 10-1; Ira U. Cobleigh, "Kinnery Service Corporation," *Parking*, winter 1963, 21.

26. "Airport Parking Company Stock on the Market," *National Parking Association Newsletter* 8 (Oct. 11, 1960): 1; "To Drive, Perchance to Park," *Newsweek* 60 (Sept. 17, 1962: 88; Bob Seltzer, "Cliches on Parking Tire Him," *Parking*, winter 1968, 12; "Delaware North Purchases APCOA," *Parking World* 10 (Nov.–Dec.), 1981: 1.

27. "Central Parking Corporation," *Better Investing* 51 (Feb. 2002): 46.

28. Rudnitsky, "Take-away Game," 51.

29. Ibid.; Gill Barnett, "Betting on a Parking Concept," *Parking*, April 1999, 36.

30. Lou Cook, "Paul Clough, Imperial Mover," *Parking*, June 1998, 39.

31. Jack Pasht, "Surface Parking Lots: Current Investment Trends," *Parking*, June 1996, 42.

32. Quoted in L. M. Sixel, "Largest U.S. Parking Lot Company to Buy Houston-Based Firm," *Houston Chronicle*, Sept. 23, 1998.

33. P. Ross Bundick, "Parking Plan to Restore Baltimore's Downtown Values," *American City* 61 (April 1946): 127.

34. "Cities: No Parking," *Newsweek* 23 (Oct. 28, 1946): 28–29.

35. Daniel W. Walls, "The Parking Problem," *Traffic Engineering* 16 (Sept. 1946): 492.

36. Walter R. Kuehnle, "Central Business District Paradox," *Journal of the American Institute of Real Estate Appraisers* 3 (Jan. 1935): 138.

37. Thomas H. MacDonald, "The Problem of Parking Facilities," *Traffic Engineering* 12 (Aug. 1941): 87.

38. Richard J. Seltzer, *Proposals for Downtown Philadelphia* (Chicago: Urban Land Institute, 1942), 38.

39. Carl S. Wells, *Proposals for Downtown Detroit* (Washington, DC: Urban Land Institute, 1942), 10.

40. "Parking Lot Economies," *American City* 51 (Nov. 1936): 91; *Street Traffic, City of Detroit, 1936–1937* (Lansing: Michigan State Highway Department, 1937), 164; Walter H. Blucher, "The Economics of the Parking Lot," *Planner's Journal* 2 (May 1936): 113.

41. Richard Longstreth, *City Center to Regional Mall: Architecture, the Automobile, and Retailing in Los Angeles, 1920–1950* (Cambridge: MIT Press, 1997), 11.

42. George Becker, "Parking Lots and Garages in Central Business Districts," *Appraisal Journal* 8 (Jan. 1940): 63–64.

43. Walter C. Behrendt, "Off-Street Parking: A City Planning Problem," *Journal of Land and Public Utility Economics* 16 (Nov. 1940): 464, 465.

44. Quoted in Blucher, "Economics of the Parking Lot," 119.

45. "Merchants Cooperate to Provide Free Off-Street Parking Facilities," *American City* 43 (Aug. 1930): 154.

46. Longstreth, *City Center to Regional Mall*, 208.

47. "The Allentown Story," press release, Allentown Chamber of Commerce, July 1952.

48. Charles S. LeCraw Jr., "Allentown Saves Its Shopping Area," *Traffic Quarterly* 3 (Jan. 1949): 68–70.

49. Hackman and Martin, *Parking Industry*, 6-2.

50. "Park-N-Shop Plan," *Business Week*, Dec. 16, 1939, 46.

51. Hackman and Martin, *Parking Industry*, 6-6.

3. MUNICIPAL PARKING LOTS

1. A. L. H. Street, "The City's Legal Right and Duties," *American City* 40 (Feb. 1929): 177.

2. Robert A. Mitchell, "Off-Street Parking Control," *Traffic Engineering* 12 (Nov. 1941): 194.

3. Ibid., 195.

4. "Cities Regulate Operation of Off-Street Parking Lots," *Public Management* 24 (Jan. 1942): 24.

5. Frank B. Williams, *The Law of City Planning and Zoning* (New York: Macmillan, 1922), 161.

6. Regional Plan Association, *Traffic and Parking Study: A Plan for Improvement of Conditions in the Central Business Districts of New York City* (New York: Regional Plan Association, 1942), 78.

7. For a thorough review of parking lot regulation by local government, see Orin F. Nolting and Paul Oppermann, *The Parking Problem in Central Business Districts: With Special Reference to Off-Street Parking* (Chicago: Public Administration Service, 1938), 11–17.

8. Catherine G. Miller, *Carscape: A Parking Handbook* (Columbus, IN: Irwin-Sweeney-Miller Foundation, 1988), 10.

9. Henry K. Evans, *Traffic Engineering Handbook* (New Haven: Institute of Traffic Engineers, 1950), 302.

10. Frank B. Williams, "Zoning and Planning Notes," *American City* 49 (Oct. 1934): 83.

11. "Zoning for Off-Street Parking," *American City* 63 (April 1948): 106.

12. Mary S. Smith, *The Dimensions of Parking* ([Washington, DC], Urban Land Institute and National Parking Association, 1993), 47.

13. Kay Mitten, "Sorry, You Can't Park Here," *Nation's Business* 35 (Nov. 1947): 87.

14. Regional Plan Association, *Traffic and Parking Study*, 78–79.

15. Gordon Whitnall, "Urban Disintegration and the Future of Land Investments," *Journal of Land and Public Utility Economics* 17 (Nov. 1941): 446.

16. Mark C. Childs, *Parking Spaces: A Design, Implementation, and Use Manual for Architects, Planners, and Engineers* (New York: McGraw-Hill, 1999), 1.

17. Richard Longstreth, *City Center to Regional Mall: Architecture, the Automobile, and Retailing in Los Angeles, 1920–1950* (Cambridge: MIT Press, 1997), 182.

18. Clarence E. Ridley and Orin F. Nolting, eds., *The Municipal Year Book* (Chicago: International City Manager's Association, 1942), 515.

19. "One-Fifth of Cities Operate Off-Street Parking Lots," *Public Management* 24 (April 1942): 120.

20. Ridley and Nolting, *Municipal Year Book*, 1946, 455; Orin F. Nolting et al. (eds.), *The Municipal Year Book* (Chicago: International City Manager's Association, 1961), 429.

21. William E. Robertson, *National Parking Facility Study* (Washington, DC: National League of Cities, 1972), 24.

22. John G. Marr, "The Parking Problem in the Business District, with Special Reference to California Cities," *Civil Engineering* 12 (Jan. 1942): 22.

23. "Legal Aspects of Municipal Parking Facilities," *American City* 56 (Sept. 1941): 93, 94.

24. Nolting and Oppermann, *Parking Problem*, 3–4.

25. *The Parking Problem: A Library Research* ([Saugatuck, CT]: Eno Foundation, 1942), 33.

26. E. S. Clark, "Parking Lots," *Traffic Engineering* 12 (June 1941): 40.

27. Fred W. Tuemmler, "Boomtown's Parking Bonanza," *American City* 68 (July 1953): 109.

28. "Getting the Most from Downtown Parking," *American City* 91 (May 1976): 78.

29. D. Grant Mickle, "What to Do about Parking," *Public Management* 34 (Sept. 1952): 200.

30. Wilbur S. Smith, "Automobile Parking Trends," *Transportation Quarterly* 37 (July 1983): 448.

31. See Arthur Pound, "No Parking," *Atlantic Monthly* 161 (March 1938): 391. For a biography of Miller McClintock, see *The National Cyclopedia of American Biography*, vol. 44 (Clifton, NJ: James T. White, 1962), 14–15.

32. William L. O'Donovan, "Auto Parking at a Profit," *Traffic Quarterly* 22 (Jan. 1968): 117.

33. Welles V. Moot, "Buffalo Parking Plan," *Traffic Quarterly* 8 (July 1954): 321.

34. Ibid., 322.

35. Robert A. Weant and Herbert S. Levinson, *Parking* (Westport, CT: Eno Foundation, 1990), 59–60.

36. Nolting and Oppermann, *Parking Problem*, 7.

37. Geoffrey Baker and Bruno Funaro, *Parking* (New York: Reinhold, 1958), 58.

38. *Parking Programs* (Washington, DC: American Automobile Association, 1954), 99, 92.

39. William C. Dennis, "Cooperation—Key to Adequate Parking Supply," *Detroiter* 47 (April 30, 1950): 1.

40. Leo H. Jacobson, "How Detroit Is Solving Its Parking Problem," *Traffic Quarterly* 20 (April 1966): 236.

41. Walls, "Parking Problem," 489.

42. "Perimeter Parking Lot," *American City* 61 (Nov. 1946): 129.

43. "Realizing Faults of Shuttle Bus Parking Service, Chicago Works Out Method to Use 6,000 Spaces," *Traffic Engineering* 17 (Feb. 1947): 235.

44. *Parking Programs*, 49–50, 52–53.

45. D. C. Hyde, "Fringe Parking," *Traffic Quarterly* 7 (July 1953): 401.

46. "Fringe Parking with a Purpose," *American City* 71 (May 1956): 157.

47. "Kelly to Head Parking Congress," *American City* 78 (Sept. 1963): 147.

48. Lonnie Hackman and Norene D. Martin, *The Parking Industry: Private Enterprise for the Public Good* (Washington, DC: National Parking Association, 1969), 2-1.

49. "Municipal Owned Lots Called Obstacle to Parking Progress," *Pueblo Star-Journal*, Dec. 6, 1960, reprinted in *National Parking Association Newsletter* 9 (Jan. 3, 1961): 4.

50. "B. M. Stanton—Founding President," *Parking*, May–June 1986, 21–22.

51. Lyman E. Wakefield Jr., "Should Cities Go into Parking," *Rotarian* 83 (Sept. 1953): 60.

52. George Berkley, "Municipal Garages in Boston: A Cost-Benefit Analysis," *Traffic Quarterly* 19 (April 1965): 214, 225.

53. F. Houston Wynn, "Downtown Off-Street Parking: Economics and Techniques," *Urban Land* 7 (July–Aug. 1963): 6.

54. David M. Freehan, "Kalamazoo Is Proof: Privatizing Parking Works," *Parking*, June 1993, 33–37.

55. Edwin M. Roth, "Private Enterprise and Municipal Parking Facilities," *Parking*, Oct. 1978, 35.

56. David Herzog, "Allentown Closes Deal with Park and Shop," *Allentown Morning-Call*, Dec. 7, 1991, B-1.

4. THE PARKING LOT AS URBAN VOID

1. Robert C. Weinberg, "For Better Places to Park," *American City* 52 (June 1937): 99.

2. Mark C. Childs, *Parking Space: A Design, Implementation, and Use Manual for Architects, Planners, and Engineers* (New York: McGraw-Hill, 1999), xxi.

3. Aileen Tatton Brown and William Tatton Brown, "Three-Dimensional Town Planning," *Architectural Review* 90 (Sept. 1941): 81.

4. E[dward] Relph, *Place and Placelessness* (London: Pion, 1976), 136.

5. Childs, *Parking Space*, 197.

6. E. Gregory McPherson, James R. Simpson, and Klaus I. Scott, *Benefits from Shade Trees in Parking Lots* (Davis: University of California, Western Center for Urban Forest Research, Briefing Paper, 1997).

7. Anne Whiston Spirn, *The Granite Garden: Urban Nature and Human Design* (New York: Basic Books, 1984), 78.

8. Henry K. Evans, "Planning Off-Street Parking Lots," *Traffic Engineering* 15 (Feb. 1945): 172.

9. Robert A. Weant and Herbert S. Levinson, *Parking* (Westport, CT:6 Eno Foundation, 1990), 155–63.

10. David J. Garber, "Effective Maintenance of Asphalt Paving," *Journal of Property Management* 51 (Nov.–Dec. 1986): 39.

11. *Asphalt: Nature's Most Versatile Product* (College Park, MD: Asphalt Institute, 1962), 4.

12. Childs, *Parking Space*, 198.

13. Garber, "Effective Maintenance," 39; *How to Design Asphalt Pavement for Open-Air Parking Lots* (College Park, MD: Asphalt Institute, 1965), 39.

14. Garber, "Effective Maintenance," 39; *How to Design Asphalt*," 39.

15. Charles M. Bolden et al., *Parking Standards Study* ([Los Angeles]: Parking Standards Design Associates, 1971), 1.

16. Weant and Levinson, *Parking*, 158.

17. Kurt S. Shelger and Louis E. Meyers, "Appraisal of Parking Lots and Garages," in *Encyclopedia of Real Estate Appraising*, ed. Edith J. Friedman (Englewood Cliffs, NJ: Prentice-Hall, 1978), 470.

18. Childs, *Parking Space*, 248; see also Richard S. Beebe and Mary S. Smith, "Parking and the ADA: Evaluation Checklist for Parking Facilities," *Parking*, Jan. 1992, 17–30.

19. Weant and Levinson, *Parking*, 172–75; Susan Chrysler, "Luminance: What the Driver Sees," *Parking*, April 1997, 36–38.

20. Edward Rusha, *Thirty-four Parking Lots in Los Angeles* ([Los Angeles]: author, 1967).

21. "Parking Capacity," *Downtown Idea Exchange Newsletter* 11 (Oct. 1, 1964): 1.

22. John Lutz, Larry W. Means, and Thomas E. Long, "Where Did I Park? A Naturalistic Study of Spatial Memory," *Applied Cognitive Psychology* 8 (1994): 439–51.

23. J. Jennings Moss, "Help for Mall Trip," *New York Times*, April 28, 1998, B15.

24. S. O. Kaylin, "What Chains Can Do about Downtown Parking," *Chain Store Age*, Oct. 1959, reprinted in *National Parking Association Newsletter* 8 (Jan. 5, 1960): insert.

25. Steve Mirsky, "Anti-Gravity: Space Invaders," *Scientific American* 277 (Aug. 1997): 24.

26. Scott E. Kangas, "The Fundamental of Parking Lot Protection," *Security Management* 40 (July 1996): 44–50.

27. Leopold Kohr, "From Vacant Lot to Car Plaza: A Proposal for Transforming the Parking Lot into an Attractive Community Square," *American City* 60 (Nov. 1945): 119.

28. "Parking Rules," *Downtown Idea Exchange Newsletter* 18 (May 15, 1971): 1.

29. *The Appearance of Parking: Washington, DC* (Washington, DC: Commission of Fine Arts, 1966), unpaginated.

30. See J. M. McCluskey, *Parking: A Handbook of Environmental Designs* (London: E. and F. N. Spon, 1987), 15.

31. See Gary O. Robinette, *Parking Lot Landscape Development* (Plano, TX: Agora Communications, 1993).

32. E. M. Whitlock Jr., "Beautification in Parking Structures," *Parking*, Summer 1963, 26.

33. "New Orleans Parking Association Does Opinion Survey," *Parking*, April 1980, 47.

5. FROM GENERAL SERVICE GARAGE TO URBAN PARKING STRUCTURE

1. "The Grafting Chauffeur and the Garage," *Horseless Age* 33 (Feb. 11, 1914): 242; "May Increase Garage Storage Rates," *Horseless Age* 31 (Feb. 5, 1913): 304.

2. P. M. Heldt, The Garage Business—Buildings, Equipment Methods," *Horseless Age* 36 (Oct. 15, 1915): 394. For a history of the Electric Vehicle Com-

pany, see John B. Rae, "The Electric Vehicle Company: A Monopoly That Missed," *Business History Review* 29 (Dec. 1955): 298–311.

3. For a detailed description of early automobile care, see "Care of Car in Winter," *Buffalo Motorist* 9 (Nov. 1916): 25.

4. James J. Flink, *America Adopts the Automobile, 1895–1910* (Cambridge: MIT Press, 1970), 218–19; Heldt, "Garage Business," 394; "Automobile Storage and Repair Stations in New York," *Horseless Age* 8, no. 1 (April 3, 1901): 17–18; 8, no. 2 (April 10, 1901): 28; 8, no. 4 (April 24, 1901): 74–75.

5. Heldt, "Garage Business," 394.

6. "Metropolitan Storage Stations," *The Automobile and Motor Review*, June 21, 1902, 2; Flink, *America Adopts the Automobile*, 220.

7. Flink, *America Adopts the Automobile*, 146.

8. For the retail petroleum industry in Pittsburgh, see Keith A. Sculle, "Pittsburgh's Monuments to Motoring: Atlantic's Fabulous Service Stations," *Western Pennsylvania History* 83 (fall 2000): 124, 126; "Pittsburgh's Motor Service Corporation's Commercial Garage," *Horseless Age* 31 (May 7, 1913): 822–23.

9. "A De Luxe Garage in Missouri," *Horseless Age* 37 (Feb. 15, 1916): 170; "Modern American Public and Corporation Garages," *Horseless Age* 33 (May 6, 1914): 714; Heldt, "Garage Business," 395; "Savage Garage, Springfield, Ill.," *Horseless Age* 31 (May 7, 1913): 834.

10. "New Garage Regulations for New York State," *Horseless Age* 34 (Sept. 30, 1914): 478–80; Heldt, "Garage Business," 395.

11. For example, see "A. C. A. Opens Its New Annex Garage," *Horseless Age* 35 (Jan. 27, 1915): 135.

12. Heldt, "Garage Business," *Horseless Age* 38 (Nov. 15, 1915): 454–56.

13. For example, see "Laying Out and Equipping the Shop," *Horseless Age* 51 (Jan. 6, 1927): 82–84; Tom Wilder, "Glass Is Much Cheaper Than Juice, Says Wyoming Garageman," *Horseless Age* 51 (June 30, 1927): 44; Tom Wilder, "A Service Garage with Filling Station and Accessory Sale," *Horseless Age* 51 (June 16, 1927): 43.

14. "A. C. A. Opens Its New Annex Garage," 135; "Philadelphia Auto Club Opens Garage to A. A. A. Members," *American Motorist* 8 (June 1916): 44; "The Grafting Chauffeur and the Garage," 241–42; H. H. Brown, "Delivery of Cars at an Owner's Residence," *Horseless Age* 35 (April 7, 1915): 463. For an explanation of the chauffeur in terms of structuration theory, see Kevin Borg, "The 'Chauffeur Problem' in the Early Auto Era: Structuration Theory and the Users of Technology," *Technology and Culture* 40, no. 4 (1999): 797–832.

15. "De Luxe Garage," 37; "A New Underground Garage," *Horseless Age* 37 (May 15, 1916): 379–380; "The Biggest Public Garage in the World," *Horseless Age* 38 (Oct. 1, 1916): 223, 236; "System in the Biggest Garage," *Horseless Age* 39 (March 15, 1917): 20–21, 128; John Edwin Hogg, "Garage and Office All in the Same Building," *Motor Life* (n.d.), reprinted in *Buffalo Motorist* 19 (April 1915): 15–16.

16. "Does It Pay to Handle Gasoline?" *Horseless Age* 38 (Sept. 1, 1916): 158–

59, 42 in advertisement section; Harold F. Williamson, Ralph L. Andreano, Arnold F. Daum, and Gilbert C. Rose, *The American Petroleum Industry*, vol. 1: *The Age of Energy, 1899–1950* (Evanston, IL: Northwestern University Press, 1963), 221–23.

17. Richard Longstreth, *City Center to Regional Mall: Architecture, the Automobile, and Retailing in Los Angeles, 1920–1950* (Cambridge: MIT Press, 1999), 14–15, 21. "Showalter and the Auto Laundry: The Idea Originated in Indianapolis," *Hoosier Motorist* 7 (July 1919): 26–27; "A $50,000 Auto Laundry," *Accessory and Garage Journal* 18 (Sept. 1928): 20, 62.

18. Harold F. Blanchard, "Ramp Design in Public Garages," *Architectural Forum* 34 (Nov. 1921): 170.

19. "The Biggest Public Garage in the World, *Horseless Age* 36 (Oct. 1, 1916), 222; "System in the Biggest Garage," *Horseless Age* 39 (March 15, 1917): 20–21; advertisement, Henderson's Garage, *Jefferson Highway Declaration*, April 1917, 27; "Big Garage in Cleveland," *Buffalo Motorist* 10 (March 1917): 49; Hogg, "Garage and Office," 15–16; Keith A. Sculle, "Still Useful after All These Years: The Hotel LaSalle Parking Garage," *Historic Illinois* 23, no. 5 (Feb. 2001): 11; "A Novel Underground Garage," *Horseless Age* 37 (May 15, 1916): 379–80.

20. John B. Rae, *The American Automobile: A Brief History* (Chicago: University of Chicago Press, 1965), 87; George Becker, "Parking Lots and Garages in Central Business Districts," *Appraisal Journal* 8 (Jan. 1940): 63.

21. "Talk the Cash Register Jingle with Public Garages," *Building Age and National Builder* 50 (Dec. 1928): 69.

22. Hawley S. Simpson, "Downtown Storage Garages," *Annals of the American Academy of Political and Social Science* 133 (Sept. 1927): 85.

23. Lee J. Eastman, "The Parking Garage Merits Encouragement as an Important Factor in Traffic Relief," *American City* 40 (Jan. 1929): 157.

24. "Garages," *Architectural Record* 65, no. 2 (1929): 178–79; Simpson, "Downtown Storage Garages," 85–88; Allan E. Parmelee, "Wanted—1,000 New Parking Garages," *Building Age* 52 (July 1930): 54; "Modern 300-Car Garage That Is Designed to Carry Three Additional Stories," *Building Age and National Builder* 48 (Sept. 1926): 134–35; C. A. Parmelee, "Old Theatre Modernized into Ramp Garage," *Building Age* 51 (March 1929): 104–5.

25. A. Raymond Ellis, "Serviceable Garages of Good Design," *House and Garden* 23 (Feb. 1913): 135; "Parking Garages Join Self-Service," *Parking*, Oct. 1973, 34; Lonnie Hackman and Norene D. Martin, *The Parking Industry: Private Enterprise for the Public Good* (Washington, DC: National Parking Association, 1969), 1-2.

26. Frank B. Williams, "Zoning and Planning," *American City* 51 (March 1936): 99. Also see *City of Chicago v. Ben Alpert* in *North Eastern Reporter*, 2d ser., vol. 13, March–April 1938 (St. Paul, MN: West, 1938): 988.

27. "Parking Cars Is Big Problem for Solution," *Buffalo Motorist* 15 (Jan. 1922): 7; "Big, Modern Garages in Business Center of City Solving Parking Space Ills and Providing Needed Facilities for Busy Business Men—Several of

Larger Establishments Now Housing Hundreds of Cars—New Buildings Near Completion," *Buffalo Motorist* 16 (April 1923): 32.

28. "Big, Modern Garages," 32.

29. Advertisement, *Buffalo Motorist* 16 (May 1923): 141; advertisement, *Buffalo Motorist* 23 (Jan. 1935): 23.

30. Longstreth, *City Center to Regional Mall*, 43–44, 210.

31. Eastman, "Parking Garage," 156–57; "Garages," *Architectural Record*, 177, 180–81, 185, 192; "Work Starts on New Fisher Building," *Detroiter* 18 (Aug. 15, 1927): 7; "Huge Building Designed for Maximum Convenience and Minimum Street Congestion," *American City* 39 (July 1928): 91.

32. Parmelee, "Wanted," 55; "Garages," *Architectural Record*, 183; Hackman and Martin, *Parking Industry*, I-2 to I-3; Regional Plan Association, *Traffic and Parking Study: A Plan for Improvement of Condition in the Central Business Districts of New York City* (New York: Regional Plan Association, 1942), 91; Austin F. MacDonald, "Planning for City Traffic," *Annals of the American Academy of Political and Social Sciences* 138 (Sept. 1927): 87; Albert O. Larsen, "An Analysis of Garage Design," *Architectural Forum* 46 (March 1927): 215; Ramp Buildings Corp., *The Modern Multi-Floor Garage* (New York: R. B. C., 1929).

33. "Garages," *Architectural Record*, 178.

34. "Putting Parking on a Somewhat Higher Level," *Literary Digest* 101 (May 18, 1929): 73; Hackman and Martin, *Parking Industry*, I-2; "New System of Parking Cars," *Motor Age* 51 (April 14, 1927): 26; "A Contribution to Car Storage," *Motor Age* 52 (Oct. 20, 1927): 42–43; "Improved Automobile Storage," *American Builder* 44 (Oct. 1927): 157.

35. "Putting Parking," 73–74; Hackman and Martin, *Parking Industry*, I-2, I-3; Shannon McDonald, "The First 50 Years of Parking Garage Design, 1910–1960," *Parking*, Sept. 1997, 38; Carl Condit, *Chicago 1910–29: Building, Planning, and Urban Technology* (Chicago: University of Chicago Press, 1973), 115; "Automobile 'Automat,'" *American City* 59 (May 1944): 105; "Commercial Parking Garages," *Architectural Record* 124, no. 3 (Sept. 1958): 187; Wayne Harding, "Mechanized Parking: The New Generation," *Parking*, May 1992, 28–29.

36. "Kent Automatic Parking Garage, New York: Jardine, Hill, and Murdock, Architects," *American Architect*, June 20, 1928, 835–37; Regional Plan Association, *Traffic and Parking Study*, 838.

37. Arthur Pound, "No Parking," *Atlantic Monthly* 161, no. 3 (March 1938): 392; Hackman and Martin, *Parking Industry*, I-4; "Garages Grow Up: Once the Ugly Ducklings of Commercial Buildings, They Put On the Architectural Dog, Start Ringing Up Profits as They Help Clear Crammed City Streets," *Architectural Forum* 98 (Feb. 1953): 122; "Small City Builds $90,000 Automobile Parking Garage," *Traffic Engineering* 11, no. 9 (Jan. 1941): 172; W. S. Wolfe, "Shoppers Parking Deck—Detroit," *Architectural Concrete* 5, no. 2 (1939): 24–26.

38. "Roof Parking to Relieve Street Overcrowding," *American City* 52 (Jan. 1937): 44; "Upside Down Store," *Chain Store Age* 16 (Jan. 1940): 16–17; "Shop-

ping Center Conveniences Feature Big Sears Store," *Chain Store Age* 18 (June 1942): 8–9; "Underground Garage to Relieve Chicago Street Congestion," *Horseless Age* 31 (May 21, 1913): 949; "Shall Motor-Cars Be Parked Underground?" *American City* 44 (Jan. 1931): 133.

39. For businessman Carlton H. Wall's critical role in the garage's inception, see "$1,500,oo Parking Space," *Nation's Business*, Aug. 1953, 40.

40. Frank J. Taylor, "San Francisco's 'Landing Strip for Motorists," *American City* 59 (Oct. 1944): 76–78; "$1,500,000 Parking Space," 40, 58–59. For a brief biography of Pansini's parking business to 1924, see "Develops Million Dollar Parking Business," *Motor Age* 46 (July 10, 1924): 16.

6. THE MATURING URBAN PARKING STRUCTURE

1. John B. Rae, *The American Automobile: A Brief History* (Chicago: University of Chicago Press, 1965), 176, 199.

2. "How Penn Harris Gets Double Profits from Parking Machine," *Hotel Monthly*, April 1955, 16.

3. Regarding the alarm for medium-sized American cities, see U.S. Department of Commerce, *Parking Guide for U.S. Cities* (Washington, DC: U.S. Government Printing Office, 1956), cited in Michael J. Gittens, "Parking," in *Traffic Engineering Handbook*, 3d ed., ed. John E. Baerwald (Washington, DC: Institute of Traffic Engineers, 1965), figure 12.1, 456. Regarding the unquestionable validity of the parking garage for handling the parking problem everywhere, see Dietrich Klose, *Metropolitan Parking Structures: A Survey of Architectural Problems and Solutions* (New York: F. A. Praeger, 1966), 11.

4. "Garages Grow Up," 120–41; "Commercial Parking Garages," *Architectural Record*, 181–88; "Urban Parking Garages," *American City* 85 (Jan. 1970): 91–93, 96–99; *The Dimensions of Parking*, 3d ed. (Washington, DC: Urban Land Institute and National Parking Association, 1993).

For a sketch of Charles T. McGavin's work to 1957, see Charles T. McGavin, "New Techniques in Downtown Parking Facilities," *Appraisal Journal* 25 (Jan. 1957): 39. For biographies of George Devlin, see Andee Seger, "Designs for One of the Country's Largest Chains, Offers a Solution to a Universal Problem," *Parking*, July 1970, 44; Fred Olmsted, "Parking Garages Join Self-Service," *Parking*, Oct. 1973, 34–35.

Shannon McDonald, "The First 50 Years of Parking Garage Design, 1910–1950" *Parking*, Sept. 1997, 34–41, provides a good architectural history of parking garage design but is very general. Neil Harris, "Parking the Garage," *Parking*, Jan. 1978, links the garage to current culture, "an artifact of our day without earlier analogues" (19).

5. "Garages Grow Up," 122, 125; "Commercial Parking Garages," 188. In "Urban Parking Garages," 93, 96, the following designers were cited where their specific work was described: E. A. Barton Associates, Cleveland; Hensley-Schmidt, Inc., Chattanooga; J. M. Hunnicutt and Merritt A. Neale, Washing-

ton, D.C.; Richard C. Rich, Detroit; and Paul C. Box and Associates, Skokie, Illinois.

6. "Urban Parking Garages," 93.

7. Anthony P. Chrest, Mary S. Smith, and Sam Bhuyan, *Parking Structures: Planning, Design, Construction, Maintenance and Repair,* 2d ed. (New York: Chapman & Hall, 1996), 1–2, 114. H. Carl Walker founded his firm in 1965; for Walker's biography, see Tom Thimes, "Carl Walker Found Life's Meaning by Helping Others," *Encore* 25, no. 5 (Jan. 1998): 8–15; Lon Cook, "H. Carl Walker: Engineering with Enthusiasm," *Parking,* Aug. 1997, 47–50; William C. Arons, "Parking Garages: How Much to Operate?" *American City and County,* July 1982, 29.

8. "Denison, Inc.," an informal history provided to the authors, Oct. 28, 1998; H. Carl Walker, "Planning Parking Structures for Future Expansion," *Parking,* Oct. 1976, 21; Robert D. Ketring, interview by Keith A. Sculle and John A. Jakle, Jan. 12, 2000. Robert D. Ketring, a vice-president of Denison, Inc., was born in 1922 in Portland, Indiana, and started work with Denison Parking Services in 1940.

9. "Garages Grow Up," 13; "Commercial Parking Garages," 181.

10. Edmund R. Ricker, *Traffic Design of Parking Garages,* rev. ed. (Saugatuck, CT: Eno Foundation for Highway Traffic Control, 1957), 1, 4.

11. Ibid., 4.

12. "Garages Grow Up," 126; "Commercial Garages," 183; Ricker, *Traffic Design,* rev. ed., 99–100.

13. Edmund R. Ricker, *The Traffic Design of Parking Garages* (Saugatuck, CT: Eno Foundation for Highway Traffic Control, 1948), 116–32; Ricker, *Traffic Design of Parking Garages,* rev. ed., 100–14; Gittens, "Parking," 484; Geoffrey Baker and Bruno Funaro, *Parking* (New York: Reinhold, 1958), 182; H. Carl Walker, "Functional Design of Parking Structures," in *The Dimensions of Parking,* 3d ed. (Washington, D.C.: Urban Land Institute and National Parking Association, 1993), 99–100.

14. "Garages Grow Up," 127.

15. Ricker, *Traffic Design of Garages,* rev. ed., 122; Weant and Levinson, *Parking,* 196.

16. Lonnie Hackman and Norene D. Martin, *The Parking Industry: Private Enterprise for the Public Good* (Washington, DC: National Parking Association, 1969), I-4; Baker and Funaro, *Parking,* 152–53; Walter Wurdeman and Weston Becket, "A One-Story Building, Six Stories High," *Traffic Engineering* 18 (May 1948): 359–60; "Urban Parking Garages," 97; Walker, "Functional Design," 99.

17. Hackman and Martin, *Parking Industry,* I-4.

18. Ketring interview.

19. "Commercial Parking Garages," 26.

20. McGavin, "New Techniques," 52.

21. Ricker, *Traffic Design of Parking Garages,* rev. ed., 11.

22. Walker, "Functional Design," 95–96.

23. Ricker, *Traffic Design of Parking Garages*, rev. ed., 30.

24. McGavin, "New Techniques," 43.

25. "Garages Grow Up," 129–30.

26. McGavin, "New Techniques," 43.

27. For example, see James McClain and William R. B. Froehlich, "The Off-Street Parking Program in Pittsburgh," *Traffic Engineering* 20 (Nov. 1949): 71; "Garages Grow Up," 132–34.

28. "Commercial Parking Garages," 186.

29. Charles J. Sharitz, Thomas J. D'Arcy, Ben W. Young, Ted R. Seeburg, Merritt A. Neale, and H. Carl Walker, "Construction Considerations," in *Dimensions of Parking*, 3d ed., 117.

30. Ricker, *Traffic Design of Parking Garages*, 59–95.

31. "Urban Parking Garages," 96.

32. Richard L. Strickland, "Parking Design for Downsized Cars," *ITE Journal* 58 (Nov. 1980): 18; Walker, "Functional Design of Parking Structures," 103.

33. Walter C. Kidney, *The Architecture of Choice: Eclecticism in America 1880–1930* (New York: George Braziller, 1974), 3, 23–24; Alan Gowans, *Images of American Living: Four Centuries of Architecture and Furniture as Cultural Expression* (Philadelphia: J. B. Lippincott, 1964), 288, 366–68, 395–413; David P. Handlin, *The American Home: Architecture and Society, 1815–1915* (Boston: Little, Brown, 1979), 269–71, 304.

34. Ricker, *Traffic Design of Parking Garages*, rev. ed., 158.

35. "Garages Grow Up," 130.

36. "Commercial Parking Garages," 50.

37. Ricker, *Traffic Design of Parking Garages*, rev. ed., 144.

38. "Steel Parking Decks," New York: n.p., 1973, 13.

39. Charles M. Boldon, "Environmental Impact on Parking," *Parking*, Jan. 1975, 28.

40. Linda Legner, "IBM Self-Park: The Garage as Sculpture," *Inland Architect* 18, no. 5 (May 1974): 16.

41. Neil I. Payton, "Architects Take a Second Look at Parking Garages," *Parking*, May 1993, 39.

42. Charles M. Boldon and Mark Vaghei, "Designing Parking Structures in Their Architectural Context," *Parking*, July 1997, 23.

43. Thomas P. Smith, *The Aesthetics of Parking: An Illustrated Guide*, Planning Advisory Service Report no. 411 (Chicago: American Planning Association, 1988), 24–31.

44. Standard Parking, An APCOA/Standard Parking Company, press release, 2000.

45. Gary Cudney, "Precast vs. Cast-in-Place: How Do They Compare? *Parking*, May 1998, 28; Sharitz et al., "Construction Considerations," 117; Walter R. Guest, "Healthcare Parking Structures," *Parking Today* 5, no. 4 (April 2000): 18.

46. Harvey L. Hurlburt, "A Fresh Idea in Parking-Structure Design," *Ameri-*

can City 76 (Dec. 1961): 80–82; Edward K. Rice and Richard W. Wickert, "Longspan Prestressed Concrete," *Parking*, fall 1961, 11.

47. R. E. Harbaugh, "Lift-Slab Construction," *American City* 77 (Sept. 1962): 143.

48. Josef Diamond, telephone interview by Keith A. Sculle, February 22, 2000; "Self-Park Structure for Dallas," *Parking*, spring 1963, 24.

49. Ricker, *Traffic Design of Parking Garages*, 141.

50. "Urban Parking Garages," 98; "Security First in This Parking Structure," *American City* 86 (Jan. 1971): 74; Charles M. Boldon, "Security," in *Dimensions of Parking*, 3d ed., 155.

51. Donald R. Monahan, "Parking Structure Lighting," *Parking*, Oct. 1991, 16–17, 19–24; Nancy Szarkowski, "How to Choose a Lighting System," *Parking*, May 1996, 34–37; "Lighting Maintenance for Safety and Profitability," *Parking*, May 1996, 28–33. For an exceptionally early article about security, see "Engineered Lighting for a 750-Car Parking Garage," *American City* 76 (June 1961): 124–25.

52. Mary S. Smith, "Security and Safety," in Chrest, Smith, and Bhuyan, *Parking Structures*, 120.

53. Mary S. Smith, Richard S. Beebe, and Thomas J. D'Arcy, "Parking and the Americans with Disabilities Act," in *The Dimensions of Parking*, 3d ed., 108–9.

54. Ricker, *Traffic Design of Parking Garages*, rev. ed., 11; "Sloping Garage Has Neither Ramps Nor Elevators," *Architectural Forum*, June 1954, 160.

55. "Urban Parking Garages," 97.

56. "Garages Grow Up," 128.

57. "Commercial Parking Garages," 184; "Urban Parking Garages," 96; "Parking Construction Hits New High," *American City* 85 (Nov. 1970): 102.

58. "Public Can Park in 11,000 Spaces in Memphis," *Parking*, winter 1964, 21–22.

59. James Alkire, "A Parking Garage Built to Give Downtown a Lift," *American City* 85 (Aug. 1970), 65–67. For a history of the garage in Bluefield, West Virginia, see "Municipality Finances Parking Building," *American City* 61 (Sept. 1946): 120; "Bluefield Makes Money on Municipal Parking Building," *American City* 64 (Oct. 1949): 139; "Bluefield Municipal Parking Building," mimeographed report [Bluefield, WV: n.p., c. 1950].

60. "Garages Grow Up"; "Commercial Parking Garages"; "Urban Parking Garages"; Richard S. Beebe, T. J. Feagins Jr., C. W. Ennis Jr., and G. Victor Brisson, "Glossary," in *Dimensions of Parking*, 3d ed., 192, 195–96. The two previous editions of *The Dimensions of Parking* carried glossaries; see 109–14 in the 1979 edition and 135–42 in the 1983 edition.

61. Chrest, Smith, and Bhuyan, *Parking Structures*; Mary S. Smith, "Functional Design," in Chrest, Smith, and Bhuyan, 54–55; "Glossary," in Chrest, Smith, and Bhuyan, 644, 645; International Parking Design, Inc., press release, 2000; Ann Carrns, "Is It Art? A Landmark? No, It's Just for Parking Cars," *Wall Street Journal*, Dec. 16, 1998, B1.

62. "Garages Grow Up," 136, 137; David A. Loehwing, "Precarious Perch," *Barron's*, Feb. 18, 1957, reprinted in *National Parking Association Newsletter* 4 (Feb. 14, 1957), insert, unpaginated; R. H. Burrage, "A Study of the Pigeon Hole Mechanical Garage at H. S. Manchester, Inc., Madison, Wisconsin," *Traffic Engineering* 24 (Aug. 1954): 407; J. M. Tippee, "Des Moines' Self-Sustaining Municipal Garages," *American City* 66 (Nov. 1951): 145; Ricker, *Traffic Design of Parking Garages*, rev. ed., 136; "Rotating Garages Provide Maximum Parking Space on a Small City Lot," *Architectural Record*, Oct. 1955, 247; Wayne Harding, "Mechanical Parking: The New Generation," *Parking*, May 1992, 27, 29; Douglas A. Yip, "An Automated Parking System for Confined Space Applications," *Parking*, March 1996, 37–40; Josef Diamond, "The President's Report," *Parking*, winter 1964, 8.

63. "Underground Garage in Los Angeles," *Traffic Engineering* 21 (Aug. 1951): 368–69, 376; Victor G. Hofer, "Chicago Park District Builds an Underground Garage," *Traffic Engineering* 23 (Oct. 1952): 14–20; "World's Largest Garage Now Being Built in Grant Park," *American City* 68 (July 1953): 128; Harry G. Cramer, "Parking 5,000 Cars a Day," *American City* 70 (June 1955): 166, 169–70; Frank A. Barcus, "Parking Problem," *Monthly Bulletin, Michigan Society of Architects* 30 (Aug. 1956): 34–35; Edmond T. Keenan, "1450 Cars to Park under Boston's Commons," *American City* 75 (Aug. 1960): 134, 137; "Newark Gets Underground Parking Garage," *American City* 75 (Feb. 1960): 137; Paul E. Heineman, "Parking under the State Capitol Grounds," *American City* 81 (March 1966): 96–97; C. D. Mullinex, "Parking under an Island," *American City* 81 (Sept. 1966): 164, 166, 168; Italo William Ricciuti, "Garages and Service Stations," in *Forms and Functions of Twentieth-Century Architecture*, vol. 4: *Building Types*, ed. Talbot Hamlin (New York: Columbia University Press, 1952), 625.

64. "Roof-Parking in Queens, N.Y.," *American City* 63 (June 1948):167; "Rooftop Parking," *American City* 65 (Sept. 1950): 143; "Public-Private Cooperation to Provide Park-Topped Garage," *American City* 65 (April 1950): 89; Ricciuti, "Garages and Service Stations," 623.

65. "The Portable Garage," *American City* 85 (Jan. 1970): 108, 110–11.

66. Paul N. Bay, "Air Rights Help Solve a Parking Problem," *American City* 82 (Nov. 1967): 84–85; "Parking Garages over Freeways," *American City* 81 (Aug. 1966): 134; "Airing a City's Parking Problem," *American City* 83 (Jan. 1968): 122; W. H. Bruder, "This Parking Garage," *American City* 80 (Dec. 1965): 98–100.

67. Harold Ellison, "First in North Carolina," *Parking*, spring 1961, 27–31; Bob Wilkinson, "End of an Era," *Parking*, Jan. 1974, 16–17; "Going . . . Going . . . Gone," *Parking*, April 1974, 16–17; M. A. Carver, "Market Square/Patten Parkway (Chattanooga, Tennessee)," National Register of Historic Places—Nomination Form, Dec. 1979; Ramp Buildings Corporation, *The Modern Multi-Floor Garage* (New York: R. B. C., 1929), 29, 33. Ronald E. Schmitt, "The Ubiquitous Parking Garage: Worthy of Preservation?" in *Preserving the Recent Past 2*, ed. Deborah Slaton and William G. Foulks (Washington, DC: Historic

Preservation Education Foundation, National Park Service, Association for Preservation Technology International, 2000), 2-193 to 2-201 argues for the preservation of a few parking garages based on an aesthetic criteria allowing for alterations in physical integrity if necessary.

7. PARKING AND DOWNTOWN REDEVELOPMENT

1. Larry Ford, *Cities and Buildings: Skyscrapers, Skid Rows, and Suburbs* (Baltimore: Johns Hopkins University Press, 1994), 13, 39.

2. Kent A. Robertson, "Downtown Redevelopment Strategies in the United States: An End-of-Century Assessment," *American Planning Association Journal* 61 (autumn 1995): 430.

3. Ibid.

4. J. T. Stegmaier, "Parking as a Factor in Business," *Institute of Traffic Engineers Proceedings* 25 (1955): 89.

5. Robert H. Armstrong, "Changing Downtown Patterns," *Urban Land* 16 (June 1957): 2.

6. Shirley F. Weiss, *The Central Business District in Transition* (Chapel Hill: University of North Carolina, Department of City and Regional Planning, Research Paper no. 1, 1957), 21.

7. John A. Miller, "Is the Downtown Shopping Area Doomed?"; reprinted in *Traffic Engineering* 16 (Nov. 1945): 58.

8. Robertson, "Downtown Redevelopment Strategies," 430–34.

9. Jane Jacobs, *The Death and Life of Great Cities* (New York: Vintage Books, 1961). See also, for example, Robert Goodman, *After the Planners* (New York: Simon and Schuster, 1971).

10. Barton Myers with John Dale, "Designing in Car-Oriented Cities: An Argument for Episodic Urban Congestion," in *The Car and the City: The Automobile, the Built Environment, and Daily Urban Life,* ed. Martin Wachs and Margaret Crawford (Ann Arbor: University of Michigan Press, 1997), 255.

11. Victor Gruen, *The Heart of Our Cities; The Urban Crisis: Diagnosis and Cure* (New York: Simon and Schuster, 1964), 124–26.

12. "Basic Plan to Vitalize Fort Worth District," *American City* 71 (June 1956): 132–33.

13. C. H. Elliott, "Long-Term Benefits of a Shopping Mall," *American City* 79 (May 1964): 91; "Kalamazoo's Permanent Mall: "Psychological Shot in the Arm," *Chain Store Age* 36 (Oct. 1960): 32.

14. See Harvey M. Rubenstein, *Central City Malls* (New York: John Wiley, 1978), 180–85.

15. For an overview of downtown malls, see Alexander Garvin, *The American City: What Works, What Doesn't* (New York: McGraw-Hill, 1996), 101–20, and Bernard J. Frieden, *Downtown, Inc.: How America Builds Cities* (Cambridge: MIT Press, 1990), 259–85.

16. "Mixed-Use Enters a New Generation," *Chain Store Age Executive* 64 (Sept. 1988): 30.

17. For an overview of themed districts or festival markets, see Roberta Brandes Gratz, *The Living City* (New York: Simon and Schuster, 1989), 314–33.

18. Dean Baim, *The Sport's Stadium as a Municipal Investment* (Westport, CT: Greenwood Press, 1992).

19. David W. Swindell et al., "The Amateur Sports Strategy," in *The Hudnut Years in Indianapolis, 1976–1991, by* William H. Hudnut III, with Mark S. Rosentraub et al. (Bloomington, IN: Indiana University Press, 1995), 143–52.

20. Charles Rutheiser, *Imagineering Atlanta: The Politics of Place in the City of Dreams* (London: Verso, 1996), 236–37.

21. Frederic A. Delano, "Skyscrapers," *American City* 34 (Jan. 1926): 1–9.

22. Ralph W. Robinson and I. S. Shattuck, "Bulky Buildings and Crowded Streets," *American City* 42 (May 1930): 157.

23. J. Thomas Black et al., *Downtown Retail Development: Conditions for Success and Project Profiles* (Washington, DC: Urban Land Institute, 1983), 15.

24. "900 North Michigan Rises on Chicago's Skyline," *Chain Store Age Executive* 63 (April 1987): 31.

25. Bernard J. Frieden, "American Business Still Wants to Go Downtown," *Wall Street Journal*, Jan. 16, 1990.

26. Robertson, "Downtown Redevelopment Strategies," 433.

27. Myers, "Designing in Car-Oriented Cities," 259.

28. Martin Wachs, "Pricing Urban Transportation: A Critique of Current Policy," *American Planning Association Journal* 47 (July 1981): 243.

29. Richard M. Robbins, "Highest and Best Use," *Appraisal Journal* 36 (April 1968): 255–56; see also Steve Thair, "What's the Use? — Most Probable Use versus Highest Use," *Appraisal Journal* 56 (April 1988): 190–99.

30. William J. Porter Jr., "Managing Parking Lots," *Journal of Property Management* 14 (March 1949): 189.

31. Jacobs, *Death and Life*, 349.

32. Jerome Gottesman, "Parking Lots Have Special Value to a City," *Parking*, Oct. 1973, 14.

33. Martin Anderson, *The Federal Bulldozer: A Critical Analysis of Urban Renewal, 1949–1962* (Cambridge: MIT Press, 1964), 73.

34. Jefferson B. Fordham, *Parking: Legal, Financial, Administrative* (Saugatuck, CT: Eno Foundation, 1956), 162.

35. Advertisement for the Manufacturers National Bank, *Detroiter* 46 (March 28, 1955): 20.

36. See Joe T. Darden et al., *Detroit: Race and Uneven Development* (Philadelphia: Temple University Press, 1987); B. J. Widick, *Detroit: City of Race and Class Violence* (Detroit: Wayne State University Press, 1989); Thomas J. Sugrue, *The Origins of the Urban Crisis: Race and Inequality in Postwar Detroit* (Princeton, NJ: Princeton University Press, 1996).

37. Donald C. Shoup, "The High Cost of Free Parking," *Journal of Planning Education and Research* 17 (1997): 11.

38. See Roger Trancik, *Finding Lost Space: Theories of Urban Design* (New York: Van Nostrand Reinhold, 1986), 98–101.

39. Hamid Shirvani, *The Urban Design Process* (New York: Van Nostrand Reinhold, 1985), 24.

40. Shoup, "High Cost," 12, 13.

8. PARKING FOR SHOPPING

1. Jo Ann Whelan (Alco Parking, Pittsburgh), telephone interview by Keith A. Sculle, Feb. 3, 2000.

2. Jane Holtz Kay, *Asphalt Nation: How the Automobile Took Over America and How We Can Take It Back* (Berkeley: University of California Press, 1997), 172–73.

3. For geography, see John A. Jakle, *The Tourist: Travel in Twentieth-Century North America* (Lincoln: University of Nebraska Press, 1985). For literary studies, see Ronald Primeau, *Romance of the Road: Literature of the American Highway* (Bowling Green, Ohio: Bowling Green State University Press, 1996); Kris Lackey, *Road Frames: The American Highway Narrative* (Lincoln: University of Nebraska Press, 1997). For histories of the automobile industries and the infrastructure supporting their products, see James J. Flink, *The Automobile Age* (Cambridge: MIT Press, 1988); John B. Rae, *The American Automobile* (Chicago: University of Chicago Press, 1965). For the South's response, see Blaine E. Brownell, "A Symbol of Modernity: Attitudes toward the Automobile in Southern Cities in the 1920s," *American Quarterly* 24 (March 1972): 29, 44. Regarding the cultural significance of the automobile in America's vast space, see Karal Ann Marling, *The Colossus of Roads: Myth and Symbol along the American Highway* (Minneapolis: University of Minnesota Press, 1984). For a history of the American highway system, see Tom Lewis, *Divided Highways: Building the Interstate Highways, Transforming American Life* (New York: Viking, 1997). For the concept of the "king's highway," see M. G. Lay, *Ways of the World: A History of the World's Roads and the Vehicles That Used Them* (Brunswick, NJ: Rutgers University Press, 1992), 64–65, 299.

4. Warren I. Susman, *Culture as History: The Transformation of American Society in the Twentieth Century* (New York: Pantheon Books, 1973), 75–85; John Chynoweth Burnham, "The Gasoline Tax and the Automobile Revolution," *Mississippi Valley Historical Review* 48 (Dec. 1961): 445–47; Kenneth T. Jackson, *Crabgrass Frontier: The Suburbanization of the United States* (New York: Oxford University Press, 1985), 288. Regarding faith in the early automobile as an effective social panacea enjoying no requirement for government intervention, see James J. Flink, *America Adopts the Automobile, 1895–1910* (Cambridge: MIT Press, 1970), 107–12. Regarding a prominent South Dakota newspaper editor's acceptance of driver licensing and speed limits, see Keith A. Sculle, "An Editor Hails the Automobile: Al J. Adams and the *Sisseton Courier*," *Great Plains Heritage* 29, no. 1 (spring–summer 1996): 45.

5. Quoted in Joseph Interrante, "The Road to Autopia: The Automobile and the Spatial Transformation of American Culture," in *The Automobile and American Culture*, ed. David L. Lewis and Laurence Goldstein (Ann Arbor: University of Michigan Press, 1980), 91, 100.

6. Martin Wachs, "Men, Women, and Urban Travel: The Persistence of Separate Spheres," in *The Car and the City: The Automobile, The Built Environment, and Daily Urban Life*, ed. Martin Wachs and Margaret Crawford (Ann Arbor: University of Michigan Press, 1992), 86–100; Paul Barrett, *The Automobile and Urban Transit: The Foundation of Public Policy in Chicago, 1900–1930* (Philadelphia: Temple University Press, 1983); Clay McShane, *Down the Asphalt Path: The Automobile and the American City* (New York: Columbia University Press, 1994), 225–26. Los Angeles leadership in decentralization has deserved Scott L. Bottles's classic study *Los Angeles and the Automobile: The Making of the Modern City* (Berkeley: University of California Press, 1987).

7. "This Is the 'Garden City' Idea," *Building Age* 51 (Aug. 1929): 49.

8. Frank Lloyd Wright, *The Disappearing City* (New York: William Farquar Payson, 1932).

9. Joseph B. Mason, "Two Fronts for Every House," *Building Age* 52 (Sept. 1929): 42–44, 106.

10. Joseph B. Hall, "What Makes the Hot Spot 'Hot'?" *Appraisal Journal* 7 (Oct. 1939): 344.

11. Richard Longstreth, *The Drive-In, the Supermarket, and the Transformation of Commercial Space in Los Angeles, 1914–1941* (Cambridge: MIT Press, 1999), 72–73; Harry E. Martin, "Trends in Decentralization of Shopping Centers," *Chain Store Age* 17 (April 1941): 39.

12. Kent A. Robertson, *Pedestrian Malls and Skywalks: Traffic Separation Strategies in American Downtowns* (Aldershot, UK: Avebury, 1994), 24, 83; E. Relph, *Place and Placelessness* (London: Pion, 1976), 132.

13. John Ihlder, "Coordination of Traffic Facilities," *Annals of the American Academy of Political and Social Sciences* 138 (Sept. 1927): 5–6; Cleland Austin, "New Life for an Old Shopping Area," *American City* 63, Oct. 1948, 106.

14. Frank R. Hawkins, "Making It Easy for the Automobile Shopper," *Chain Store Age* 4 (April 1928): 17. For an example of a business manager who not only acknowledged but documented how he learned that drivers preferred driving longer distances to arrive at empty parking spaces rather than driving a shorter distance and hunt for a parking space, see F. R. Henry, "Changing Buying Habits Set Our Location Policies," *Chain Store Age* 10 (July 1934): 18.

15. R. E. Wood, "Space for Head-in Parking Relieves Congestion and Facilitates Suburban Street Widening," *American City* 40 (Feb. 1929): 127; Richard Longstreth, *City Center to Regional Mall: Architecture, the Automobile, and Retailing in Los Angeles, 1920–1950* (Cambridge: MIT Press, 1997), 46–47.

16. J. C. Nichols, "Developing Outlying Shopping Centers," *American City*, 42, July 1929, 99. The best history of J. C. Nichols's real estate developments leaves unexplained the reasons for his prescience about the automobile's commercial potential and the ways of providing for it at Country Club Plaza; see

William S. Worley, *J. C. Nichols and the Shaping of Kansas City: Innovation in Planned Residential Communities* (Columbia: University of Missouri Press, 1990), 80, 254–55.

17. "All-Chain Shopping Area," *Chain Store Age* 6 (Dec. 1930): 58; "Taking Business out of Traffic," *Chain Store Age* 15 (Dec. 1939): 23.

18. J. C. Nichols, "Developing Outlying Shopping Centers," *American City* 41 (July 1929): 98–101.

19. E. E. East, "Los Angeles' Street Traffic Problem," *Civil Engineering*, Aug. 1942, 437. For a generalized description, see Gerald J. Foster and Howard J. Nelson, *Ventura Boulevard: A String-Type Shopping Street* (Los Angeles: Real Estate Research Program, Bureau of Business and Economic Research, University of California, Los Angeles, 1958), 7.

20. L. Deming Tilton, "Roadside Control through Zoning," *Civil Engineering* 10, no. 1 (Jan. 1940): 11. For an example of shopping center growth on the west side of Cleveland, see "How Searstown Grew," *Chain Store Age* 24 (Sept. 1958): 35.

21. Longstreth, *Drive-In*, 46–47; Chester H. Liebs, *Main Street to Miracle Mile: American Roadside Architecture* (Boston: New York Graphic Society, 1985), 10–13; M. S. C., "Shop Fronts Must Advertise," *Building Age* 52 (Jan. 1930): 40.

22. "A Program for Community Conservation in Chicago and an Example: The Woodlawn Plan," ([Chicago]: Chicago Plan Commission, 1946), 49.

23. "Looking Backwards: 25 Years of Super Market Progress," *Super Market Merchandising* 20 (1955): 68–69.

24. Howard L. Preston, *Automobile Age Atlanta: The Making of a Southern Metropolis* (Athens: University of Georgia Press, 1979), 131.

25. H. S. Wright, "Locating Grocery Stores," *Chain Store Age* 1 (Aug. 1925): 54–55.

26. "Now Comes the 'Automarket,'" *Chain Store Age* 4 (June 1928): 49–53; "MacMarr Develops the 'Drive-In' Store," *Chain Store Age* 6 (Oct. 1930): 59–60, 62, 72.

27. For example, see Andrew Williams, "Super Markets to Endure Must Excel in 5 Ways," *Chain Store Age* 13 (Aug. 1937): 18; "All the Most Modern Red and White Food Store in the United States (Today)," *Red and White Hy-Lites*, Aug. 1940, 3; "Include a New Store Front in Your Post-War Plans," *Red and White Hy-Lites*, Jan. 1945, 6; "Tom's Quality Market," *Monthly Bulletin, Michigan Society of Architects* 23 (March 22, 1949): 3; Samuel Shore, "How We Planned Our New Providence Unit," *Super Market Merchandising* 15 (March 1950): 43; "Supers Continue Forward March, Part I," *Super Market Merchandising* 19 (Feb. 1954): 41.

28. "Supers Emulate 'Great White Way,'" *Super Market Merchandising* 19 (July 1954): 55.

29. H. W. Underhill, "What It Costs to Build a Modern Super Market," *Super Market Merchandising* 19 (Sept. 1954): 62–63, 66; "What Do You Think?" *Super Market Merchandising* 17 (Feb. 1952): 124–25; "Shopping Centers—A

Neighborhood Necessity," *Urban Land: News and Trends in City Development,* Sept. 1944, 4; "The 1964 Model," *Super Market Merchandising* 33 (April 1965).

30. For an excellent overview of the long-term tension between elitist and vernacular aesthetics along the roadside, see Daniel M. Bluestone, "Roadside Blight and the Reform of Commercial Architecture," in *Roadside America: The Automobile in Design and Culture,* ed. Jan Jennings (Ames: Iowa State University Press, 1990), 170–84. For a perceptive appreciation of the strip's competing meanings, see Richard P. Horwitz, *The Strip: An American Place* (Lincoln: University of Nebraska Press, 1985).

31. J. M. Bennett, *Roadsides: The Front Yard of the Nation* (Boston: Statford, 1936), 165.

32. Robert Venturi, Denise Scott Brown, and Steven Izenour, *Learning from Las Vegas: The Forgotten Symbolism of Architectural Form* (Cambridge: MIT Press, 1997), 3.

33. "Tourist Hotel Project Includes Maintenance and Accessory Sales," *Buffalo Motorist* 15 (Aug. 1922): 30–31.

34. Warren James Belasco, *Americans on the Road: From Autocamp to Motel, 1910–1945* (Cambridge: MIT Press, 1979), 139.

35. George Thomason (Downtowner architect, 1958–c. 1971), interview by Keith A. Sculle, Memphis, May 22, 2000.

36. For example, see "Bank Caters to Motorists Curb Service for Depositors," *Hoosier Motorist* 18 (May 1930): 15; "'Drive-In' Bank Opens New Field," *American Builder* 60 (Feb. 1938): 52–53.

37. "Ticket Office for an Airline," *American Builder* 77 (Aug. 1955): 144–45; "'Drive-In' Retailing Setting New Trend?" *Chain Store Age* 33 (July 1957): 32–33.

38. "Something New in Selling Used Cars," *Accessory and Garage Journal* 19 (Aug. 1929): 39. The history of the automobile dealership has focused heretofore either on its architectural history or largely on its commercial practices. For the former, see Liebs, *From Main Street to Miracle Mile,* 75–93. For the latter, see Henry Dominguez, *The Ford Agency* (Osceola, WI: Motorbooks International, 1981), and Robert Genat, *The American Car Dealership* (Osceola, WI: MBI, 1999).

39. "Ways of Controlling Automobile 'Graveyards,'" *American City* 41 (Oct. 1929): 171. Also see "What Disposition of 'Junked' Automobiles," *American City* 43 (July 1930): 114.

40. C. G. Stoneburner, "The Development of Off-Street Parking in Arlington, Va.," *Traffic Engineering* 15 (May 1945): 309, 311; "Adequate Parking Holds Big Regional Retail Trade," *American City* 67 (Nov. 1952): 155; Harold C. Frantzen, "The Speculative Stop-and-Shop," *Appraisal Journal* 17 (Jan. 1949): 98; Howard T. Fisher, "Can Main Street Compete? *American City* 65 (Oct. 1950): 101; Preston, *Automobile Age Atlanta,* 130.

41. For the historical context of the suburban shopping center, see Meredith L. Clausen, "Northgate Regional Shopping Center—Paradigm from the

Provinces," *Journal of the Society of Architectural Historians* 43 (May 1984): 144–45; Jackson, *Crabgrass Frontier*, 257–61; Howard Gillette Jr., "The Evolution of the Planned Shopping Center in Suburb and City," *APA Journal* 51 (autumn 1985): 449–60; Richard Longstreth, "The Diffusion of the Community Shopping Center Concept during the Interwar Decades," *Journal of the Society of Architectural Historians* 56 (Sept. 1997): 268–70; Longstreth, *City Center to Regional Mall*, 145–53; Lizabeth Cohen, "From Town Center to Shopping Center: The Reconfiguration of Community Marketplaces in Postwar America," *American Historical Review* 101, no. 4 (Oct. 1996): 1,050–53.

42. "ISCS: 20 Years Worth of Memories," *Chain Store Age Executive* 53 (May 1977): 67.

43. Homer Hoyt, "The Status of Shopping Centers in the United States, October 1960," *Urban Land* 19 (Oct. 1960): 5.

44. Victor D. Gruen, "The Planning of Shopping Centers," *Monthly Bulletin, Michigan Society of Architects* 26 (Feb. 1952): 15–17, 19, 21; Victor D. Gruen, "What to Look for in Shopping Centers," *Chain Store Age* 24 (July 1948): 61–66.

45. Pietro Belluschi, "Shopping Centers," in *Forms and Functions of Twentieth-Century Architecture*, ed. Talbot Hamlin (New York: Columbia University Press, 1952), 129.

46. Neal R. Peirce, "Shopping Center's Inventor Disowns His Progeny," *Parking*, Jan. 1979, 31.

47. Urban Land Institute, *Urban Land: News and Trends in City Development* 2, no. 4 (Sept. 1944).

48. Belluschi, "Shopping Centers," 127.

49. Urban Land Institute, *Technical Bulletin no. 30: Shopping Centers Re-Studied," (1956)* (Washington, DC: Urban Land Institute, 1956), 51.

50. Jim McCluskey, *Parking: A Handbook of Environmental Design* (London: E. & F. N. Spon, 1987), 121. Also see Willard L. Thorsen, "Mini Malls," *Urban Land* 33 (Oct. 1974): 12.

51. Urban Land Institute, *Shopping Centers: An Analysis*, technical bulletin no. 11 (Washington, DC: Urban Land Institute, 1949), 15.

52. "Planning Advice Given to Shopping Center Developers," *American City* 69 (May 1954): 185; Kenneth C. Welch and Bruno Funaro, "Parking Plans for Shopping Centers," *Traffic Quarterly* 6 (Oct. 1951): 419; "Parking Lot Survey," *Super Market Merchandising* (April 1953): 42.

53. "Choosing Your Shopping Center Wisely," *Super Market Merchandising*, April 1953, 39.

54. Victor Gruen, "Parking Lots," *Chain Store Age*, Aug. 1952, 44.

55. Victor Gruen and Larry Smith, *Shopping Towns USA: The Planning of Shopping Centers* (New York: Reinhold, 1960), 124–25.

56. Harry E. Martin, "Parking Points That Make the Difference," *Chain Store Age* 30 (May 1954): 21.

57. "Parking," *Chain Store Age* 41 (April 1965): E27.

58. Nicholas Ordway, A. Alexander Bul, and Mark E. Eakin, "Developing a

Visibility Index to Clarify Shopping Centers," *Appraisal Journal* 56 (April 1988): 233.

59. "Bellevue Shopping Square," *American Builder* 68 (Nov. 1946): 75.

60. "One-Stop Centers Continue Growth," *Chain Store Age* 22 (Sept. 1946): 24.

61. "Thirty-Three Cars to a Store," *American Builder*, June 1947, 111.

62. "Framingham Picked as New Shopping Center Site," *American City* 63 (Feb. 1948): 135.

63. Welton Becket, "Parking Poses Perennial Problem," *Chain Store Age* 27 (July 1951): 62; Welton Becket, "Shopping Center Traffic Problems," *Traffic Quarterly* 10 (1955): 166.

64. Geoffrey Baker and Bruno Funaro, *Shopping Centers: Design and Operation* (New York: Reinhold, 1951): 84–85, 169; "They Raised the Center above the Parking," *Shopping Center Age* 2 (Jan. 1963): 22–23, 29.

65. Welch and Funaro, "Parking Plans for Shopping Centers," 421–22.

66. Ordway, Bul, and Eakin, "Developing a Visibility Index," 241.

67. Josef Diamond, "Our National Parking Association," *Parking*, summer 1963, 7.

68. Homer Hoyt, "Status of Shopping Centers in the United States, October 1960," *Urban Land* 19 (Oct. 1960): 4.

69. John W. Combs, "The Future of Shopping Centers," in *Urban Land Institute*, "Trends and Prospects in Shopping Centers—A Symposium," March 1962, 8.

70. Cynthia Davidson-Powers, "Architecture and the Shopping Center," *Inland Architect* 31, no. 3 (May–June 1987): 61; Joel Garreau, *Edge City: Life on the New Frontier* (New York: Doubleday, 1988): 245; Michael Berwick and Robert Cervero, *Transit Villages in the 21st Century* (New York: McGraw-Hill, 1997), 234; E. Relph, *Place and Placelessness*.

71. Thorsen, "Mini Malls," 12; Bruce N. Wright, "America's Largest Shopping Complex, the Mall of America, Opens on the Outskirts of the Twin Cities," *Inland Architect* (Nov. 1992): 49; Howard L. Green, "The Changing Population . . . And How It Affects Retailing," *Chain Store Age Executive* 51 (Sept. 1975): 87; "Trend Shifts from Traditional Malls," *Chain Store Age Executive* 57 (Dec. 1981): 46, 49, 51; "Growth of Car-Care Malls Accelerates," *Chain Store Age Executive* 65 (Jan. 1989): 33, 37.

72. William F. O'Dell, "Market Strategy for CDBs," *Urban Land* 31 (June 1972): 18–19; Daniel Locitzer, "A Parking Garage Helps Revitalize a Deteriorating Downtown," *American City* 85 (June 1970): 94; "Many Centers Switch to Parking Garages," *Chain Store Age Executive* 65 (May 1989): 94; "Survey Discloses Shifts in Shopping Center Chains," *Chain Store Age Executive* 61 (May 1985): 70; "Illuminating the Parking Lot," *Chain Store Age* 32 (Sept. 1954): 38–39; William Koelling, "Parking for Lighting," *Chain Store Age* 38 (Sept. 1962): E11; Charles Bolden, "Security," in *The Dimensions of Parking*, 3d ed. (Washington, DC: Urban Land Institute and National Parking Association, 1993), 156–57.

73. Quoted in *Design for Modern Merchandising: Stores, Shopping Centers, Showrooms* (New York: F. W. Dodge, 1952), 166.

74. For example, see advertisement of Meyers Brothers Wash 'n Shop Sales, Inc., *Chain Store Age* 44 (Oct. 1968): E4.

75. "Find Revenue in Parking Areas," *Chain Store Age* 45 (Sept. 1969): E67.

76. "Punching Up Profits on the Periphery," *Chain Store Age Executive* 60 (May 1984): 68–69.

9. PARKING FOR INSTITUTIONS, AIRPORTS, RECREATIONS, AND INDUSTRIES

1. Wilbur S. Smith, *Access and Parking for Institutions* (Saugatuck, CT: Eno Foundation for Highway Traffic Control, 1960). No biography of Wilber S. Smith has been written, but information about his practice can be obtained from the following sources: Smith, *Access and Parking for Institutions*, v; "Bibliography" in Edward M. Whitlock, *Parking for Institutions and Special Events* (Westport, CT: Eno Foundation for Transportation, 1982), 53–56; Wilbur Smith Associates, "History," http://www.wilbursmith.com/index.ctm (accessed April 21, 2000).

2. Charles S. Le Crow Jr. and Wilbur S. Smith, "Zoning Applied to Parking," *Appraisal Journal*, July 1947, 403–7.

3. Smith, *Access and Parking for Institutions*, 36.

4. Whitlock, *Parking for Institutions and Special Events*; Robert A. Weant and Herbert S. Levinson, *Parking* (Westport, CT: Eno Foundation for Transportation, 1990), 109–19, 144–48. Fairs were one of the important activities suffering inadequate parking yet overlooked in Smith's report; see Louis Silver, "Parking Difficulties of Fair Shared by Other Displays," *Memphis Commercial Appeal*, Oct. 16, 1959, 17, 1–7.

5. Smith, *Access and Parking for Institutions*, 2, 5, 3.

6. Whitlock, *Parking for Institutions and Special Events*, vii.

7. Weant and Levinson, for example, cite Whitlock, *Parking for Institutions and Special Events*, p. 109, note 16, regarding vehicle occupancy at special events, and p. 110, note 17, regarding the commentary on hospitals and medical centers.

8. George E. Kanaan, *Parking and Access at General Hospitals* (Westport, CT: Eno Foundation for Transportation, 1973) 1, 9, 14–16.

9. Jerome Gottesman and Marc Gellman, "Hospital Parking," *Parking*, Oct. 1977, 25.

10. Whitlock, *Parking for Institutions and Special Events*, 5; Weant and Levinson, *Parking*, 146; Kanaan, 85; Gottesman and Gellman, "Hospital Parking," 25.

11. Crane and Gorwic Associates, Inc., Planning and Urban Design Consultants, *A Development Plan for a Youngstown Health Center* (Detroit, c. 1960).

12. "The New Prescription for Hospital Parking," *Carl Walker: Parking, Planning, Engineering, Restoration Newsletter* (Sept. 1999): 3; Whitlock, *Parking for Institutions*, 12.

13. Walter K. Guest, "Healthcare Parking Structures," *Parking Today* 5, no. 4 (April 2000): 14. Also see Dennis Cunning, "Metropolitan Hospital Parking Can Be Complex," *Parking Today* 5, no. 4 (April 2000): 20.

14. *Parking Programs for Universities* (n.p.: University Facilities Research Center, 1961), 2; L. H. Csanyi, "Parking Practices on College Campuses in the United States," Bulletin 181 (Ames: Iowa Engineering Experiment Station, 1958): 14, 16; Robert E. Dober, *Campus Planning* (New York: Reinhold, 1963), 4, 159, 161, 163.

15. Alan Charles Freeman and James Alfred Zavagno, "Mitigating University Parking Problems," *Parking*, May 1995, 34–37.

16. Dober, *Campus Planning*, 12–14, 159, 16; John Nolte, "Balancing the Diverse Needs of University/Hospital Parkers," *Parking*, Feb. 1995, 37; Susan A. Kirkpatrick, "A Changing Parking Paradigm at the University of Michigan," *Parking*, Aug. 1995, 32–36.

17. "One School of Thought on College Parking," *Parking Today*, April 2000, 47.

18. Smith, *Access and Parking for Institutions*, 3; Paul Gonzales, *Campus Safety Journal*, cited in *Parking Today* 5, no. 4 (April 2000): 45.

19. Betsy Braden and Paul Hagan, *A Dream Takes Flight: Hartsfield Atlanta International Airport and Aviation in Atlanta* (Atlanta: Atlanta Historical Society; Athens: University of Georgia Press, 1989), 122; John Walter Wood, *Airports: Some Elements of Design and Future Development* (New York: Coward-McCann, 1940), 3–14.

20. Paul Barrett, "Cities and Their Airports Policy Formation, 1926–1952," *Journal of Urban History* 14 (Nov. 1987): 113.

21. Nory Miller, "Can We Save O'Hare Field from Itself?" *Inland Architect* 17, no. 8 (Aug. 1973): 18; Richard J. Daley and Milton Pikarsky, *Chicago Public Works: A History* (Chicago: Rand McNally, 1973), 172, 174; Harry Weese, "Troubled Allies at O'Hare," *Inland Architect* 27, no. 6 (1983): special "Take Out" section, 2–3.

22. Weese, "Troubled Allies at O'Hare," (1); "O'Hare Main Parking Garage," http://www.city.ofchicago.org/Aviation/Ohare/Parking (accessed April 16, 2000).

23. Weant and Levinson, *Parking*, 144; Wood, *Airports*, 64; Bill Girgash, "Edwin M. Roth: King of Airport Parking," *Parking* (Nov.–Dec. 1985): 37–38.

24. "Headache Clinic," *Parking*, summer 1963, 34–35; Girgash, "Edwin M. Roth," 38; Jeff Diersen, "A Sophisticated Revenue Control System Speeds Transactions at Lambert Airport," *Parking*, June 1996, 38–41.

25. "Headache Clinic," *Parking*, 35; Car Barn advertising folder, 2000.

26. Richard C. Rich, "Airport Parking Design," *Parking*, Nov.–Dec. 1985, 51–53; "Airport Parking Steers toward 'Wheel' Growth," *World Airport Week* 4, no. 42 (Oct. 21, 1997), available at http://www.lexis-nexis.com (accessed Dec. 6, 1998).

27. "Municipal Auditoriums and the City Plan," Information Report no. 7,

Planning Advisory Service, American Society of Planning Officials, Oct. 1949, 14, 18, 4.

28. Technical Council Committee Report 6A5, *Traffic Engineering Magazine*, June 1975, cited in Whitlock, *Parking for Institutions and Special Events*, 34.

29. "Cobo Hall," *Michigan Society of Architects, Monthly Bulletin* 34 (Oct. 1960): 20–21; Harold Burris-Meyer and Edward C. Cole, *Theatres and Auditoriums*, (New York: Reinhold, 1949), 20; Ivan J. Miestchovich and Wade R. Ragas, "Stadium Parking Attracts Office Developers in New Orleans," *Urban Land* 45 (June 1986): 14–17.

30. Whitlock, *Parking for Institutions*, 35; Weant and Levinson, *Parking*, 145–46. Disneyland's exceptional size dictated unique requirements as noted in "Effective Parking Management at Disneyland Keeps Guests Coming Back," *Parking*, spring 1982, 61, 63, 65.

31. "Special Parking Considerations for Super Bowl XVI," *Parking*, spring 1982, 69, 71; Weant and Levinson, *Parking*, 146.

32. Museum of Science and Industry new releases, 1997, 1998; Blair Kamin, "A Subterranean Parking Garage Reveals a Museum's Beauty and Excitement," *Chicago Tribune*, July 16, 1998, sec. 2, pp. 1, 4; "Discover the Getty," brochure, 1998.

33. *Parking for Recreation: A Primer on the Techniques of Parking Vehicles at Public Recreation Centers* (Wheeling, WV: American Institute of Park Executives, 1965), 5, 34–36.

34. James J. Flink, *The Automobile Age* (Cambridge: MIT Press, 1988), 134; "Parking Facilities for Industrial Employees," *American City Magazine* 31 (Sept. 1924): 239; "Assembly Plant Under Way," *GMC News and Views* 16 (Feb. 1936): 32; "New Plant for Buffalo," *GMAC News and Views* 17 (April 1937): 27; "A Tale of Three Cities," *Automobile Facts* 3 (April 1940): 3; "Busy Highways," *Automobile Facts* 3 (March 1940): 7; "U.S. Gears Working Efficiency to Motors," *Automobile Facts* 3 (Oct. 1940): 1; "Use of Automobiles Spurred by Defense," *Automobile Facts* 3 (Jan. 1941): 1; "Industrial Plant Parking," *Traffic Engineering* 29 (March 1959): 25–30, reprinted in *Urban Land News and Trends in City Development* 18, no. 5 (May 1959): 3–7; *Parking Facilities for Industrial Plants* (Washington, DC: Institute of Traffic Engineers, 1969); Weant and Levinson, *Parking*, 119.

35. J. L. Donoghue, "The Role of Park and Ride Facilities in Energy Conservation," *Parking* (Oct. 1980): 31.

36. Austin F. Macdonald, "Parking Facilities outside the Traffic Zone," *Annals of the American Academy of Political and Social Sciences* 138 (Sept. 1927): 79.

37. "Philadelphia's Parking-Riding Plan Extended," *American City Magazine* 35 (July 1926): 7; Macdonald, "Parking Facilities outside the Traffic Zone," 79.

38. Macdonald, "Parking Facilities outside the Traffic Zone," 79.

39. Ibid., 79–80; G. J. MacMurray, "Parking Places at Electric Railway Stations Help to Relieve Downtown Congestion," *American City* 43 (Dec. 1930): 142–43; Leon R. Brown, "Suburban Parking Stations, with the Street-Car or Limited Bus Service, as Aids in Solving Parking and Traffic Problems," *American City* 40 (Feb. 1929): 81–82.

40. Carl Feiss, "Commuter Parking," *House and Garden* 76 (Oct. 1939): 36–37.

41. Percival M. Bland, "Summit Plan Grapples with Parking Problems," *American City* 69 (April 1954): 114; Percy Sprague, "Commuter Parking in Valley Stream, N.Y.," *American City* 69 (Jan. 1954): 147.

42. "Shoppers Park at Gasoline Stations," *American City* 151 (Sept. 1955): 187; Leslie Williams, "Wanted in Memphis, Tenn.: More People and Fewer Cars Downtown," *American City* 70 (Jan. 1955): 151, 153; "HHFA Approves Commuter-Parking Lot Grant," *American City* 78 (June 1963): 131; Cary C. Burnett, "A Parking Mall That . . . ," *American City* 82 (Jan. 1967): 74–76. For a shuttle bus operation in North Bergen, NJ, see "New Commuter Parking in New York Area," *American City* 70 (Dec. 1955): 115.

43. "Free Bus Service Allows Elderly to Shop with Ease," *American City* 88 (June 1973): 28; Sam R. Nakib and Joseph F. Ligas, "A Park 'n Ride Program for the Chicago Area," *Traffic Engineering* 15 (March 1975): 14–16; Donoghue, "Role of Park and Ride," 31, 34; Joseph E. Robertson, "Park Ride Plan Gives Commuters a Break," *American City* 89 (Dec. 1974): 86.

44. Barbara Quinn, "Country Congestion," *American City and Country* (Feb. 1988): 58.

45. Michael Bernick and Robert Cervero, *Transit Villages in the 21st Century* (New York: McGraw-Hill, 1997), 138.

46. I. Paul Lew and Abraham Graham, "Parking: A Key of Any Intermodal Facility," *Parking*, March 1999, 29.

47. Charles E. Bowler, Errol C. Noel, Richard Peterson, and Dennis Christiansen, *Park-and-Ride Facilities — Guidelines for Planning, Design and Operation* (Washington, DC: Federal Highway Administration, U.S. Department of Transportation, 1986), cited in Weant and Levinson, *Parking* (Westport, CT: Eno Foundation, 1990), 104.

48. Weant and Levinson, *Parking*, 105.

CONCLUSION

1. Mark C. Childs, *Parking Spaces: A Design, Implementation, and Use Manual for Architects, Planners, and Engineers* (New York: McGraw-Hill, 1999), 17.

2. Catherine G. Miller, *Carscape: A Parking Handbook* (Columbus, IN: Washington Street Press for the Irwin-Sweeney Foundation, 1988), 1.

3. Childs, *Parking Spaces*, 16.

4. Edward Relph, *Rationalistic Landscapes and Humanistic Geography* (London: Croom-Helm, 1981), 95–103.

5. Victor Turner's theory of liminality, but one result of his prolific career, was a lifelong work whose antecedents date back to 1908 with Arnold van Gennep's publication of *Rites de Passage*. Turner explained his theory of liminality in many works, but the most complete discussions are given in *Dramas, Field, and Metaphor: Symbolic Action in Human Society* (Ithaca: Cornell University Press, 1974), and *Process, Performance and Pilgrimage: A Study in Comparative Symbology* (New Delhi: Concept, 1979).

6. Theodore Goldberg, "The Automobile: A Social Institution for Adolescents," *Environment and Behavior* 1, no. 2 (Dec. 1969): 164–65.

7. "Handling Noise in Your Drive-In," *Drive-In Magazine* 21, no. 8 (Aug. 1957): 18; "What Makes the Teenager Tick?" *Drive-In Magazine* 23, no. 10 (Oct. 1959): 10; "St. Louis Drive-In Operators Meet to Share Ideas, Tell Problems, Find Solutions," *Drive-In Restaurant*, 28, no. 1 (Jan. 1964): 26–27; "Drive-In Closes Because of Rowdyism," *Drive-In Restaurant*, 28, no. 1 (Jan. 1964): 27; Don C. Gibbons, "Explaining Juvenile Delinquency: Changing Theoretical Perspectives," in *Critical Issues in Juvenile Delinquency, ed.* David Shichor and Delos H. Kelly (Lexington, MA: Lexington Books, 1980), 9; James Gilbert, *A Cycle of Outrage: America's Reaction to the Juvenile Delinquent in the 1950s* (New York: Oxford University Press, 1986), 183, 12–14, 143–61.

8. "The Kids Tried to Haze Us," *Drive-In Restaurant*, 26, no. 4 (April 1962): 8; "A Drive-In's Program for Juvenile Adult Control," *Drive-In Restaurant*, 28, no. 8 (Aug. 1964): 16–17; "San Bernardino's New Drive-In Ordinance," *Drive-In Restaurant*, 28, no. 11 (Nov. 1964): 20–21.

9. Brian Butko, "Car Hoppin' at Eat n Park," *Western Pennsylvania History*, 82 (summer 1999): 92; Goldberg, "Automobile," 170.

10. Calvin Trillin, "Hail to the Suburban Devils," King Features, July 7, 1995; Andrew Jacobs, "No Broadway for Devils, But Plenty of Parking," *New York Times*, June 13, 2000, B5; Andrew Jacobs, "Devils and Fans Say the Place to Party Is Wherever the Stanley Cup Is," *New York Times*, June 14, 2000, C30NE).

11. Carl Bernstein and Bob Woodward, *All the President's Men* (New York: Simon and Schuster, 1974), 72, 76, 130, 134, 172, 195, 244.

12. David Obst, *Too Good to Be Forgotten: Changing America in the '60s and '70s* (New York: John Wiley, 1998), 244–48.

13. Roberta Brandes Gratz with Norman Mintz, *Cities Back from the Edge: New Life for Downtown* (New York: John Wiley, 1988), 104.

14. Andres Duany, Elizabeth Plater-Zyberk, and Jeff Speck, *Suburban Nation: The Rise of Sprawl and the Decline of the American Dream* (New York: North Point Press, 2000), 97.

15. For a critique of reformers divining a monolithic past and proposing a monolithic future, see Diane Barthel, *Historic Preservation: Collective Memory and Historical Identity* (New Brunswick, NJ: Rutgers University Press, 1996), 35–53.

16. Stefanos Polyzoides, foreword to Childs, *Parking Spaces*, xv.

17. Clay McShane, *Down the Asphalt Highway: The Automobile and the*

American City (New York: Columbia University Press, 1994), 194; Kay, *Asphalt Nation*, 149; *Childs, Parking Spaces.*

18. Polyzoides, foreword, xii.

19. Duany, Plater-Zyberk, and Speck, *Suburban Nation*, 12.

20. Kay, *Asphalt Nation*, 64.

21. This useful concept comes from Mark Childs. See Childs, *Parking Spaces*, 115.

INDEX

Pages in boldface indicate illustrations.